"R.A.B."—STUDY OF A STATESMAN

"R.A.B."

Study of a Statesman

*

GERALD SPARROW

The career of
Baron Butler of Saffron Walden, C.H.

ODHAMS BOOKS LIMITED
LONG ACRE, LONDON

First Published 1965

To the Young Men of the Twenties—
The Last of the "Heaven-Born"

Made and Printed in Great Britain by
Odhams (Watford) Ltd.,
Watford, Herts.
T.1065.P.

Contents

Illustrations

Foreword

THIS BIOGRAPHY is an attempt to answer questions that the public have been asking for many years concerning that part of the recent political history of Britain in which Richard Austen Butler has played a prominent role, questions which have remained to a great extent unanswered so that we are now confronted with unexplained chapters in the life of our nation.

Among these questions are the following:

How was it that Mr. Macmillan was able to by-pass Mr. Butler and secure the Office of Prime Minister for himself when Butler was so clearly the heir-apparent?

And, stranger still, what, exactly, happened in 1963 when Sir Alec Douglas Home emerged as the temporary Tory leader?

What part did Butler play in the tragedy of Suez? And in the earlier drama of Munich?

Then, apart from these questions, the basic question has to be answered: was this a man of massive achievement in many fields? Had he a vision and, if so, what was it? How will his contemporaries and history regard him? How should we regard him? Has he served us well?

At this point it might be said: "Only Butler, himself, can answer questions such as these."

My assessment of his character, which is at once simple and sophisticated, is that he will never do so. It may well be that, with more leisure, eventually, from the secluded and sheltered precincts of Trinity College, Cambridge, an auto-biography or reminiscences will emerge. But its hallmark will be its restraint and its dignity. It will tell us nothing we should not know.

I last met him a week ago in his house in Smith Square. Sitting there on a sofa he talked of autobiographies that have recently appeared. "Many of them seem so bitter. It is enough to put one off writing one's own story." Lord Kilmuir's book was mentioned. "It even lost him some personal friends."

This man will never reverse the form of forty years of public life to become the indiscreet extrovert who tells the whole truth in a book that must in some quarters give offence. As I left him he looked up at the great church being restored in the square and said: "Such a pity. Lady Parker means well, but it was such a lovely ruin. . . ."

If it is true that Lord Butler, himself, will never tell us the whole story we may be certain that we shall not get it from other figures intimately concerned. Mr. Macmillan, Sir Alec Douglas Home, Lord Salisbury are not going to disturb the peace. Sir Winston has gone to his rest to join the immortals. The part played by the Queen is to some extent protected by the secrecy that shrouds the remnants of the Prerogative.

Only one consideration impels me to write this book—apart from the fact that writing is my life—it is that, in a democracy such as ours, the people are entitled to know what has happened and why it happened. In this task I shall make use of the weapons that experience has put in my hands and pray that I do a good job.

I have been a barrister for forty years with some judicial experience. I can, I think, weigh evidence. I have had facilities during 1965 for getting to know the truth. At the most formative period of his life, when he was twenty-three, I spent seven weeks with RAB touring the universities of the United States and Canada. We were together night and day as members of the Cambridge Union Debating team. The only other member was A. P. Marshall, now a High Court Judge. RAB was not on his guard then, but the signposts of his career were already well indicated. He had just preceded me as President of the Union. His Toryism had already assumed its liberal aspect—and he had met and fallen in love with Sydney Courtauld.

His approach to life was already mature, formed. He was already dedicated, having achieved his Double First in History and Modern Languages at the expense of a near-breakdown. He had then, as he has now, that attribute which the late Lord Birkenhead so greatly admired, an absolutely first-class brain. He was elegant as the young men of his period—Charles Cavendish, Mervyn Clive, Geoffrey Lloyd and David Horner—were elegant. They were a well-heeled, carefree generation of English undergraduates, whose ideal was effortless mastery—the last of the "Heaven-born". He already had that individual speaking voice and that surprisingly high-pitched laugh, at times a chuckle, that has since disconcerted his worried opponents on the floor of the House of Commons. He already grasped most realistically the kind of world into which we had been born. "The Butlers," he said to me, "have always been able to earn good salaries, but we have never had any real money. . . ." He was proud of the great family of civil servants and headmasters from whom he came.

And, even then, everyone called him "RAB". Today, forty years later, his family, his friends, his acquaintances, his colleagues and even the public use the abbreviation. He signs himself in this way when writing to friends. Only one other politician of recent times has achieved this kind of universal intimacy—"Nye" Bevan. So much a part of the fabric of British life has RAB Butler become that it is hard to think of him as Baron Butler of Saffron Walden. Yet, in spite of this, he has remained our most elusive public figure.

The questions that I have posed in this foreword can only be answered fully and truthfully if we are able to probe the character of this man. That will not be easy, but it should not be impossible. Certainly he is complex and his character and personality present contradictions. But I am imbued with the idea that this probe will be very well worth while. We are not dealing here with a man who has any small or mean aspect.

It is certain he has never betrayed a friend. Roaming for forty years in what Hugh Dalton once described to me as the green-eyed jungle of Westminster, RAB Butler has never shown envy, jealousy, malice or mortification. His faults are part of his mental make-up, his virtues are part of the man that life has made him.

No one yet has penetrated effectively the urbane armour of this man. That is the challenge he presents to us. But before we begin our investigation we can say this of him : that in his candour and his native caution, in his calculation and his charm, in his immense dedication and his dignity, he is a very English man.

GERALD SPARROW.

Brighton, September, 1965.

I

The Adventure Begins

THE SUBJECT of this biography, Richard Austen Butler, known to generations of Englishmen as "RAB", and only very recently, and perhaps superfluously, disguised as Baron Butler of Saffron Walden, is surely one of the most intriguing and fascinating figures of contemporary British politics and recent history.

His career is one of spectacular achievement yet he was twice denied the Premiership. Why?

We have to seek the explanation not only in the long and distinguished record, in the speeches, the debates, and the tortuous struggles of politics; we have to look into the character of this man, probing his heart and mind, his innermost faith, his inherited and acquired opinions, his prejudices, and his methods of combat.

This will not be easy, but it should be worth while. RAB Butler rose with almost unchecked success until he reached the last golden door of number ten Downing Street. Although he was, for twenty years, at the nerve centre of the Tory Party, although he exercised more influence over a longer period than any living Englishman, entry, which, it seemed, was his by right, was denied him.

With the choice of Sir Alec Douglas Home as the temporary leader of the Tory Party in October 1963 the Conservative leadership seemed to have rejected RAB and all he stood for permanently. Yet, within two years, by replacing Sir Alec by Edward Heath, it would seem that the progressive type of liberal-conservativism to which RAB dedicated his career has triumphed in the end and is unlikely to be cast aside.

The drama does not reside in the fact that, on both occasions, when RAB was by-passed for the leadership, he was often deputizing for the outgoing Prime Minister. It arises from his massive achievements over four decades. The Butler Education Act is one of the four great landmarks in the advance of British education. His Penal Reform White Paper is the basis of penal reformation today. He recreated the Tory philosophy immediately after the war, bringing it into a new, intensely competitive, highly mechanized age. He dominated the financial thinking of England in four Budgets. He played a significant role in both Munich and Suez. He made an immensely valuable contribution to the story of India, and he left his imprint on the continuing foreign policy of Britain and the Commonwealth.

And yet, in the last resort, he was turned down, first for a man of equal abilities though far smaller achievements, and, on the second occasion, for a man who, whatever his merits, was a much smaller man if measured by the standards we use in judging our Prime Ministers.

This adds up to high drama. And in this book we shall see the political swords drawn and the daggers being used. For man is an aggressive and acquisitive animal and when it comes to seizing of great power the urbane, even convivial scene of British politics vanishes for a week or more to reveal the naked struggle in which no holds are barred.

What is the criterion by which a biography such as this should be judged? What, exactly, are we setting out to do? Not, I think, to photograph a life. Our job is to paint a portrait. Of course the panorama of this man's life must emerge clearly, but the real test will be: Have we brought our subject to life? So that we feel we know him, understand why he did what he did, how he was able to accomplish so much and yet perhaps lacked some vital fibre for complete success? Animation is our business. The adventure that was his must be shared by us. We have to start out with him on the voyage and walk with him on the journey through the four decades that followed his youth. As we come to the immense strains and challenges that fate presented to him, as we come to the final awful frustration, we must be there, knowing his mind, feeling as he did, making the decisions, living his life.

This is the only way in which we can hope to understand and appreciate the story of RAB Butler. It should not be dull. At times it should be unnervingly dramatic. It is part of the English story, some of it very familiar, but also containing unrevealed chapters, hidden because of the strange shroud of secrecy that, a relic of our feudal past, still drapes the exercise of supreme power in British politics.

In order to embark on this adventure ourselves we have to go back to the beginning. Our roots are always important. But in the case of RAB they were exceptionally strong. His background, his family, his early environment made him the man he was to be. He never changed. Essentially at sixty-three he is what he was at twenty-three and this continuity is revealed perhaps most in his voice which is at once young and fastidious, individual and wholly distinctive, now, as it always was.

The beginning is India in 1902. His father, Sir Montagu Butler, was a distinguished British civil servant, who became Governor of the Central Provinces. Curiously the early background is almost identical to that of Hugh Gaitskell whose father was a civil servant in Burma then administered—quite irrationally—as a part of our Indian Empire. These two men, each of whom has left his mark on British public life, were children of the Raj. And the British Raj in India was based not so much on force—though that existed—as on the absolute assumption of British superiority, collectively and individually. It is a trait that was to come out in RAB discreetly from time to time and forms a tantalizing contrast to his liberal, political philosophy. And the two men had this in common. Hugh Gaitskell was never a Socialist, always a radical; Rab was never a Conservative in the narrow meaning of the term but always a liberal in the broadest sense of that phrase.

I took the trouble to visit the house his father lived in for many years and it was not difficult to recreate the atmosphere —the guard at the gate, the army of sweepers, the men who drew the water, the ponies, the dogs, the household servants, the Ayah who cared for the children; the routine of administration, the "bridge" parties—to get to know the Indians— the sport, shooting and polo and cricket, the short, sparkling winters and the long devastatingly hot summers, with the move to Rawalpindi.

RAB's father, like all the Butlers, could and did invoke much affection and respect from those who knew him. Very recently speaking to a roomful of Elders and Civic dignitaries in Peshawar, I was asked : "Why did not Mr. Butler become your Prime Minister? Why was he stabbed?" It was a Pathan who asked the question—and the Pathans know all about daggers. And, as the meeting ended, the chairman said : "When you see him tell him we remember. We had a regard for his people."

I told him. He smiled that tolerant smile of his. And as he did so I remember reflecting : yes, he can inspire loyalty among those who know him—but he has not let people know him, not the public, not even the Tory Party as a whole.

The life of the British in India and of the upper civil service hierarchy in particular, was a strange life. The Indian Civil Service—the "heaven-born"—were the best paid and the ablest civil service in the Empire. Less than two thousand of them "ran" a country of over three hundred millions of people of more than twenty races and a dozen major languages. From the fair Pushto speaking Pathan in the high north-west to the dark agile Madrasi of the south, from great princes to miserably impoverished peasants, they all were ruled ultimately by the small cadre of English "gentlemen" who formed this great service and who directly were responsible to the Viceroy and so to the Secretary of State and the Emperor in London.

It was not possible for a boy to be born in this background of imperial magnificance without some of the glamour and the glory leaving its mark on him. For although young RAB was soon sent home to school in England, his father, after a spell as Governor on the Isle of Man, was chosen as Master of Pembroke College, Cambridge, where RAB had been an undergraduate. So the family links with the Indian Empire lingered on in talk, in correspondence and later, markedly, in the early political life of RAB himself.

If he acquired any arrogance from his Indian contacts it was quickly lost and replaced by a very firm confidence in the whole Butler family and, of course, in his own abilities. The success of the family in many fields was an inspiration to him.

The family had fairly bloomed with Headmasters since the 18th century. A George Butler was Headmaster of Harrow from 1805 to 1827. Sir Henry Montagu Butler, who died in 1918, was Headmaster of Harrow and Master of Trinity College, Cambridge, a position RAB has inherited nearly fifty years later. Another Butler was Headmaster of Haileybury. The Butlers were linked to the Church as Deans and Canons. One of them, more catholic than other members of the clan, actually went to Oxford *and* Cambridge and, indeed, founded his own College at Oxford, Butlers Hall, which, however, did not survive.

So the other impact on RAB's early life was a strong sense of the importance of academic distinction. To be second-rate intellectually was anathema to this family. All the Butlers had first-class brains or if they hadn't they managed to give the impression they had. In this respect RAB was lucky. He had no need to pretend. His intellectual gifts were exceptional even in this rather awesome family.

RAB did not follow the family trend and go to Harrow. The fees at Marlborough, where he did go, were almost identical and in any case this was not a point that was considered. RAB himself chose Marlborough perhaps because he thought he would be stifled by the terrific Butler presence at Harrow. And there was a link with Marlborough, too. Young Charles Sorley, the poet, later killed in the first World

War, had been to Marlborough and he was a cousin of RAB through his mother. Sorley was the son of the Professor of Moral Philosophy at Cambridge. As we trace the Butler convolutions we see them everywhere, not at the summit of power or wealth, but holding important positions and moving with urbane omniscience through the quiet parlours of the two Universities and the major Public Schools.

RAB did not like Marlborough. Or rather he was not happy there. Perhaps he was never quite juvenile enough to be a schoolboy. But he worked reasonably hard, took to amateur painting and went for long walks on the downs. He made a few well chosen friends. He left with relief and as soon as he set foot in Pembroke College, Cambridge, at the age of eighteen, he started to expand. This was the atmosphere in which he throve. Cambridge immediately claimed her child and, forty-five years later, she called him home. In the interval he took a great part in the English story and became the best known Butler of them all.

I first saw him sitting sprawled on a couch with his friend Geoffrey Lloyd in Lloyd's rooms in Trinity Street. Geoffrey Lloyd, like so many of his contemporaries, had great charm. He devoted much of his time to hunting and the Pitt Club, but there was strength behind the languor. A few years later, as a political candidate—Tory, of course—in Birmingham, he invented "Lloydies", the first political use of cigarette cards, then at their zenith, to tell the lucky voters of the merits of their good-looking young candidate. It was late in the evening and they were sharing a bottle of champagne. RAB was an elegant young man of medium height with fine hands. His eyes were slightly hooded. His nose was strong, if plebeian. He had a firm mouth and jaw. When he spoke he spoke with calculation. One felt the brain behind the conversation. I spoke about the matter I had come to see him on and left them, the rather indolent Lloyd, and young RAB who appeared to have all the gifts, including the most precious gift of all, what we should now call The Knack. For he had fallen in love with Sydney Courtauld, the most attractive and vivacious of the undergraduates then in residence.

Shortly after this, with consummate ease, he became President of the Union to be followed by A. P. Marshall, David Hardman, Patrick Devlin and Michael Ramsey. It was not a negligible vintage and it was a measure of his stature that in it RAB stood out, not head and shoulders above the rest, but notably for his remarkable gifts of concentration, urbanity, charm, when he chose to exert it, and savoir faire.

It is never entirely fair to recall in detail the decisions and activities of public figures when they were young. Youth and indiscretion may go merrily hand in hand. But, in the case of RAB, everything that is revealed points not to irresponsibility but to maturity. And his tenure of office at the Union provides an instructive and sometimes amusing commentary on his character.

The Oxford and Cambridge Union Societies are unique institutions. They hold debates, run on Westminster lines, once a week in term, formerly on a Tuesday, now, usually, on a Thursday. The motions for these debates are chosen by the President as part of his "prerogative". He does not have to consult his committee and does not do so. So the debates during his term of office show the way in which this young man's mind is working.

Elections to the post of President are strenuously contested. RAB beat the brilliant W. L. Perlzweig comfortably by over a hundred votes. Later the author was to have a similar majority over the persistent but unlucky Mr. Perlzweig. It never occurred to me at the time but since I have wondered whether some unrecognized anti-Semitism played its part in these Elections. However this may be, the Elections were conducted with great decorum. The candidates usually left Cambridge on Election Day, going to London to see a play or to Newmarket if there was racing there.

RAB's tutor was worried lest his preoccupation with the Union in an Easter term would interfere with his taking a first in his Tripos for the examination was held at the same

time of the year. RAB was able, by pushing himself to the
limit, to conduct a remarkable term of office and to get his
coveted first in the Honours list.

At his first debate in the Chair the House debated a Motion
which read: "That this House has the highest regard for
rhetoric." Winston Churchill was to be one of the visitors
supporting the Motion. Stanley Baldwin spoke fourth in
opposition. Churchill was prevented from coming and the
fluent and eloquent lawyer, Mitchell Banks, took his place.
When Baldwin got up to speak he said that it had been his
intention to say—pointing to Churchill—"Look at him. He
is the living proof of the danger and delusions of eloquence."
History was to provide an ironic answer to this criticism.
Baldwin went on to suggest that more wars and miseries had
been provoked by rhetoric than by any other human gift. It
was indeed the harlot of the arts.

But when the Union came to vote, two hundred and ninety-
seven members voted for the Motion and two hundred and
ninety-seven voted against. The new President had to give
his casting vote. He gave it—in favour of the Motion—which
was duly carried.

A Motion calling on the Government to "deal with strikes"
did not reach these heights, but another deploring the
"invasion of England by America" was lost after some brilliant
debating.

Oddly enough RAB chose two American Motions during
his term. A Motion urging that "America should join the
League of Nations without delay" was carried by a large
majority, A. P. Marshall and J. W. G. Sparrow scoring as a
supporting team on this occasion. In the twenties it was
regarded as quite in order for Britain, or at least the older
British Universities, to admonish and correct the junior
partners in the world hierarchy who, naturally, had not her
great wisdom and experience. How these kindly rebukes
were received by their targets one can but imagine.

RAB contrived an amusing debate on a Motion urging
undergraduates to devote themselves to the intellectual

pursuit of knowledge and not fritter away their time on journalism, politics and other "elusive entanglements". Again there was a draw in the voting and again the President gave his casting vote for the Motion.

He invited Oswald Mosley to defend the Labour Government in a straight political debate and the man who later was to rally half a million fascists in prewar Britain towered above the other speakers that night, a bird of very brilliant plumage, persuasive, ironic, handsome, one would have said: "This man, one day, must be Prime Minister. . . ."

Finally, at his last debate, RAB opposed with wit and some vehemence a Motion that gloomily declared the emancipation of women to spell the doom of civilization. This was, of course, the typical undergraduate motion tossing the hare into the air, catching it, and tearing it to pieces. It was not intended to be taken seriously, nor was it. Women were not going to be manacled again or veiled again even if the Cambridge Union decided that they should be. The Debate was merely a vehicle for verbal acrobatics—fun. But then, in the twenties, fun was regarded as worth while in itself.

As secretary before becoming President, RAB wrote up the minutes in the Debating Book. His signature followed the same pattern as it does now—the R. A. B. being separated from the "utler". But the restriction in his right hand now causes him to write with the pen sloping inwards and this has made his writing change. Incidentally, he ignores this so successfully that many persons who have met him are quite unaware of it.

The peculiar, "parliamentary" atmosphere of the Union suited RAB. He was in his element here, happy, assured.

In the autumn of 1925 a Cambridge Debating team was invited to visit the eastern universities of the United States and Canada. It was the best "beat". An Oxford team, which included Malcolm MacDonald, were covering the western universities and the Middle-West. This vast area was much more out of touch then than it is now. But our hosts in the east were lively, vivacious, avid for culture, and, as hosts, great fun. It was a memorable outing for three young men embarking on life.

The team consisted of RAB, Archie Marshall and myself. We were complete contrasts. Marshall, who had been in the Navy during the war, was older than either of us. He was a stern non-conformist. When we entered our first New York hotel there was a pretty girl soliciting in the foyer. Marshall was horrified. "In the Old World one expects this kind of thing but I had not expected to find it in the New!" I said it was one world; and RAB gave his curious high-pitched laugh, detached and tolerant, which gave me the impression that at such moments he resembled an experienced manipulator laughing at his own puppets.

I think that perhaps this was one of the happiest periods of RAB's life. He had become engaged to Sydney Courtauld and she came to Southampton to see him off on the Mauretania. She gave him a locket with her photograph inside. He still has it. I watched from the rails of the great ship as they stood there, talking, the young man with the world before him and the girl he loved. From their quiet absorption and devotion I knew even then that this was no transient affair. They were going to be together until death parted them.

Five days later we were steaming into New York. RAB said: "It's not beautiful. It's almost ugly. But it's immensely impressive." At Columbia University we met the immensely public figure of the University President, a namesake of RAB's, whom I recall as a round red apple of a man, very alive, very aware, with a genial aplomb, adroit in conversation, a man whom no one had ever managed to pin down.

And from New York we started our seven-week schedule mainly by train. We had what in those days was called a "drawing room". It was a compartment for four and just held three with their luggage. It was not uncomfortable. All the service was provided by Negroes dressed to look like English butlers. The food was gargantuan but rather tasteless. There was, at first, no liquor. We were in the Prohibition era. This pleased Archie Marshall but had less appeal for RAB and myself.

At the Princeton "prom", a University dance, the girls swarmed in from New York and Washington. The prom started decorously enough. The young men looked incredibly clean and cropped and vigorous and the girls seemed equally clean and cropped and suitably seductive. This went on until around midnight. Then the bubble burst. There were far fewer couples on the floor dancing to the three bands. RAB said: "Where have they gone?" We went to investigate. They were making love in the cars down the great driveways that led to the ball-room. And each couple had a bottle of bootleg gin. The practice was to drink half the bottle and then start doing what came naturally.

This must have been a routine at this time for many of the girls whom one might have expected to be drunk and dishevelled would suddenly sit up in the car, powder their noses and return with their escorts to the dance floor. Occasionally a girl would take a fancy to a man in the band, in which case she insisted on dancing without moving very close to the band, making gestures that seemed to indicate that she would not be adverse from love that night from the object of her predatory affections.

We looked round and RAB said: "Where's Marshall?" He was not with us. Unhappy and disappointed by the drink and the loving he had gone to bed. How fortunate it is that he is not now a Divorce Judge, and how unlucky Stephen Ward was in having this incorruptible man to preside at his trial. . . .

I drank some of the bootleg gin and found it quite drinkable provided one did not sip it. RAB drank very little. He was charming to the young women but even the most lovely —and there were some really beautiful girls there that night— could not slip under his defensive armour. It was absolute. He was in love already.

You cannot spend six weeks in the company of a man night and day without getting to know him quite well. Even very old friends over a long period are seldom kept together for weeks in close proximity and working together as a team. My impressions of RAB began to form quickly and, looking back, I do not think I was mistaken. My first thought was: This is a man who must make his mark. He has everything. Background, influence, looks, good manners, first-class brains, a most formidable combination. He also had a complete awareness of social values and a strong basic ambition. I do not know whether he believed in God but in so far as God could be said to be a Patron of the Tory Party and a good friend of the Butlers, I think he did admit that there was some divinity somewhere. After all, so many Butlers had served God well in His Church and a little reciprocity was only to be expected.

He had a certain streak of rectitude and even non-conformist propriety which he may well have inherited from his mother. It was overlaid by his urbanity and his worldliness but it was there. He had not, I think, at this stage defined the rigid rules by which later he was to play the political game but rules, unwritten rules, there were and these were his code. He would never cheat, he would never—intentionally—be rude, he would never intrigue. He was, as we said in the twenties, a gentleman. Not of course an aristocrat, but a gentleman. We shy away from this term now but still in Africa, in India, in Europe and even in Russia and China, they know exactly what we mean by it.

His mood changed with the way he felt and the success or failure of a debate. He could be detached and even disdainful but as a rule he was warm and friendly, amused, tolerant, often witty, a good companion. I think that secretly he thought Archie Marshall a bore but not by the most elusive suggestion of a word could one have detected this. The only indication was that strange laugh that would ring out unexpectedly and sometimes disconcertingly.

We debated every kind of subject from the NEW WOMAN to the old Adam, from democracy to dictatorship, from love to lust. And RAB was ready to take either side on any question. This did not mean that he did not have his opinion, even his conviction. It was the mode and manner of the day. The young intellectual was supposed to be able to argue both sides of an issue. If he could not do so there was something wrong with his mental equipment. Marshall, of course, felt passionately about nearly everything, so he said, but I had the odd impression that it was RAB who had the most solid convictions forming and not the fat, twinkling little evangelist orator that was Archie Marshall.

Looking back now I find that my first assessment of RAB during the early part of our American invasion may have contained some pointers for the future that lay ahead.

For instance, his apparent flippancy enabling him to speak with equal ease for or against a Motion on the League of Nations. Was this manner carried on into public life where it was wholly inappropriate and was sure to be misunderstood?

The fact that he was a gentleman as opposed to an aristocrat. Was this to explain his unwillingness or inability to cope with the leadership intrigues many years later?

Had he in fact failed to adapt the manners and modes of a fashionable young intellectual of the twenties to the grim, dark, desperate politics of the thirties, the forties and the fifties?

The affection he inspired in his close associates and the indifference and even hostility that he sometimes provoked in those who did not know him, but who would decide his fortunes, was this accounted for by the fact that, even as a very young man, he prized his intellectual independence, and never pretended to be anything but what in fact he was?

As we come to the great hurdles and obstacles of his career these questions will occur to us again and we can then apply them to the actual conditions prevailing. They should bring us nearer to RAB Butler than writers have been able so far to penetrate. If they do not the fault is mine.

We debated at Yale and Princeton but not a Harvard. We went to a number of minor Universities each bursting with newly acquired tradition, and we realized that the American undergraduate was as much a creature of fashion as we were at Cambridge. It was RAB who pointed out that there was one notable distinction and difference. Whereas the American ideal was the "regular fellow", the British ideal, in more sophisticated circles, was the irregular fellow. The American chairman, introducing RAB, would say: "R. A. Butler, known as RAB, a regular fellow. . . ." It was the highest compliment he could pay. But home at Cambridge it was the men who defied rather than the men who complied who were the intellectual heroes.

To some extent RAB complied. He was a Conservative Party man then. He has been now for forty years. He will be always. He was not in my opinion ever a conservative. His mission was to be to turn a Conservative Party into a Progressive Party. And this he did. But all this was accomplished within the framework of party machinery and party loyalty. It was inconceivable that RAB would ever, whatever the provocation or the circumstances, change his political allegiance. Just as Hugh Gaitskell, a radical, tore Socialism out of the Labour movement and made it a mildly radical party, so RAB tore reactionary conservatism out of the Tory Party and made it a liberal party of the people. He really represented the English professional "upper class" who would carry with them millions of the middle classes, the technicians and workmen.

I find a strange similarity in the methods of RAB and Hugh Gaitskell. Both men turned their Party to their own pattern, and both men looked at the Party that they themselves had recreated and found that it was good.

You may say that this represents a sublime arrogance. Most men confronted with a Party that does not adequately represent their own views assume that they must look elsewhere. Not so either of these two men. Both set to work to mould the party to fit in with their own convictions, ideals and aspirations. Both were convinced that they were right, and both, at the height of their power and prestige, were irresistible. But there the similarity ended. Whereas Hugh Gaitskell had to achieve his revolution openly with all the bitterness and acrimony that this entailed, because this is the nature of the Labour Party, RAB was able, over the years, to achieve his drastic changes by working mole-like from within. He was always there at the very centre of Conservative power close to the Premiership, the 1922 Committee, the Conservative Central Office, and the Research Department. It was perhaps inevitable that when, years later, he acquired a London home it should be in Smith Square, so near the nerve-centre of English power politics as represented by the Tory Party Headquarters, Transport House, Parliament, and the other ramifications and tendrils of actively exercised power in Britain and the Commonwealth.

We went on a camping holiday—two days off—in Maine and shot rapids and fished and camped in that wonderful state —Scotland on a grand scale. RAB was reasonably cautious in adventure. I do not think he was a man who courted physical danger. In this I had complete sympathy with him. Marshall of course did not mind. It was all in the hands of Almighty God on whom apparently he relied in matters both great and small.

From Maine we crossed the border into Canada. There was a contrast here which RAB, always the most quickly perceptive of our party, immediately noted. Whereas in Pittsburg we had stayed with a local millionaire and each was given a Negro valet to look after us—who stood behind our chairs at meals—here in Canada they were nearer the simplicity of the great western adventure. Here the debates took on a very down-to-earth tone. Flippancy was not encouraged. Wit, I think, made the audience uncomfortable. The belly laugh was allowable but not the cynical smile. RAB sensed this but did not change his approach unduly. At Montreal after he had toyed with an idea being debated, undecided, it seemed whether to accept or reject it, he eventually stopped his verbal acrobatics and took the Motion into his argument. A young Canadian opposing us got up and seizing the opportunity presented by a pause said: "Do you mean that? Do you really believe it?"

RAB looked at him and I thought that we were going to hear that laugh of his or at least an amused chuckle. It was not so. He looked at his interrupter as if he was something that had crawled out of the woodwork, looked at him with smiling toleration and said: "Yes, I believe it, but perhaps I do not parade my faith as effectively as you do. . . ."

He was very quick at seizing small, fleeting points. I got up to speak. We were all in tails as was the custom—tails and white ties and usually white waistcoats though a fawn or lavender waistcoat was allowable—when one trouser leg remained hitched up. I suppose the incongruity of the immaculate young man and the trouser out of position amused the audience because they laughed. I did not know why they were laughing. RAB pointed to my trousers and whispered: "Say, you must have a word with your tailor about this. . . ." I said the line and it went down very well.

This trick of always being with the situation of the moment remained with RAB all through his political career. He had a lightning response to any novelty, anything unexpected. He was always a dangerous man to heckle. He was already at twenty becoming a complete politician and tactician. He was not eloquent. He had little rhetoric. He spoke too fast, but what he said impelled attention. And at this time he was so young, so confident and so engaging, that it would have been a disagreeable critic who did not capitulate to so compelling a personality.

All good things end far too soon and our American adventure was soon over. The golden American fall—the maples in Canada were unforgettable—bid us farewell. The *Toronto News* did a page of caricatures of our party. Looking at them recently I noticed that though they hit off Archie Marshall and myself completely and effectively, RAB had eluded them. They just could not "get him". He had avoided capture by the cartoonist's pencil. The deep lines, the eye pouches, the look of utter disillusionment that was to give the cartoonists their hold later were not yet there. The English Pimpernel had slipped home.

Back at Southampton, Sydney met RAB. Marshall and I travelled up to London together. We talked about our experiences and quite naturally the conversation turned to RAB. "I don't know what to make of him. Sometimes I feel I know him and then he seems far away in a world of his own. . . ." It was Archie Marshall's verdict. I felt I knew him a little better than this, making allowance for his complexities and apparent contradictions. And we were both quite sure that he had summed us up in the neat, analytical categories of his mind.

Each of us now returned to the path we had chosen. Marshall and myself to the law, RAB to that academic post for which his talents and achievements so obviously fitted him. I am sure that already he had a vision and it was an ambitious one. But immediately ahead of him were two turning points in his life—marriage and the quiet quadrangle period which was to be a prelude to one of the busiest, longest and most varied political careers of our time.

II

Young Man of the Twenties

WHEN RAB had completed his undergraduate life in 1925 the world it seemed was his oyster. He had all those prerequisites that in the twenties were regarded as assuring success in the Tory Party; and an influential, closely-knit family firmly behind him. He was good-looking without being disturbingly handsome, he had first-class brains and a double-first to prove it, and he was a most engaging young man.

The present Chief Clerk of the Union, who was an office boy at the Union in 1924 when RAB was President, gave his impressions of the young Butler recently on a Panorama programme of television. He said that he did not think that RAB was the kind of man to take much notice of a junior clerk. "He was always a little aloof."

Panorama asked me to give my impressions of RAB at the same time and I recalled only his grace and wit and a rhyme attributed to him that was sung at a Conservative ball in Cambridge:

> *Land of Hope and Glory*
> *Mother of the Free,*
> *Keep on voting Tory*
> *Till Eternity. . . .*

I think it may be that both impressions had some validity. I do not think that RAB at this stage had developed the compassion that later lay at the root of his political philosophy. It would have been strange had he done so. The path had, on the whole, been a primrose path. True, he had had to work to the point of complete fatigue and exhaustion to achieve his brilliant degree, but in doing this his ambition drove him on. He had seen remarkably little of the other England where men work for a weekly wage with their hands. But the railway strike and the General Strike, the fantastic depression of the thirties when Britain walked to the edge of Revolution and, not liking what she saw in the abyss, struggled back again, were only just ahead. It was a decade that was to change not only RAB but all his generation. The halcyon days were coming to an end. Even the most insensitive were never to be the same again.

But, in 1925, the magic was still there. The first World War had not really changed the fabric of English society. It had killed nearly half a million young Englishmen. Perhaps because of this a blindness overtook the twenties. The menace of the murder of the Tsar and the Soviet revolution was ignored. The people who ruled England did not want to look back and they refused to look forward. Today was to be enjoyed. There was the transient prosperity of war gratuities and Cambridge, like Oxford, was made more mature, more sophisticated and gayer by the fact that young men who had survived the last years of the great conflict were with us as undergraduates.

RAB, at this time, by no means immune to the dictates of fashion, swam with the current. But he took the steps that his head and his heart dictated. He was offered a Fellowship by Corpus Christi College and he accepted; lecturing on the Third Republic. In 1926 he married Sydney Elizabeth Courtauld, the daughter of the great industrialist, Samuel Courtauld. She was his only daughter. RAB's only brother had been killed in the war, though he had two sisters. As a honeymoon they went round the world.

I met Sydney Courtauld at this time. She was one of the rather rare women who combine feminine attraction with mental activity and ability of a high order. This was a love affair. The fact that the marriage gave RAB complete financial independence did not enter into its motivation. RAB married Sydney because he loved her and that love endured to the end. I may, perhaps, be forgiven for reflecting that he was extremely lucky in love. Today, forty years later, he still is.

He was at Corpus over three years. They represented a backwater in his life to which he always looked back with pleasure. The world was young and gay and fresh and beyond the quadrangle opportunity beckoned.

He mastered his subject of the Third Republic with enthusiasm for he had always had a love of France and French culture. The French political story fascinated him. And Corpus Christi was, as it still is, one of the fascinating smaller Colleges of Cambridge, its first Courtyard, with its splendid array of flower beds, being more attractive than the rectangular austerity of Trinity or the wide grandeur of Kings.

RAB was a good lecturer. His grasp of the subject and his ability to elucidate stood him in good stead. Understanding his subject and its background completely he was able to impart his own knowledge and interest to his young listeners. The standard at Cambridge in lecturing was high. Keynes was emerging as a new force in economic thinking, and the Coles were immensely popular and effective in spreading Socialist thinking in the minds of a new generation of under-graduates and young graduates at Oxford.

An undergraduate who remembers RAB during this period says of him: "I thought at the time that this man could have graced any great position. He could have become a states-man, a Governor, an Ambassador, a Bishop. He had all-round excellence. . . ." And it was that all-round excellence that was to emerge in the busy and sometimes bitter years ahead.

To commemorate his connection with Corpus Christi, RAB and his wife gave the Combination Room of that College a very lovely Directoire Clock. It was the apt and charming gift of the lecturer on the Third Republic.

At this time all young Cambridge Conservatives came under the influence of Sir Geoffrey Butler, RAB's uncle.

Sir Geoffrey Butler occupied a unique position not only in Cambridge but in the wider life of the Tory Party. He was the Conservative scholar and thinker then very much in vogue. He took, as was natural, a particular interest in his brilliant young nephew persuading him to found his Tory faith on those who historically had played a part in creating conservative thinking and in others who had shaped British life and policy. So RAB became immersed in history, in the two Pitts, in Bolingbroke, in Disraeli. It made an academic and intellectual background for his political thinking.

In practical modern politics it never seemed to me that Sir Geoffrey Butler was as great an innovator as his friends declared him to be, but he had a great gift for winning the confidence and friendship of young people. For instance when the great Lord Curzon (who had been by-passed by Stanley Baldwin) came to speak at a Conservative Association dinner run by Patrick Devlin and myself Sir Geoffrey realized that, with the cruelty and reality of youth, we had already "written off" Curzon as a factor in the new Toryism. Very gently he reminded us of this man's great services in India and elsewhere. It was just as well for that night he was taken ill. We took him flowers to his room. He received us with charm, almost with majesty. He was facing death but he was not afraid. The following day he returned to London and in two days he died.

This gift for understanding and guiding the youngest men in the Party made Sir Geoffrey Butler RAB's natural mentor and friend. Unfortunately he died at the age of forty-one in 1929. But by that time RAB was beginning to form his own political philosophy that envisaged a property-owning democracy. This idea, now so much taken for granted, was I think, very much RAB's development of his uncle's historical precedents and rather cautious progressive planning. Once the idea had taken hold it was, of course, a modern development of the ideas with which Lord Randolph Churchill, had he lived, might well have introduced progressive Toryism into British public life forty-five years earlier.

The General Strike of 1926 came as a test for many young politicians. It drove men like Hugh Gaitskell into the Labour Party. Under the influence of the socialist dons of his day Hugh Gaitskell drove a car for the strikers and from that experience his deep feeling for the workers of Britain dates. RAB felt no such impact. He lent his services for a time to the "authorities". But this was the year of his marriage and perhaps we should not expect the desperate political crisis to have aroused in him the compassion and the practical action which it might well have done ten years later.

I have tried to indicate the atmosphere in which the young men of Cambridge lived in the twenties because RAB flourished in this rather unheeding, fashionable world; in his manner of thinking and his mode of speaking, the whole outward and visible signs of the man were to some extent to bear the hall-mark of the twenties. His critics would say he never lost this aspect of his character. Over-detachment, an apparent, though not a real, flippancy, the quiet assumption of an effortless superiority, these were acceptable in the twenties. They were less acceptable in the thirties and in the forties and fifties they became anachronistic. As RAB's story develops we will see this vein of weakness reveal itself from time to time.

There is of course another side to this comment. There is a certain amount of hypocrisy and acting that goes down very well with the conventional British electorate. They seem to expect their political leaders to be a little pompous. The acceptable "image" changes constantly. At the moment the middle-class, red brick, grammar school, slightly kitchen-sink background is very much appreciated in both Labour and Tory circles. RAB was incapable of playing up to this appetite. He was always completely natural. He was never simple and often he was apt to be tortuous, but a humbug he never was.

After his marriage, his wife, Sydney, was perhaps the only person to exercise a great impact on RAB. The Courtaulds were not merely rich English industrialists. They were Huguenots who had settled in England to develop their traditional crafts in the 18th century. And they brought with them their traditional merits. The family were hardworking, God-fearing, intensely aware of social justice—and therefore of injustice—enterprising, completely honest and with abounding energy.

Sydney Courtauld had all these traditional qualities. As long as she lived she was the flame that guided RAB and encouraged him. She believed in his destiny. She believed in his talents and in his star. With such a woman by his side and with the children she gave him a very happy and lively family circle was always there for RAB to retreat into. He kept that circle away from the glare of publicity and controversy. It gave him constant moral support and his young family kept him in touch with a generation that was perhaps further removed from his own than any new generation has been this century.

Sydney Courtauld died in 1954 and a Memorial Service was held at St. Margaret's, Westminster. The whole Butler family and a far wider public realized that RAB had lost a great support and a wonderful influence on which he had greatly relied. Recently he married again. The present Lady Butler (previously married to the late Augustus Courtauld) has that complete devotion and admiration of RAB that this strange man is able to inspire in all those who are close to him.

In 1953 RAB's father's will was published and contained this passage quoted by the press: "My son Richard has expressed to me his desire that, having regard to his circumstances, he does not wish to benefit under my will pecuniarily, but only to receive my Orders, Medals and certain of my chattels and personal effects. I desire to place on record that it is only owing to this expressed wish that I am not including him as one of the participants in my residuary estate on its division on the death of my wife, and desire to express my appreciation of his characteristic generosity."

This generosity was no rich man's solitary whim with RAB as we shall see later when we come to the loan of his country house to Essex University. He was and is genuinely generous in small matters as well as in larger affairs. And that generosity extends to political opponents with whom he has battled on the great arena of British and Imperial politics.

Now, in 1928, the young tiger was poised to pounce and he did so with considerable encouragement from the Circus masters. The Secretary of State for Air, Sir Samuel Hoare, in particular, took a step that was of the greatest importance to RAB. He made him his unpaid private secretary.

A General Election was looming ahead and was to take place in May, 1929, for Mr. Baldwin's Government had run its somewhat smug, uninspiring course, very clearly out of touch with the tremendous unrest in the country of which the Coal Strike had only been one of the outward and visible signs.

Sir Samuel's timely help gave RAB the entrée into politics just before the election. Now he could slip in and out of Westminster at will. He saw all the figures of the period performing. He watched as the Prime Minister answered questions at three o'clock. He heard the last Baldwin Budget. He lunched and often dined in the House listening to the best informed political talk of the day. All this before he had won an election.

RAB was already becoming known to the powers that be. Young Butler was very much a man on whom Ministers and even Prime Ministers had an eye.

But of course, RAB could not fulfil political ambitions unless and until he became a Member of Parliament. So he had to find a Constituency, if possible a Constituency near London, near Cambridge, and with a respectable Conservative majority.

Discreet soundings were made not fifteen miles from Cambridge—and fifteen miles nearer Westminster—at Saffron Walden. It was the heart of rural Essex which is perhaps as near the heart of rural England as one can imagine.

It was an immensely fortunate choice for RAB. Although at times his majority dropped to become almost marginal, although there were tough determined Labour and Liberal minorities, fortunately at first almost equally balanced, Saffron Walden remained true to RAB for thirty-five years, till he himself withdrew. It was so remarkable a marriage be-

tween a man and the people he represented that it bears
much closer inspection. As one takes the London road out of
Cambridge, just after leaving the town one branches off to
the left and fifteen miles farther on the country market town
of Saffron Walden, a Borough of respectable antiquity, greets
the traveller through the rolling Essex arable farming land
ripe in late summer with barley and oats and wheat.

Saffron Walden is the centre of the Constituency and the
Constituency is not an ordinary one. Although RAB held it
without interruption for the whole period of his effective
political career the tradition of East Anglia was not Tory but
radical. If at any time during RAB's long tenure the Liberal
and Labour Parties had combined in Saffron Walden RAB
would have been in jeopardy except in the National Government Election when his majority was abnormally large.

For a right-wing Tory to stand for Saffron Walden would
even today be disastrous. The farmers, the labourers, and the
industrial workers who, apart from the squirearchy, form the
voting population are all for progress. RAB coming to them
as a very young man represented that progressive idea. Perhaps few constituencies in Britain were happier than Saffron
Walden to have a very young candidate who was on the
move.

But RAB had another very powerful motive for seeking to
become the M.P. for Saffron Walden. The southern and
eastern portion of the county was the place chosen by the
Courtaulds to start their great spinning and textile business
and they still have works at Dunmow and at Braintree. The
Courtaulds, for long established here, had done much for the
Essex that supplied their work people. They may have been,
by modern standards, too paternal, but they were, admittedly,
enlightened, benevolent, progressive.

So that RAB was assured of a personal following not only
among the well-to-do and the middle classes and the agricul-
turists but also in the factories and on the factory floors. He
inherited an immense amount of prestige and goodwill from
this Courtauld connection. In the thirty-five years of his ser-

vice as the Member for Saffron Walden he added to this a
body of support for himself on his merits as one of the most
constituency-minded members of Parliament.

RAB might be the great Minister, ex-Directory, in London
but in Saffron Walden anyone could ring his house, Stansted
Hall, and if he was at home, he was quite likely to answer
himself. The people here felt that in RAB they had a friend.
If he was by nature sometimes restrained, even withdrawn,
they liked it that way. They thought it only natural in a man
who carried much responsibility. To the end he always
found time to encourage and thank his supporters. On
October 22nd, 1964, after the election, he wrote his supporters this charming, and unpompous note of thanks:

October 22nd 1964.

"Dear Friend,
     I write to thank you for the part you played in helping to win
the seat for me in this constituency. It was entirely due to the
devoted service of our supporters and our organization that we
kept up the level of our vote in 1959. The Socialist swing was
less here than in most places and our cause triumphed against
a strong attack. We must now keep ready for the next challenge.
     It is most inspiring for my wife and myself to be able to rely
on so many devoted friends and we are constantly grateful to
you.
     I look forward to continuing to serve you as your M.P.
Yours sincerely,
R. A. BUTLER."

To find out what the men and women he had represented
for so long felt about their member I spent many days in
Great Dunmow, Halstead, Saffron Walden, Broxted—where
RAB lived for a time before acquiring Stansted Hall—and the
little villages off the main roads where the old Essex survives
almost unchanged.

A market gardener, a spry, straight man in his mid-forties
told me that his father had been a Liberal. "We always were
Liberal. But I voted for Butler. Why? Well he was as near
a Liberal as one gets these days. And he did things. He didn't

just talk. If he took a matter up he pursued it to the end. They could never unseat him. He was just too good. . . ."

A young apprentice in Courtaulds Dunmow factory struck quite another note. "Count me out," he said, "I would be glad to see the whole lot go. Mr. Butler, the Courtaulds, their friends and relations, they represent something that should be dead—but isn't." I asked him what he meant? "Paternalism. I can help you, my man. We are all in this together. Vote Tory and we'll see you through." I liked the angry young man, but he did not seem to be at all typical.

A successful arable farmer with over five hundred acres told me he voted for RAB because "he really understands agriculture". And when he said this I recalled that Michael Ramsey in the chapter he contributes to the history of the Cambridge Union says that "RAB was apt to make speeches on agriculture". Too earthy a subject perhaps for the modern Church to be bothered with? And he has been making speeches on agriculture ever since. But the speeches did reflect a real knowledge as the farmer said. They were not theoretical. They were practical, informed.

I talked to women young and old and middle-aged about him. Their responses were surprisingly similar. They thought he was so "sensible". Not wise, that was not the operative word. Just sensible so that as long as RAB was there with a finger in the pie or an office in the Cabinet "they" would not do anything too stupid—or dangerous. He inspired this confidence easily and naturally.

The centre of political Tory power in Saffron Walden was and still is the headquarters next to the Conservative Club and enjoying the romantic name of the Old Armoury. It is here that, over a period of nearly four decades, the campaigns were planned, the strategy conceived, the tactics thought out. Every time the seat was contested, though RAB always started favourite in the betting, there was a feeling that it was a very real contest. And this feeling stemmed from the knowledge that unless RAB held the allegiance of the descendants of the old Radicals he was lost.

He held it. And he had not to strain his convictions to do so. They were willing to elect a Tory only if he pursued liberal policies. RAB did just that. He has grown older with Saffron Walden but when he first came to them he was a becoming cavalier.

On May 30th, in the gay weather of an early English summer, RAB at the age of twenty-seven was returned to Parliament as the Member of Parliament for Saffron Walden.

The figures were:

R. A. Butler	(C)	13,561
W. Cash	(LAB)	8,642
A. M. Matthews	(LIB)	8,307

Although this gave RAB a majority of around five thousand it was clear that in an exceptional year the turnover to put either the Labour candidate or the Liberal candidate in would be under three thousand votes. And, in addition, the combined Labour and Liberal vote was more than five thousand above the Tory vote. If Labour were not to put up a candidate what would happen then?

But these speculations were not to prove necessary. The result was taken as it stood. The general verdict in all parties was that one of the most brilliant and promising young men in England had been returned to Parliament by a substantial majority that showed him to be at a very early age an effective and formidable campaigner.

RAB's fortunes were waxing. His star was rising rapidly. He was on his way.

III

Office and India

RAB COULD hardly have entered politics at a more opportune moment. Had 1929 been a year of Conservative victory he might well have been swamped for years in the onrush of a new wave of young Party men, and the scramble of the old guard to return to office and power.

But, unexpectedly, it was Labour who greatly increased their representation at Westminster—from 190 to 288 seats —and were thus able to form a Government. The Liberals still had a very substantial party in the House having fifty-nine members. So the Tory Party had its back to the wall. Its whole philosophy and way of life was being challenged and there were new men at Westminster.

Ramsay MacDonald was Prime Minister with Philip Snowden as his Chancellor. Lord Sankey was Lord Chancellor. Foreign Affairs were in the hands of Arthur Henderson and J. R. Clynes was at the Home Office. Agriculture was looked after by Noel Buxton of the old Liberal family and Sir C. P. Trevelyan was at the Board of Education.

In view of the cry that had been raised—but not by RAB —that Labour could not form a Government, or would be a Government of ignorant nonentities, this formidable team came as a surprise to the Tories and as a reassurance to the public.

Just as F. E. Smith on an earlier occasion had shot into the Tory firmament by a brilliant aggressive maiden speech designed to rally a dispirited Tory Party so RAB was presented with the opportunity of making a very early impact by his first speech. It would not of course contain the fireworks that delighted the House when they listened to "F. E." but by its careful presentation, its reasonableness, its novelty and its over-all persuasiveness might achieve a similar result by different methods.

At this time Private Members day included Wednesday as well as Friday as it does now. The backbencher had twice the chance of being heard and although this cut down Government time it undoubtedly made the House of Commons more what it was intended to be, a vehicle for hearing all its members rather than a tool designed primarily for the implementation of Government business.

Then, as now, the House was a most sophisticated audience. Any suggestion of condescension on the part of a new member damned him—or her—in the eyes of the House. There were no "stars" among the new entry. Let them say what they had to say, and provided they sensed the tradition and manner of the House, they would be given a polite hearing and an appropriate murmur of applause when they sat down.

Now RAB sensed one danger. He had been President of the Union, a brilliant double first, was a protegée of the former Air Minister. He was in fact a marked man, destined for preferment in the Tory hierarchy. He had by marriage acquired great wealth. None of this must reflect itself in any way in his manner to the House. One hint of over-confidence and he was doomed. He made no such mistake.

His manner was quiet—though he could be heard—his delivery, if over rapid, a fault he never cured, was agreeable. He had a sense of humour, not sparkling perhaps but well attuned to the spontaneous smile and chuckle of Westminster.

He chose his subject with great skill. The subject being debated was a motion calling on the Government to prevent injury to British agriculture caused by the dumping of German grain on the British market. It was a subject designed to engender a certain amount of heat and prejudice for the British had not forgiven the Germans for World War I, any more than they have now forgiven them for World War II.

RAB avoided all the obvious points and any suggestion of jingoism. He represented Saffron Walden, the most agricultural of constituencies, he called attention to the wretched housing conditions of some farm labourers in his constituency and the sufferings of the rural unemployed no less than the urban unemployed.

Then he turned to possible cures. He suggested that the old remedies might be out of date. Protection might not be the inevitable or unavoidable answer with all its possibilities of retaliation and inevitable reciprocity.

He called for an International Conference to study world farm commodity prices and a review if necessary of the Gold standard.

Now this suggestion, though made with the decorous tentativeness thought to be suitable to a new Member, was in fact a bold one. It turned the Tory Party agricultural thinking away from the past and suggested possible new lines of approach in the future. But it did more than this. It challenged the whole fiscal policy that had been stoutly maintained for four years by the previous Tory Chancellor of the Exchequer—and the previous Chancellor of the Exchequer who had restored the Gold Standard in 1925 and maintained it with characteristic obstinacy and courage was—Winston Churchill.

The general consensus of opinion among all parties at the time was that Churchill then and there took a gusty dislike to the intrepid newcomer. Churchill's father, Lord Randolph, had been prevented from introducing his Budget which he drew up on two sheets of Club note-paper, and it had been Winston's pride and joy to be a resounding success in the sphere in which he thought his father might well have been remembered. If in fact the whole Churchill-fiscal policy for nearly five years had been based on a fallacy; if that fallacious thinking had contributed to the deplorable situation in which both British agriculture and industry now found itself, if it had been, even in part, responsible for the appallingly high rate of unemployment in England, Scotland, Wales and

Ulster, then indeed one chapter in the Churchill story was a bleak and not a brilliant one.

Churchill had not yet risen to the heights of vision and faith which destiny later was to thrust upon him. He was still very much the tough aristocrat. His personal friends were the hard core of old families who tended to swing the Tory Party their way when it came to a show-down—the Cecils with Lord Salisbury at the head, the Cavendishes with the Duke of Devonshire, a family into which a promising young Tory, Harold Macmillan, married, and the still influential Tory landowners of whom Lord Halifax was a prominent example.

If Churchill had in fact been wrong, if his policy had been ill-conceived and if he had clung to it against the rational arguments of the economists such as Keynes, the brilliant Cambridge don whose influence on RAB was considerable, then Churchill's chances of dominating the Tory Party were reduced. And if this had been done by the first speech of a newcomer to the House then Winston might well feel that it would have been more tactful if RAB had been less controversial.

The Churchills were always capable of animosity. Lord Randolph had told the urbane and conciliatory W. H. Smith "To go back to his damned books". And Churchill now felt resentment at the oblique attack on his record. Perhaps he never quite forgot it, as this book will show when we reach great turning points in RAB's career.

But if RAB had offended an outstanding and powerful figure in the Tory hierarchy he had won much approval. The Conservative Party were as adroit then as they are now. Dispassionate observers in the party councils knew that to shake the Labour majority a new approach was necessary, necessary in the industrial field, necessary in the agricultural sector and essential, perhaps, in realizing the dependence of Britain on closer economic and political relationships with the rest of the world, with Europe and America in particular. The talent-spotters at Party Headquarters made a laconic note that RAB was a man to watch and might be destined for office, perhaps even, one day, for the highest office of all. And the Press, with whom from the start RAB cultivated friendly informal relations, noted the newcomer with approval.

It was not a dynamic entry into the arena; it was a very characteristic one—carefully planned, quietly executed, extremely effective.

In the opinion of many experienced observers the Tory Party had thoroughly deserved their defeat at the Polls. Mr. Baldwin, the Prime Minister, had gone to the country on the slogan of Safety First! It was a slogan well suited to warn a committee of Trustees charged with the investment of private funds—though in fact the old Trustee investments were to prove the most disastrous in the years to come, with the depreciation in the value of money. But it was not a slogan to encourage a great Empire or a great power. It seemed to stress out of all proportion the tenacious conservatism of the Tory Party. What it meant in effect was that Mr. Baldwin, if he had been returned, would have done as little as possible in an era that demanded strong, resolute and daring innovation. So he was not returned to power.

But although Stanley Baldwin was still the leader Neville Chamberlain was now the dynamo in the Tory Party. And Chamberlain realized that there was a lot wrong. What was wrong essentially was that the Tories did not have a modern policy. They still stood, in the public estimation, for King and Country, for Empire and big business, for the Church and the Public House—usually in Britain to be found in close and happy proximity the one to the other.

There was nothing wrong about Empire, King or Country but it was not enough. The Party had to demonstrate effectively that it had vision as well as a gift for the nostalgic cultivation of past glories. It must be a Party that looked forward prepared to suggest modern solutions to modern problems as well as being the traditional party of might, majesty, dominion and power.

Chamberlain saw that the Conservative Central Office was an office dedicated, in the main, to tactics. They were always concerned with how to win immediate political advantage and this consisted largely in attacking Labour policies and in preparing for the next By-Election or General Election. They were not a thinking office. Chamberlain realized the Party needed to think again, to mould entirely new policies based on a cogent and modern philosophy. The strategy and basic conception of Conservatism had to be thought out anew and then explained to the electorate in terms which it could understand.

Chamberlain persuaded Stanley Baldwin to allow the setting-up of the Conservative Research Department in Old Queen Street with a political chairman—the first being Chamberlain, himself, and a permanent paid head. This step was to pay rich dividends in the future and it is pleasant to record today, when only his part in Munich seems to be remembered, that Neville Chamberlain had the foresight and the energy to introduce this novel planning office into the Conservative Party complex.

RAB was immediately attracted to Old Queen Street and became one of its most assiduous supporters contributing notes, papers, memoranda and his personal impact from the start. This was to foreshadow his long and fruitful association as political head of the Research Department so that for twenty years after World War II Butler and his "backroom" boys became legendary in the Tory Party and the country.

And today the Old Queen Street office is dominated by photographs and portraits of RAB whose spirit seems to linger over the place. One hardly notices, yet, that Mr. Edward Heath has been allotted a cubby-hole on the second floor next to the Committee Room.*

At this time though RAB was often at Old Queen Street, and often attending functions in his constituency, he was keeping up a good record of attendance in the House and learning the complicated rules of procedure. He said to a

---

* This paragraph was written just before Edward Heath was elected leader.

friend at this time that the methods and regulations of debate presented no difficulties to him. Perhaps his long training in the Cambridge Union helped him in this. Both the Cambridge and Oxford Union had much the same procedural tradition as the House of Commons, which was of course their pattern. Their attitude to new speakers was almost identical, their response to wit and rhetoric very similar. There was only one small difference. The Unions each had a cross-bench put in when a member of the Royal Family was an undergraduate so that he should not appear to take sides. RAB in fact was immersed in the tune and temper of the House before he entered it and the absorption of the rules was very easy for him.

His speeches at this time were listened to attentively not only by his Tory fellow members but noticeably by the Government Labour Party as well. Perhaps he made less appeal to the Liberals for the fortunes of the Tory Party depended on reverting to a two-party Government of Britain, in fact to strangling the Liberal Party and substituting the Labour Party in its place.

Then came crisis. And it was an economic crisis of the first magnitude. It did not have the horrifying and chaotic results of the American depression but it shook the British economic empire to its foundations. Ramsay MacDonald agreed to negotiate with the Tories on the foundation of a National Government. This was called an act of betrayal from which it took the party years to recover. But at the same time it may well have seemed to MacDonald to be in the best interest of Britain, a patriotic decision overriding party advantage . . .

Neville Chamberlain and Sir Samuel Hoare negotiated the deal on behalf of Mr. Baldwin, and their secret conversations took place not at Conservative Headquarters in Smith Square but in the Research Department offices in Old Queen Street, where there was much less publicity, for the Press had not wholly been alerted to the new importance of Old Queen Street as a Tory stronghold.

The Election came in October 1931. The result was a tidal

wave of all parties who supported the National Government. The Electorate accepted the thesis that this was a national emergency, that a national party alone could save the economy and assure future prosperity. Over five hundred and fifty members returned supported the National Government and only sixty were left to form a most inadequate, but by no means subdued, opposition.

Young Mr. R. A. Butler faced the electors of Saffron Walden again but the Liberals, sensing defeat, did not put up a candidate. And RAB walloped his Labour opponent by 16,000 votes. It was an overwhelming victory, but, of course, it only reflected, perhaps in a rather exaggerated form, the decision and the judgment of the country as a whole.

The National Government tidal wave of popularity affected RAB in two ways. It greatly decreased his chances of distinguishing himself on the floor of the House for the competition from the Government side—many of whom had to sit on the Opposition side of the House for there was no room for them behind their leaders—was much greater and RAB was but one of a number of rising satellites.

But in another direction the National Government victory led RAB to his first important office. Sir Samuel Hoare, his patron, had noted with delight that his protégé had already made his mark when the Conservative Party was in opposition, and on returning to Westminster, Sir Samuel was given the important post of Secretary of State for India. In his turn he made RAB his Parliamentary Private Secretary. There could hardly have been a more suitable or fortunate appointment for RAB who had been versed in Indian affairs since his schoolboy days by his family who had played so large a part on the Indian stage. RAB himself had toured India extensively and carefully though privately since his Cambridge days. His quick, alert, inquiring mind had already formed certain conclusions as to the eventual outcome of the Anglo-Indian relationship. And those conclusions were not at all those which Winston Churchill harboured and which that great man was to advance with so much tenacity and skill both at this time and after World War II.

But, of course, at this stage in his career, RAB did not formulate policy. He might be becoming a key man in Old Queen Street. He might be regarded as a bright light of the New Toryism. But the decisions were not in his hands. It was his task to further and explain policies made by others. And this he did most effectively. His loyalty to his party and to the party leaders was seen to be characteristic of him at this time. It remained one of his most prominent traits throughout his long career. As we shall see there were times to come when emphatic and determined protest might have benefited Britain—and incidentally assured RAB the leadership of Britain. But he was not that kind of man. He worked quietly, diligently from within. Never extravagantly, rebelliously from without.

In the first onrush of measures to restore financial stability to Britain, RAB, under his new chief, applied himself to the long and extraordinary story of the British in India, to the resurgent nationalism typified by a strange, little Indian lawyer—Mahatma Gandhi—a leader of genius, and to the path that Britain was to follow in shaping her Imperial destiny and perhaps bringing her role as an Empire to a satisfactory end. How could that be done? RAB had no doubt that the eventual answer was a great expansion of the Commonwealth of free nations. And if this totally altered the nature of the Commonwealth? Change was acceptable. It was inevitable. It was part of the dynamics of politics, and of RAB's own philosophy.

RAB was not yet thirty and no one, not even this sanguine young man himself, expected that he would be made a Minister before his thirtieth birthday, but this is what was to happen and the story of his appointment is so characteristic of that combination of nepotism and realistic exercise of power by individual ministers that it is worth recording.

The Tories found themselves by far the most powerful

party in the National Government. The electorate, told that there was a crisis of the first magnitude, as indeed there was, had turned to the Tory Party as the most experienced and in some directions the most down-to-earth party in the State. Lloyd George split the Liberal Party by his formation of the National Liberal Group backed by his massive funds largely accumulated by the award of honours during his Premiership. The Labour members under MacDonald were presumably National Labour members and the opposition were independent Labour and Liberal members. The Tories were in theory National Conservatives but they soon started to operate as if the Tory Party, in all its glory, had been returned at the Polls. Perhaps this was not such a refutable presumption as it seemed to be.

A fight developed at Westminster as to the best measures that should be taken to cure the economic ills of Britain in a permanent sense. We could not afford to limp along any longer crippled by an adverse trade balance and a frightening unemployment situation. That way disaster and possibly revolution lay.

Faced with this situation the larger part of the Tory leadership decided to scrap the free trade basis of the economy. A bill was introduced into the House and passed into Law— the Import Duties Bill. It was frankly protectionist, and in this same year of 1932 the Government sent a strong delegation to negotiate new Commonwealth trade and Preference agreements in Ottawa.

There was uproar among those Liberals who had been assured by Lloyd George that their backing for the National Government would not entail any breaking of their fundamental Liberal faith. This seemed to be a genuine and possible assurance. If the National Government was to be truly national presumably the balance would be held somewhere between the Labour Prime Minister and his Tory supporters —and in that balance the Liberals should have occupied a central and even a commanding position.

Some Liberals of principle resigned, including the dedicated and visionary Marquess of Lothian who was Sir Samuel Hoare's Under-Secretary of State of India. This left Sir Samuel in a very unenviable position. The Government of India Bill which was to bring a large measure of self-government and enfranchisement to the Indian sub-continent was a measure of the utmost complexity.

Here was a Bill that sought to transfer in instalments a framework of democratic self-government to the Indian masses. But those masses consisted of many races, at least half a dozen major languages, and two major religions which traditionally were intolerant of each other to the point of madness.

Moreover by no means all the Conservative members agreed with "constitutional reform" in India. They argued that "India" had been a creation of the British Raj. That before the British there had been no India, merely a collection of feuding, fighting states interrupted by long tyrannies such as those of the Mogul Emperors. They said that every act of social justice, every act of religious toleration, every act of peaceful security had been directly due to the strong, paternal and entirely incorruptible rule of the British who, up to now, had not doubted their destiny as masters of the whole of India and Burma. They predicted that once this authority was corroded, as in this India Act, or eventually replaced by self-government as it was to be by the independence act of 1947, there would be bloodshed and terror in India and that India as we knew it and as we had made it would cease to exist.

These right-wing "reactionaries" were not as far out in their prophecies of woe as their critics liked to think. Independence was followed by the murder of nearly a million innocent men, women and children. India had to be split into two weaker states, India and Pakistan, and the remaining "India" was so weak that a comparatively small force of Chinese regulars was able in 1963 to cross the Indian border and inflict on the Indian Army a humiliating defeat such as they had never suffered in the days when British and

Indian officers controlled together the magnificent Indian Army.

Leading this critical Tory minority, though now outside the Party Whip, a great and lonely wolf at Westminster, was Winston Churchill; he thundered against the Bill at all its stages just as he was later to denounce the Independence Act as an act of handing over our Indian Empire "to the Brahmins"—a picturesque but quite inaccurate description of the Indian Congress Party.

So though in principle there was ample Government support for the India Act on which Sir Samuel Hoare had set his heart, though its provisions had been painfully hammered out over several years with Indian leaders, the Bill was in fact explosive as well as extremely intricate. Its multiplicity of clauses demanded complete mastery if it was to be piloted successfully through the House of Commons and receive the assent of the House of Lords. And it should perhaps be recalled that, at this time, during the last two years of a Government's life, the House of Lords by its powers to delay legislation, in fact exercised a veto on any Bill* with which they were not satisfied or which they simply disapproved of or disliked.

Sir Samuel Hoare could hardly have been faced with a graver situation than was caused by the departure of Lord Lothian. The complexity of the proposed Bill arose from the complexity of India herself. The Indian Empire was divided into British India with eleven major provinces each of which was already exercising a degree of autonomy and self-government, five minor provinces including the capital Delhi, the seat of the Viceroy, five hundred and sixty-two Indian Princely States varying from small territories governed by tribal chiefs to great countries such as Hydrabad, Kashmir, Mysore, and Travancore, and states that fell between these two divisions and were grouped into Agencies such as Gujarat and Rajputana. Then there were very special areas such as the tribal areas of the North-West Frontier, politically

* Except money bills.

vital, peopled by a fair Aryan people who spoke Pushtu and were, in certain respects, far removed in background and outlook from their neighbours.

On top of this great and bewildering complex of races, languages, customs and power rode the two greatest religions of India, Hinduism which was a caste system as well as a religion, and Islam, a strong, vigorous proselytizing faith—and the followers of Islam hated their Hindu neighbours collectively with an undying hatred, which was heartily reciprocated by the Hindus. This burning but latent antagonism had been kept dormant for over a century—the period of absolute British domination in India—and for over a century before that during which British influence and power had constantly waxed.

The British domination of India rested on an Army of some sixty thousand men, mostly Indian, and an elite corps of civil servants normally under two thousand in strength. The judiciary also played an important role, as did the foreign trading communities.

How was it that the Tory Pary had decided to introduce Home Rule for India gradually instead of leaving well alone? The answer lay in the concerted advice of those who knew India best and this included the advice of such men as RAB's father and uncle, both of whom had had long and distinguished records of service in India as Governors. With the rise of overt Indian nationalism it was realized that the highly intelligent educated Indian was determined to share and eventually to control his country's destiny and the Tory Party, much to its credit, came down on the side of reform and freedom resisting the very real temptation to continue government by forceful persuasion indefinitely.

Sir Samuel Hoare, looking around for possible replacements for Lord Lothian, had no doubt that in his Parliamentary Private Secretary he had the ideal man. He needed a man with a mind that could be applied exclusively and analytically to the manifold and diverse problems of the Bill. He needed an advanced member of the Tory ranks who was acceptable to the great middle-of-the-road following at Westminster and in the country constituencies. And, himself a first-class brain, he favoured a man, however young, with mental powers to match his own.

RAB's background of intimate family connexion with India told greatly in his favour and the fact that he had already demonstrated a mastery of the subject as Parliamentary Private Secretary. And then, of course, as so often in British politics, there was the personal touch which the enemies of the establishment called nepotism. Sir Geoffrey Butler had been one of Sir Samuel's closest political friends and advisers, and Sir Geoffrey had been quite sure that RAB could tackle any political problem however complex.

Even so it was not easy. Baldwin hummed and hawed. Was there not a rather older, more experienced man available? The Party were not enthusiastic it seemed in promoting RAB as quickly as this. Let the young man wait a bit. Wait and see. Sir Samuel dealt with this opposition in a delightfully oblique but effective manner. He sent Mr. Baldwin the very latest drafts of the Bill asking for his detailed comments and ideas. Mr. Baldwin had an ingrained dislike of all "foreign affairs". They quite frankly bored him.

He capitulated. RAB, at twenty-nine was "in". A Minister in charge of one of the greatest and most controversial Statutes ever to be passed by the British Parliament.

On this occasion the instinct that sometimes seems to haunt the Tory hierarchy to this day, leading them to appoint the wrong man at the wrong time was defeated. In spite of gloomy predictions that RAB would not be up to the immense task that now fell on him—during an illness of his chief he carried the whole burden—he came out triumphantly. He was wise, firm, conciliatory, completely master of his subject.

He kept Churchill at bay, he kept the main bulk of Tory opinion in the House and in the country happy. He had excellent relations both with the Indian Princes and with the new political leaders of India.

The Bill of over three hundred and fifty clauses, considering its debatable nature and the innumerable opportunities it gave to delaying tactics, had a remarkably smooth passage. The Committee stage was prolonged, but then it had to be. The Lords' amendments were dealt with and in some measure adopted. When the Bill was published in January, 1935, and finally became law, it was a major measure with which the name of R. A. Butler was linked to an extent at least equal to that of Sir Samuel Hoare. And this was just, for RAB had not only done much of the spade work. He had, more than anyone else, been responsible for the success of the entire operation.

The conduct of this great undertaking by RAB was not cleverness, diligence and applied power alone. The Bill reflected his inner convictions. He was, as I have already mentioned, essentially a liberal. He genuinely believed in change as inevitable and in progress as desirable. It was in this appetite for change that he differed so markedly from the typical Tory of the day.

A hazard occurred just before the India Bill was completed. Ramsay MacDonald ceased to be Prime Minister and he was succeeded by Mr. Stanley Baldwin. Baldwin moved Sir Samuel Hoare to the Foreign Office and moved the former Foreign Secretary, Sir John Simon, to the Exchequer. The Marquess of Zetland became Secretary of State for India. Now Lord Zetland had not had the opportunity of becoming familiar at first hand with the immense plethora of problems and their solutions that made up the India Act. So his Under-Secretary, more than ever, was the man really in charge.

RAB welcomed responsibility. He had complete confidence in his own ability to grapple with any political question, and for years now he had lived with the great political field that was our Indian Empire. It could already be said of him by a Tory backbencher that he knew more about India than any living Englishman. The comment of the old judge to the young Mr. Bethell, then a junior barrister: "As always, Mr. Bethell, you completely understand the matter . . ." could certainly be applied to RAB at this time. As he was later to say of himself—somewhat surprisingly—referring to his job as Chancellor—"the honourable gentleman should realize that I am on top of my job."

Of course, the background and the connexions had been a great help. The Butler Governors, the ubiquitous and lively Sir Geoffrey who twinkled at Westminster after being returned as one of the members for Cambridge University, Sir Samuel Hoare, who had taken the young man under his wing, even the phlegmatic Mr. Baldwin, who had warned RAB against becoming an intellectual on his visit to Cambridge, they all helped. But RAB, it can be fairly said, at this stage, owed his growing reputation, at home and abroad, to one fact above all else. He owed it to the fact that he was a first-rate man.

In grasp of a subject, in tact, in loyalty, in vision, he had few equals. The golden but fitful sun of power was shining for him and he walked confidently forward, well prepared to meet whatever the future might hold.

IV

Path to Munich

ENTRENCHED, it seemed, at the India Office, RAB could survey the entire political scene and calculate his chances of becoming a Cabinet Minister in the not too distant future. He had completely mastered the complicated affairs with which his office dealt from day to day. India, it was clear, was on the road to independence and it gave RAB personal satisfaction that he should be the member of his family to take a part in that historic voyage.

He was highly regarded by the main body of Conservative opinion, including the 1922 Committee, a body we shall hear more of in this book. True, he had made some major enemies, or rather some powerful Tories had taken a dislike to him. These included that lonely eagle Winston Churchill and the Cecil family, Lord Salisbury in particular.

The clash with Churchill had arisen out of RAB's new ideas on an economic policy entailing criticism of the Gold Standard, Churchill's extravagant child* The lack of enthusiasm of the Cecil family for RAB was partly political principle, as when the late Lord Salisbury sided with Churchill over the India Bill, and both men privately portrayed RAB as a

* Lord Boothby, Raconteur Plenipotentiary of Britain, recently defended Churchill against charges that the Gold Standard was his favourite fiscal child. "That policy was decided by the Governor of the Bank, Mr. Montagu Norman, Baldwin, and Snowden before he took office as Chancellor of the Exchequer.

"I subsequently became Sir Winston's parliamentary private secretary and I know he never liked it.

"He once said to me characteristically after a conference on the Treasury: I wish they were admirals or generals. I can speak their language and I can sink them if necessary. But when I am talking to bankers and economists, after a while they begin to talk Persian, and then they sink me instead."

dangerous appeaser. And partly it arose from accident, the
fluctuations of office. When Anthony Eden resigned as
Foreign Secretary in February, 1938, his Under-Secretary,
Lord Cranborne, the member for South Dorset, resigned with
him. The admitted reason for these resignations was a complete and irrevocable disapproval of the Foreign Policy carried on over the head of the Foreign Secretary by Neville
Chamberlain who had succeeded Baldwin as Prime Minister
in 1937. RAB Butler stepped into the vacated office of Under-
Secretary of State for Foreign Affairs, thus making it quite
clear that he agreed with the Prime Minister's policy—or—as
some critics quickly said, was more keen on office than on
principle.

We shall deal with the great divisions, passions and situations that led to Munich later. It is enough here to indicate
that today the retired Lord Butler of Saffron Walden takes
the view that Chamberlain, in the circumstances, was right;
while, much later, over Suez, while admiring the courage of
Sir Anthony Eden, he thinks he lacked judgment at this
juncture and, on the whole, was wrong. These are the two
life and death matters we will test RAB's character by before
we come to his most constructive periods as Minister of
Education and as Chancellor and before we come to the
strange events whereby first Harold Macmillan, then Sir Alec
Douglas Home, were able to seize the Premiership, ousting
RAB from what appeared to be his rightful reward, until it
was too late and he had retired to the inviting academic
shadows of Cambridge once more.

When from the India Office RAB reviewed the political
scene, what were his reactions? He was never excitable or
over sanguine but he had the right to believe that nothing
except an act of God could stop him. Saffron Walden was
becoming an increasingly enthusiastic ally. True, his overwhelming majority of sixteen thousand dropped to ten thousand during Mr. Baldwin's Premiership, but this was still a
fine majority. Later it went down to around five thousand,
a third of its former glory, but RAB had a personal following

in the division, utterly devoted and loyal, of perhaps two thousand men and women, many of them active workers in his cause. So he expected to hold Saffron Walden to the end, which he did.

How much did the distrust and veiled hostility of such families as the Cecils and the Churchills count? I think RAB underestimated them. In the day-to-day conduct of Government they hardly counted at all, but they always had access to number 10 Downing Street. They were, until 1965, always near the centre of power politics in Britain. Having no say over minor appointments, when it came to choosing the party leader, the actual or potential Prime Minister, they made themselves felt. That they were able to do this was the result of the mystical process which, until 1965, the Tory Party adopted whereby the Party leader "emerged", a kind of immaculate conception, that was treated with becoming reverence, it being considered very bad form to inquire who the parents were. RAB was a son of a civil service family who, on the whole, had been promoted on merit. He found it difficult to realize that merit could be over-ridden in the most important choice of all.

Perhaps he inherited another strong trait from those Butlers who had made such urbane and excellent Governors of great territories in India. The tradition never to resign and never to complain. Both attributes were excellent, indeed indispensable, to a civil servant. His not to question why but to soldier on, doing his best within the terms of reference laid down by his political masters.

But RAB now was one of those political masters and to them the public applies a more rigorous code of behaviour. They expect their political leaders to resign if they do not agree. They expect them to complain and take the public with them if things are going wrong, if the destiny of Britain —as opposed to the fortunes of a particular political party— are being jeopardized. Was RAB to stand up to this test? The supreme character test of political crises? Or did his loyalty to the Conservative Party, which no one has ever questioned, override his other loyalties? Was he over-fond of office as office? Did he dread the wilderness? Was he so absorbed and happy in the daily game and excitement of Westminster that he did not want ever, for whatever reason, to leave it? These are the questions we are now approaching, and the answers, of course, will measure the weight and value of RAB Butler in the scales not only of Westminster, but of England.

The foreign scene was gradually taking a new and sinister shape. In Germany an odd-looking little man with appallingly bad breath but with a streak of fanatical madness akin to genius had imposed his will on the German tribes. The German people had gone back to their old war-gods and were conducting their fantastic war-rites on an ever-increasing scale of grandeur and of menace. In Italy Mussolini had spearheaded a fascist revolution and from the Baltic to the southern Mediterranean the underlying decencies of democracy, the kind of world RAB Butler understood and which he represented, had been ruthlessly discarded.

So the seas were stormy and the undercurrents treacherous in 1936. But RAB had still no reason to doubt his own ability to ride the storm. His judgment of his contemporaries was not harsh. He liked Stanley Baldwin and the terrible neglect of Britain's security, of which Baldwin as Premier was guilty, made little impression on him. But then at the time this was the general trend. Only Churchill thundered his warnings and he was alone, a distrusted turncoat in the opinion of many both at Westminster and in the country.

So RAB could count himself an "in" man. He stood for the new Tory thinking that favoured progress, increased educational facilities, a reformed Empire, moderate and flexible fiscal policies, a house-owning democracy—and peace, peace first and last, peace almost at any price. To a man as sophisticated as RAB war seem the ultimate, incalculable, irrational horror that politicians and statesmen were intended to avoid. The bomb, the shell, poisonous gas, the bayonet, could these really be the ultimate argument in 1936? If they were in danger of becoming so it was obviously the duty of political leaders to exert themselves to the utmost to avoid this madness.

Appeasement? What did that mean? It meant, literally, to pacify. It indicated any action towards peace. It was the policy of peaceful persuasion. It was the triumph of the mind over the mad urgings of ambition and the lust for conquest. No one who knew him would have expected RAB to throw in his lot except with those who most obviously were striving to reach an accord with the new powers in Europe. He had a sense of history. He knew something of the culture of Germany and of the far older and more diverse culture of Rome. He could not believe that it was impossible to reach an understanding with Britain's potential enemies. So, later, we shall see him closely allied to Neville Chamberlain, becoming one of his most effective supporters both in the House and in the country.

RAB had still one more step to take before he reached the upper echelons where real power lay at Westminster. He was still a very junior Minister. He was perhaps leading the younger Tory group except for Anthony Eden who was older and one step ahead of him in the political preferment stakes.

The Baldwin era came to an end in May, 1937. Baldwin received an earldom and retired. Neville Chamberlain, for long the driving power behind the scenes, took over as Premier. He made RAB Parliamentary Secretary to the Ministry of Labour. This might have been regarded as a demotion. It was certainly calculated to abate any jealousy that might have been aroused by RAB's very early appointment as Under-Secretary in the India Office.

RAB made no complaint, and started to learn his new job. He had no chance of playing any major role for Ernest Brown, the Minister, was a strong, extrovert character, outspoken and respected. If there was any limelight going Mr. Brown saw to it that it was turned on him. The Press forgot about RAB for a while. They were not to forget him for long.

There is no doubt that this post, though it was out of the political highlight, served RAB well. Up to now he had been

identified with India and had had no experience of a
domestic department. Under Ernest Brown he saw just how
such a Department should be and could be run. And he
started to acquire skill and knowledge in the extremely difficult field of labour relations that were to stand him in good
stead later. Moreover, RAB had through his marriage
acquired an intimate knowledge of one great business, the
textile firm of Courtaulds, whose directors looked upon him
as extremely shrewd and wise in business. RAB's academic
background is so strong, and recurs in his story with the
inevitability of Greek drama. This may be the reason why his
considerable financial acumen was not more noted at this
time. Later, when he became Chancellor, this acquired skill
was to reveal itself.

When, in 1938, Sir Anthony Eden and Lord Cranbourne
resigned from the Foreign Office, Neville Chamberlain
replaced Lord Cranbourne with RAB and Lord Halifax took
over the now vital portfolio of Foreign Affairs. This was a
turning point in RAB's career. If Eden was right to resign,
then it could be argued that RAB was wrong to support
Chamberlain by accepting the second post in the Foreign
Office. If Chamberlain was right, then, of course, RAB was
right, too.

We can only form a judgment if we follow the sequence of
events as they occurred and the part that RAB played in
them.

The hard core of the nightmarish situation in Europe
really centred around one's estimate of the character and
intentions of Adolf Hitler. Was he, as Churchill declared,
preparing avidly for war? Or was he still capable of reason?
A visionary whose real quarrel was with Communism and
not with Europe and certainly not with Britain? Certainly
reports from Berlin were not encouraging. Sir Nevile
Henderson, our very able and imperturbable Ambassador,
drew an extraordinary picture of Hitler. A demoniac,
dynamic man often hysterical to the point of madness. The
British Government must have known exactly what the

German Führer was like. But events, though they moved fast enough, were absorbing and consuming. As each fresh crisis arose the Prime Minister, his Foreign Secretary, and RAB, himself, were caught up in the maelstrom and tackled the ever-changing scene as best they could. The Prime Minister had a great belief in his own powers of persuasion and was apt to intervene whenever matters became critical. RAB was used to explain to the House what was going on.

It is not, I think, fair to judge these men as one would statesmen who had ample time to reflect. They had no time. They were constantly confronted with new and alarming situations to which they had swiftly to react. They were creatures of the great turbulence caused by the most dreadful European revolution of all time—the angry, arrogant rise of the two great fascist dictatorships.

Britain, as a democratic state and Empire, was at a great disadvantage. The dictators had to consult no one. They could act with lightning speed, and they had done so ever since in 1935 Mussolini had defied world opinion, the British Navy, and the League of Nations, to storm into Ethiopia and capture it as a new prize in his rapidly expanding African Empire.

The invasion and conquest of Ethiopia by the Italians set a precedent. If they could indulge in naked aggression against a sovereign state, and transport thousands of troops and equipment through the British-controlled Suez Canal, the dictators must have argued that they could get away with anything. Britain gave refuge to Hailé Selassie, the tough, resilient little Lion of Judah. Before the storm blew itself out many more heads of State were to seek refuge in London, and it is to the credit of the Foreign Office team that they were all made welcome. London began to play its role of a sanctuary in the drama that was unfolding.

The attack on Ethiopia revealed another point of menace. How strong was the Italian Navy? Was the Mediterranean really as Mussolini claimed "mare nostrum".

Churchill continued to flash the red light in the House of

Commons and it was RAB's job to counter the effect of his speeches. But in fact the House was not taking Churchill seriously at this time although his sincerity, his vehemence, and his matchless oratory still drew the members into the Chamber. The House remembered his reactionary attitude towards the India Bill, and his brave but ineffective intervention in the Abdication crisis. All but a few of the more thoughtful members had written Churchill off. He had had his day. He was no longer "in touch".

Hitler, not Mussolini, was always the man to watch. When he marched into the Sudetenland and reunited the Sudeten Deutsch with the Third Reich he could have been stopped by swift Anglo-French action. But was there a moral case for stopping him? These people were, for the most part, Germans. They desperately wanted to rejoin the motherland. The German troops were welcomed with carefully encouraged but nonetheless real enthusiasm. The British Government made no effective counter-move. Nor did the French who could have acted immediately with the Treaty sanction to support them.

Now the drama had begun in earnest. Hitler cast his predatory eye towards Czechoslovakia and Poland. Chamberlain refused to believe that he would court war by these tremendous invasions.

The Chamberlain-Halifax-Butler team must get all the praise and all the blame for the months that led up to war. The great debate that raged week after week in the House of Commons was made more bitter by the fortunes of the Spanish Civil War. The legitimate Government of Spain was being attacked in a civil war of great horror by the Fascist General Franco and his Italian supporters. In this war the Chamberlain attitude was that His Majesty's Government was neutral. But, in fact, neutrality played into Franco's hands. It allowed the Italians and the Germans to aid him while the Spanish Government received no aid except that represented by some devoted individual volunteers from many nations. If, as in fact happened, the fascist creed and ideology was firmly planted in Europe for thirty years in Spain, outlasting the regimes of Germany and Italy, then Chamberlain, Halifax and RAB must take part of the responsibility.

On the other side of the scale, the Government did achieve their Anglo-Italian Agreement of April 16, 1938. At the time, perhaps, it seemed worth while, but very soon the rush of events were to show how worthless it was. Those who witnessed the historic debates in the House remember the Labour members tearing into the attack on RAB day after day and the detached coolness with which he met the onslaught. Always in command of his brief, always courteous, he was a most valuable member of the triumvirate of the Prime Minister and his two Foreign Office chiefs. Of course, the fact that the Secretary of State was in the House of Lords greatly increased the importance of RAB's work in the Commons. He was, in many ways, an essential member of the team, perhaps in relation to the House of Commons its most vital link. Certainly the Labour Party attacked him as if the policies were *his* policies. This was inevitable. The fact was that they were policies that had his full support.

Once more the defence of the agreement arrived at fell on RAB. He did his work with extraordinary skill, showing patience, restraint, complete grasp of his subject. To attack him must have been frustrating, for nothing, it seemed, could shake his composure or his conviction. The fury of the Opposition broke all over him and he was still there, cool, never stung into indiscretion, using to the utmost the fact that the responsibility was the Government's, not the Opposition's, and stating that the Government alone knew all the facts.

Was, he, at this time, as his severest critic declared, merely in the position of a lawyer who, regardless of his personal opinion, defends his client? In this case the Government? Or was he moved by a deep conviction that the Government was right? If the first was the true interpretation RAB becomes a much smaller man. If the second is correct he increases in stature. There seems to be a danger in applying the simplification of an "either or" to politicians engaged in heated and grave controversy. The record seems to show that RAB was genuinely convinced that the Munich policy was right both in its ultimate objective of peace and in its very important subsidiary advantages of gaining time for military preparation and Imperial unity. But from day to day he was out in the fight. To ask a fighting soldier what his principles are may sometimes be out-of-place. He is too busy to attend to you. And so, one feels, it was with RAB. But there is considerable evidence that, whereas the Prime Minister was convinced that he could bring it off, succeed in the whole project of securing a peaceful solution, RAB more realistic, less emotionally involved, was deeply concerned with the buying of time.

This was not an argument that he could advance in the House. It would have been taken as proof that the Government distrusted and suspected the dictators with whom they were negotiating. It would have torpedoed Chamberlain's chances of winning peace. But it was a view that RAB stressed privately. It is also a view that fits in very well with his mental make-up. He always looked ahead. However immersed he was in controversy, however stormy the debate and heated the argument, he always had this capacity for looking into the future. And he had one more invaluable asset. After the most gruelling session in the House, defending the Government policies, he could always throw off the cares of office as soon as the House rose. He could retreat, unscathed and imperturbable, into the happiness of his family circle. He was at the very height of his mental and physical powers at this time. Though later he was to achieve far greater influence and more important office there is no period in his career when his outstanding abilities were more clearly revealed. Chamberlain and Halifax might well have been sunk without RAB. RAB at this time appeared to be unsinkable.

There was, of course, drama in the story. When Neville

RAB partners his wife at a Conservative Agents' Ball held in October, 1963; possibly less polished a performer than on the floor of the House but enthusiastic none the less.

RAB with Quintin Hogg, then Viscount Hailsham, at the fateful
Conservative Party Conference, held in October, 1963. Mr. Hogg
flashed briefly in the Tory pan, then faded. . . .

RAB photographed in the rose garden, where in the world of
fashion is to be found a welcome, if fleeting, respite from the
increasing burdens of Cabinet office.

Chamberlain, in many ways the typical decent British business man complete with Homburg and umbrella, was on his way to meet Hitler in his stronghold, the German crowds cheered him and the cheers were heard by the dictator himself. According to some eye witnesses he did not like that. What most offended him was that large sections of the crowds that lined the route were clapping their hands instead of giving the Nazi salute. He need not have worried. It would be many years before Germany was to hear this degenerate, democratic gesture of applause again.

The triumvirate Chamberlain, Halifax, RAB, stood out at this critical time, partly because the other members of the Cabinet who held essential posts were not men of the kind who make much public impact. Hore-Belisha, the brilliant Minister of Defence, was an exception. But one could not expect the public—or the cartoonists—to wax enthusiastic about Sir John Simon, Sir John Anderson, Sir Thomas Inskip, Duff-Cooper, Kingsley Wood or Lord Stanhope. The most that could be said of them was that they were an able if unexciting team. So the Prime Minister and his two Foreign Office henchmen carried the burden of the day. Theirs the glory if they won. Theirs the blame if they lost.

And there was one very promising Tory who did not go along with the Chamberlain-Halifax-RAB axis at all—Harold Macmillan. When sanctions against Italy were abandoned and it became clear that a deal with Italy was to be the objective of the Baldwin Government, in 1936 Harold Macmillan defied a three-line whip and voted for the Labour censure motion that "His Majesty's Government by their lack of a resolute and straightforward foreign policy have lowered the prestige of the country, weakened the League of Nations, imperilled peace, and thereby forfeited the confidence of the House".

This was a most daring and courageous act of defiance. And it could well be argued that just as, over the much later Suez crisis, RAB was right and Macmillan was wrong, so now on the road that led to Munich RAB was wrong and

Macmillan was right. But there was one big difference. The
coming of Churchill was to sweep the anti-Munich men back
into favour. RAB over Suez was to have the benefit of no such
helpful tidal wave. The men of Suez were to pull the strings
for many years to come—and RAB was not forgiven.

Macmillan carried his revolt to the point of resigning from
the Government Whip and taking the position of an independent Conservative Member. This was a very bold step.
His letter to the Prime Minister was received most coldly.
Baldwin wrote:

> My dear Macmillan,
>   I have received the letter telling me that you feel unable any
> longer to receive the National Government Whip. I regret the
> decision you have thought it necessary to take.
> Yours sincerely
STANLEY BALDWIN.

Macmillan then was lined up in the Churchill camp. He
was a powerful ally, for he represented a younger generation
of Tories and he had first-rate abilities. RAB, watching events,
must have felt that Macmillan had made a blunder of the
first magnitude, but the choice of when to resign and when
not to resign is one of the perpetual puzzles of politics. The
only answer seems to be that RAB's policy, which seemed to
be never to resign, is not the one that reaps the highest
reward. Probably the test is first did the man resign on a
point of principle, in itself important? Did he passionately
believe he was right? And, politics being the science of
success, was he vindicated by events? We might add, did his
friends and colleagues forgive him or did they hold it against
him in perpetuity?

These being all the factors involved, Harold Macmillan
was brave and bold in his decision. It is, one feels, a decision
that RAB would not have taken. It may well be that RAB
had the weakness of identifying too closely the interests of
the Tory Party with the interests of England. It may even be
that by his nature, always as much a civil servant as a politician, he regarded his loyalty to the team he was working

with as of paramount importance. However this may be, Harold Macmillan was carving out a path for himself as a tough, able Tory who could not be swept along with a tide. The impression got round, as early as this, that the two men, obviously ascending stars in the Tory firmament, were opposites by nature—Macmillan bold, decisive, vain, immensely able. RAB, dedicated, urbane, cautious, somewhat calculating. It may have been a superficial judgment, but it stuck. Butler's part in the negotiations that led to Munich are only understandable if we know something of his chief, Lord Halifax. This Yorkshire aristocrat, born to great wealth and position, was one of the least self-seeking of politicians. He had nevertheless made a success of that most challenging of all great posts in Imperial Britain—he had been an outstanding Viceroy of India. Certainly he did not want to become Foreign Secretary. He thought that Eden should never have resigned and he took up the post with considerable reluctance.

The very fact that he did not understand the full reason for Eden's resignation suggests that at this time he was not really familiar with the fast-developing pattern of Europe. But he was a tenacious learner. He quietly realized that, in RAB, the Government had a valuable asset and he left far more to RAB than it is usual for a Minister to leave to his Under-Secretary.

Prime Ministers are notoriously apt to interfere in foreign affairs. Lloyd George did it, Churchill, of necessity, revelled in it, Macmillan certainly was guilty of it, as is Harold Wilson. It may be unavoidable so closely interlinked, these days, have overall policy and foreign policy become. Who, for instance, can separate the interplay on policies and interests that the United Nations, the International Monetary Fund and the defence of Britain, have one on the other? Who can say, precisely: this is an overall question of policy for the Prime Minister, and this, on the other hand, is exclusively a Foreign Office matter?

Certainly Chamberlain interfered in Foreign Affairs. And

he used a close confidant, Sir Horace Wilson, as his messenger
and reporter on Foreign Affairs at home, giving him a room
at number ten. This was altogether objectionable. One can
imagine Lord Curzon's ironic wrath if such an unofficial post
had been created when he added lustre to the post of Foreign
Secretary. There was no doubt that RAB disliked the Wilson
prowling commission, but as his chief did nothing about it, it
was beyond RAB's power to make effective protest. In any
case the work overlapped and RAB was too busy to become
upset by minor matters. He believed that Chamberlain was
right. Halifax believed that, too. It was enough. The three
men worked together in accord.

Chamberlain, Halifax and their able lieutenant made the
best prodigious efforts to secure peace. It was all of no avail.
It became sickeningly clear that Hitler was only interested in
negotiation if by it he could get without loss the prizes of war.
If and when the fruits of blackmail stopped he would go to
war confident that nothing could frustrate or stop him. The
seizure of the whole of Czechoslovakia was followed by the
invasion of Poland and that called for the British ultimatum
to Germany.

The policy of Chamberlain and Halifax was in ruins and
it is a tribute to the sincerity that the public attributed to their
efforts that the Government did not crash there and then.
Chamberlain carried on but obviously his days were num-
bered. When he had to go it was RAB, the diligent Under-
Secretary, who negotiated with the Labour Leaders as to
whether they would join a Coalition Government under
Chamberlain. The answer was: NO. It must be Halifax or
Churchill. Lord Halifax was appalled at the idea that he
might be forced into the position of being Britain's war
leader, a post for which his reflective and scholarly approach
ill-fitted him. He realized that it must be Churchill whose
active, grasping mind, great powers of oratory, indefatigible
energy and deep knowledge of the art and science of war
made him outstanding as a potential leader of Britain in the
appalling years of struggle that lay ahead.

Looking back on this tragic period, the prelude to war, one is appalled by the large part that individual opinion and prejudice played in the approach, the moves, and the result. Chamberlain never got anywhere near understanding the kind of man Hitler was. And when Hitler and Halifax met they clearly moved in different worlds. RAB had not to conduct meetings at the top and so was apt to get his personal impressions second-hand. But in any case, he brought his typically liberal and gentlemanly approach to this problem of what to do about the most appalling political thugs and gangsters who had ever enslaved a great nation. Only Churchill understood the kind of men we were up against. How it came about that he had this intuition as to evil as well as good we cannot say, but had it he did. And the men of Munich lacked it entirely.

Perhaps of the trio RAB was the least misled. He watched the military preparations being made, not nearly as urgently as the times required. He saw that the great Dominions were ranging themselves on Britain's side. And he saw that opinion in the United States, though still determined to keep America out of "the European War", was turning, in sympathy at least, to Britain and her allies, a trend which the large German population of the States was powerless to stop.

RAB's judgment of his contemporaries was not always as shrewd as one would have expected this to be. In his estimation Stanley Baldwin and Lord Halifax stood out as exceptional politicians who attracted him very much. But events were to prove that Baldwin, however attractive his personality, was a disastrous Prime Minister, allowing England to stray to the edge of revolution at home, and refusing to recognize any of the danger lights abroad which resulted in a neglect of Britain's defences that might well have proved fatal. Similarly the career of Lord Halifax at the Foreign Office was not really the resounding success that his admirers would have us believe. He was often woolly, deceived, and at times, inflexible. Probably both men appealed to RAB as men and the fact that he liked them

induced him to think of them as politically much more
effective than they were. RAB was attracted to reflective,
scholarly men who appealed to the academic side of his
complex character. The human dynamos held much less
attraction for him.

There is no doubt that RAB reached a new stature during
these gruelling months. Suddenly he was young no longer.
He was mature and very serious. The Parliamentary battle
had taken its toll. He greatly needed rest. With the advent
of Churchill he was not sure that he would be in the Government at all. But Churchill was too wise to drop the man who
had moved so near to the new core of Tory thinking and
who had such a large following among the new technocrats,
and the younger generation who now would be the armies
of Britain.

When war came RAB was sure that the Government, in
spite of failure, had followed the right path. We might have
had a great war a year earlier and lost it if a less conciliatory
policy had been followed. If that estimate is correct then
indeed the men of Munich, and RAB not least of them,
performed a public service.

On September 1, following the German invasion of Poland,
an ultimatum was handed to Hitler from the British Government. This was ignored. A final ultimatum, emphatic in its
terms, was delivered early on Sunday morning, September 3.
Unless the Germans called off their Polish venture the British
Government would consider itself at war with the German
Government forthwith.

RAB never left the Foreign Office during this crisis. He
waited for the reply that might reprieve Europe—and
humanity. It did not come. He walked across the road to
tell the Prime Minister that there was no reply. Shortly
afterwards the Prime Minister went on the air to tell the
people of Britain that they were at war with the German
Reich. Almost as soon as the Prime Minister had finished
speaking the first air raid warning sounded. It was a sound
to which Londoners were to become only too familiar in the

dangerous and tragic years ahead. But this was a false alarm.

In one sense the policies of Chamberlain and his faithful lieutenant had crashed around them. It was only too easy to say now that the dictators had never had any intention of stopping their aggression, that their aim had always been world conquest. Perhaps it had, but Hitler, at any rate, viewed a war with Britain as a disaster to his own diplomacy. It was not going to make any real difference, of course, but how much better, how much more suitable it would have been if the great Anglo-Saxon races had been allies and friends.

Churchill did not say: "I told you so." He was soon back at the Admiralty, too busy for recrimination.

Although there were many, perhaps the majority, who thought that all appeasement had been a mistake, there were others, at least equally well informed and responsible, who said that, by buying time, Chamberlain had enabled the British Army to have at least basic equipment for a modern war, that it had been possible to bring into the conflict with Britain the members of the Commonwealth as a united and resolute force, that the United States had seen that the British rulers had indeed sought peace and pursued it before taking up arms; and that the Royal Air Force, small, but superbly manned and equipped, had been placed on a war footing.

Apart from these very practical arguments in favour of "Munich" it may perhaps be said that many millions of men and women of all parties, faiths and trades were assured and strengthened by the extraordinary exertions of the British Government to avert war which it regarded not as heroic and holding glittering prizes but as the last resort when opposing the increasing madness of a megalomaniac with a frightful dream of a master race ruling a world of slaves.

An interesting side-light on possible alignments within the Government in June, 1940, was given recently by Mr. Bjorn Prytz, formerly Swedish Minister in London, during a broadcast in Sweden on September 8, 1965.

Mr. Prytz said that Mr. Butler, then Under-Secretary of State under Lord Halifax at the Foreign Office had assured him that "die-hards like Churchill" would not be allowed to dictate British Foreign policy, and that no opportunity would be missed of securing a compromise peace.

Mr. Prytz said that their talk was interrupted by RAB being called to Lord Halifax who sent him back to assure the Minister that "common sense, not bravado" would dictate British Foreign policy.

As RAB has pointed out all this happened a very long time ago. A fair comment seems to be that the Swedes, who were determined to follow their policy of profitable neutrality, were being assured that the Foreign Office in Britain was not swayed by passion or war hysteria.

The conversation took place on June 17—the day France capitulated. It was reported by Mr. Prytz in a telegram to his Government. The publication of this telegram was for years suppressed.

It may well be that Churchill resented the "open mind" on peace negotiations (said to have been initiated in great detail at this time by Hitler—German colonies in Africa were to be restored, India governed by a German-British co-dominium according to the proposals) which was attributed to Halifax, Simon, Hoare, and RAB.

The following month, on July 4, 1940, Churchill issued to all Departments an extraordinary document under his own signature. The statement said:

NOTE.—Mr. Prytz was not a career diplomat. He was closely concerned with Swedish industry and Big Business. He was regarded as one of the ablest and most forthright envoys in London at this time. A man of pungent and persuasive personality, he has now retired to live in Portugal.

The former Rumanian Minister in London, Dr. V. V. Tilea, who was instructed by his Government to sound the British Government on peace proposals, has now stated that RAB, after consulting Lord Halifax, stated that complete withdrawal of German troops from all conquered territories would be necessary before negotiations started.

Moreover, Lord Birkenhead has pointed out that there is evidence that Churchill himself at the time had not entirely excluded the possibility of a negotiated peace.

"The Prime Minister expects all His Majesty's subjects in high places to set an example of steadiness and resolution."

The innuendo of all this appears to be that RAB may once again have incurred the Churchillian displeasure.

RAB's feelings during the period of false calm that preceded the unleashing of the Nazi blitzkrieg in the West were shared by many of his countrymen.

With the dreadful slaughter and hideous aftermath of the First World War long forgotten, it is easy, after twenty-five years, to condemn the so-called "Men of Munich". Many and varied were the motives that inspired those who continued to counsel conciliation even after hostilities had begun. Many motives were high-minded, some were less worthy. It is to the undying credit of Churchill that when all seemed lost, when brave men everywhere might doubt the possibility of continuing the struggle, the stout-hearted warrior rallied the nation with these words:

> "What has happened in France makes no difference to our actions and purpose. We have become the sole champions now in arms to defend the world cause. We shall defend our Island Home and with the British Empire we shall fight on, unconquerable, until the curse of Hitler is lifted from the brows of mankind."

The radio carried this message to millions, and it quite literally inspired the ordinary people of Britain with the inflexible determination to stand fast; death *was* after all to be preferred to servitude and dishonour.

In 1940, RAB might feel that, in the long run, the British people would say that, though he had failed, he had tried, and that the attempt to avert World War II, pursued with great tenacity and courage, was some measure of his stature as a politician. The public were beginning to have a respect, almost an affection for this detached, cool man.

He was no longer the successful shooting star of the Tory firmament. He was securing for himself a place in the fabric of British life. He was becoming a Statesman.

TLB/1812—C*

V

Revolution in Education

THE DISTASTE which Hitler felt at the idea of being at war with Britain and the inability of the allied forces to invade Germany led to the first quiescent months of the war. But, with the invasion of Holland, Belgium and Norway, the war flared into action. It was seen that a national Government was a dire and immediate necessity. Mr. Amery used an historic phrase in the House of Commons saying to Mr. Chamberlain: "In the name of God: go!" He went, not without the respect and admiration of his closest colleagues.

The choice of Premier lay between Lord Halifax, the Foreign Secretary, and Winston Churchill. There was a strange confrontation and it was clear that whereas Lord Halifax was not willing to grasp power Winston Churchill was. With the prayers of England, her Commonwealth and the free world, Churchill took over his gigantic task.

It was thought that his first step would be to "purge the Government of the appeasers". But he was not a man to be impressed or deluded by political clap-trap or slogans. He retained Lord Halifax at the Foreign Office until sending him, in February, 1941, to Washington which had become overnight the most vital British diplomatic mission. And RAB was retained as Under-Secretary until July, 1941.

This meant that, for over a year, he was working first under Lord Halifax, then under Sir Anthony Eden, the new Foreign Secretary, and it meant that in the final months of this association the triumvirate of Halifax in Washington and Eden and Butler in Whitehall were very close to one another and could supply at a moment's notice Churchill's demands to have accurate and complete information on all phases of Anglo-American relationships. Later his direct exchange of letters with the President made this less necessary.

RAB had never been busier. Eden often had to make trips abroad. Legitimate Governments in exile were flying into London, all extremely touchy, though grateful for the sanctuary London provided. The head of the Free French was the outstanding émigré and he contrived to carry on a running quarrel with Churchill himself, no mean accomplishment considering the circumstances. But RAB—perhaps because he spoke really excellent French and understood every nuance of the language—managed to maintain the friendliest relations with General de Gaulle, as he did with the Poles, the Dutch, the Norwegians, the Czechs and the other Governments evicted by Hitler.

It was not a spectacular period. The Press reported little of RAB's daily work, for there were events abroad that overshadowed the smooth working of the Foreign Office, but it was a fruitful period.

In July, 1941, Churchill reshuffled his Government and RAB left the Foreign Office. He did not say like General MacArthur on a famous occasion: "I shall return." But he had this much in mind.

He was offered the Presidency of the Board of Education. This meant that he would take little or no part in the prosecution of the war which was Churchill's only concern.

It was not an appointment that excited much comment, though one or two of the more prescient newspapers commented that the appointment was appropriate bringing a man of academic distinction, whose family had long links with education at all levels, to an office that might reshape the pattern of young Britain after the war.

When Winston Churchill made RAB the offer of a post abroad or the Board of Education at home in his administration, there was never any doubt in RAB's mind which he would choose. He did not want one of the great diplomatic posts which, in times of crisis, are sometimes held by politicians outside the diplomatic service. The practice might be admissible in posts such as Moscow and Washington in order to maintain at the highest level our relationship with our most important allies, but, on the whole, these posts were adequately filled by the Ambassadors themselves. If RAB had accepted such a post he would have made a career mistake. It would have been taken at Westminster as a sign that he could, at least for the time being, be written off, and it would have been very difficult for him to rejoin the race without losing his position.

Nor, more importantly, did he think that he could serve his country better abroad than at home. To Churchill the offer of the overlordship of education in time of war was not an accolade. RAB would not be concerned with war direction and that was, quite rightly, the only matter with which the new Prime Minister was concerned. But to RAB it was a golden opportunity. He might have been trained for this very post. His first-class scholastic honours, his academic family background, his period as a don at Cambridge teaching—it all seemed to pave the way for the appointment. He realized that education in Britain was in a state of flux, that the great changes that were needed and were pending demanded expert direction and immense drive to put them on the Statute Book.

The time to do this work was not in the chaos of post-war reconstruction but now so that, when Victory came, and this was the presumption on which somewhat illogically the whole Cabinet worked, education could move ahead swiftly and with assurance into a new age in which science had outstripped the humanities, and brains were going to win their rewards, if backed by character, without the hazards of nepotism.

In the immense task which RAB undertook he had the support of one of the finest educationists of the day, James Chuter Ede. The two men understood one another and worked together as a team, Chuter Ede preserving his independence of judgment, RAB benefiting greatly from the fact that Chuter Ede had all his life been connected with the National Union of Teachers. In order to commemorate the outstanding contribution of Chuter Ede to the cause of education the N.U.T. instituted the Chuter Ede Lectures; the idea being that each year a public figure would lecture on education from the point of view of Society as a whole. The Lecture was not to be delivered by anyone currently engaged in educational reform. It was to sustain the highest level of general assessment.

It is not surprising that the inaugural lecture was delivered by RAB in the Assembly Hall, Hamilton House, on Thursday, March 22, 1962. Chuter Ede was present and the much respected James Griffiths was in the chair.

In the opinion of many who have followed his career and read all his speeches, RAB never presented a subject with more clarity and force than he did developing the theme of education in this lecture, and one might add with more humour and insight. He was speaking to a highly intelligent and largely expert audience but his theme was one that all could follow.

In introducing RAB, James Griffiths said that on entering the House as a new Member a friend had said of him: "Watch that man. He can make you believe you are receiving a gift when he says, 'The answer is in the negative.'"

Griffiths made the very good point that most of the major educational revolutions had come during or just after a period of intense crisis. He cited the Balfour Act after the Boer War, the Fisher Act after the First World War and the Butler-Ede Act in the midst of the Second World War. There seemed to be a connection between the struggle of a nation to survive and the determination to assure the enlightenment of its people.

"It is as if during the crisis the nation suddenly realizes how prodigally wasteful we are of the gifts and talents of our children and decides to make amends and to create a system of national education that will be worthy of our people and adequate to the needs of the nation. . . ."

James Griffiths as chairman struck exactly the right note. This was to be an impartial comprehensive survey and RAB took his cue skilfully. This is how "the Secretary of State for the Home Department" advanced his argument: "I am very proud to have been asked to give the first Chuter Ede Lecture.

"Mr. Ede and I worked very happily together in the main reforms of the Education Act, 1944. These were the reorganization of education, the reform of the Dual System and the overhauling of local government in the sphere of education. Mr. Ede is, in my view, a very worthy object of the honour you have done him, both for his association with the National Union of Teachers and for his outstanding contributions to the cause of education in this country.

"He was first appointed Parliamentary Secretary to the Board of Education in May, 1940—Britain's "finest hour". He was invited by Sir Winston Churchill to accept promotion, in the course of his political career, as Parliamentary Secretary to the Ministry of War Transport, two years later in 1942. It was typical of Chuter Ede that he declined Sir Winston's offer—and remained to help me and the cause of education.

"I should like to make two points about Mr. Ede—one personal and one political. We share close ties with Corpus Christi College, Cambridge, where he was an undergraduate and I a don, though not at the same time—otherwise he might be a better man. And, incidentally, Sir Will Spens, whose name is well known in education, was later Master.

"Secondly, although we are, and have been, political opponents and he has kept me up as late as any other member of the Opposition, we are educational allies. The 1944 Act was a true child of the war-time Coalition spirit. When I look back on that period I am reminded of the other great personalities involved—Cardinal Hinsley, Dr. William Temple, Sir Granville Ram, and not least the able and efficient and devoted civil servants of the period—Sir Maurice Holmes, Sir Robert Wood and others.

"Looking through my notes of those days, it is interesting to find that Sir Robert Martin was asking for a 75 per cent grant for the Church Schools in the early 1940s. Cardinal Hinsley was asking for very much more. When he wrote his letter to *The Times* early in 1941, Sir Winston Churchill sent for me and drew my attention to it. He said I was dealing with a master and that I must not get the Government involved in the sort of disputes that had taken place in 1902. It must be remembered that this was at the very outset of Sir Winston's career. He jumped into it with the utmost gusto and it left an indelible impression of friction and difficulty in his mind. I have a note of May 25, 1943, which runs as follows:

"It is interesting to reflect that, politically, the Nonconformists are now going to receive satisfaction 40 years after their anxieties and tribulations over the Balfour Act of 1902—thanks to the concession that a Head Teacher in a Church of England School, which assimilates itself to use by the local Council, shall be appointed by that Council. This means that Nonconformist children can thrive in a non-Churchy atmosphere."

"That satisfied him:

"At the same time we satisfy the Church people by reserving special teachers to give Denominational teaching to those children who desire it."

"I go on to describe what we did equally for the Roman Catholics.

"Sir Frederick Mander was my great teacher at that time and on one occasion he took me aside to inform me—I was a younger man 20 years ago—that I would be unable to sustain a series of public meetings in the country if I did not take lessons from him. I did take lessons from him and I was able to sustain a series of public meetings in the country. He was always quite firm that if the N.U.T. were to expect reform of the Dual System which was due so much to the mediation of William Temple, then they must have the kernel of their own green book included in the

Bill, namely a statutory re-definition of the different stages
of education and free secondary education for all, at least.
Those of you who look back to those days of education reform
will remember that there were two green books—one I
inherited when I took over the Ministry, which was a source
of great controversy at the time; the other a sager-looking
document which was produced by the National Union of
Teachers. I use 'sage' in the colour sense. This sage book
of the National Union of Teachers demanded a statutory
re-definition of the different stages of education and free
secondary education for all, at least.

"The negotiation of the Religious Settlement, the history
of which will be written one day, I feel sure, derived from
William Temple's realization that it was impossible to bring
into anything like a sound and modern condition the
hundreds of dilapidated Church Schools. He therefore
grasped at the proposal made by Mr. Chuter Ede and myself
for a controlled school—which I think has proved a pretty
successful experiment—coupled with the option of the aided
school. The then Bishop of Chichester, Dr. Bell, was the
advocate of the aided school in which he said the children
would be Church members.

"Both Dr. Temple and Sir Winston Churchill were
fascinated by the agreed syllabuses of religious teaching,
and the latter asked me whether I was starting a new State
religion like Zoroaster. I was able to take him through the
syllabus, much to his edification and satisfaction.

"Looking back, I think we did the right thing by introducing compulsory religious teaching. As I shall be saying
before I conclude, however, I do not think the content of
this education has had sufficient influence on the morals and
behaviour of children of our day. In fact, it is not only in
the sphere of religious education and morals, but on the
whole question of what a national system of education may
be expected to achieve, that I shall be expressing some
thoughts in the latter part of this lecture.

"Meanwhile, let us run over some of the physical achievements and describe how we are facing up to them in this hour and day. I can not only report progress but also philosophize a bit about each—Reorganization, Teacher Supply, Continuing Education, Technical Advance, and so forth.

"I remember that my first service to the cause of education was in 1927, when I served on the Dunmow District Sub-Committee. We were responsible for recommendations in regard to teachers—for their morals and everything else to do with them—for the upkeep of the schools. We had no proper secretarial assistance and of course the work was entirely voluntary, very long and difficult.

"It is interesting to compare these little District Committees with their wide powers, their anxieties and problems about unsuitable head teachers, their devotion to detail—such as the colouring of a wall in some lonely rural school—with the final massive divisional executives suggested by Sir Granville Ram, the draftsman of the Education Bill. It is remarkable to recall now, so many years later, how much this great craftsman influenced the final form and wording of the Act. In fact, the two Ministers barely recognized their child when they had sent it to 'Woolworths'—namely the Parliamentary Counsel—to be dressed up. When one goes to look at the up-to-date offices on the Divisional Executive as well as the County level or the Borough level, one realizes how much administration in education has come into its own. I want to counter that a little in this lecture.

"If I had been speaking before an audience of the N.U.T. 20 years ago, the chief interest would have centred on the reorganization of the schools, and we must remember that today. The White Paper of 1943 was based on the Hadow and Spens Reports published respectively in 1926 and 1938. After the White Paper came the Norwood Report, which recommended the tripartite system of grammar, technical and modern secondary schools.

"The Bill took account of these reports, but wisely—I think, as we see today, very wisely—did not tie development down to the tripartite system but enacted that secondary education should be organized according to the age, ability and aptitude of the pupils. To achieve this objective, reorganization clearly had to have the first priority. And, in achieving it, how important it is to have a variety of secondary experiment today such as we are getting under the various authorities.

"Realizing the backlog from the Hadow Report, published in 1926, I said at the time that a generation would pass before the Bill could be fully implemented—and this chimes in, Mr. Chairman, with something you said in your opening remarks. Now, more than 30 years after Hadow, and almost 20 years since the Education Bill was conceived and thought out, the Crowther Report restates and reaffirms the objectives of the Act with its recommendations for raising the compulsory school (leaving) age to 16 and its references to further education, to which I shall return.

"As for reorganization, the position is that only 1 in 25 children of secondary age is still at an all-age school compared with 1 in 4 in 1947. All-age schools have been reduced in number from 8,755 in that year to just over 1,000 in 1961. The proportion of all senior pupils who are in all-age schools is now 3½ per cent. Three-quarters of all the building needed to complete the reorganization is now in hand. This stems from the 1958 White Paper (Cmnd.604) 'Secondary Education for All'.

"This proposed a £300 million school building programme designed to bring existing secondary schools up to modern standards, to complete reorganization and to meet the needs of the new housing areas. In spite of the economic stringency of the time we look forward to the completion of reorganization within a span of 25 years after the passage of the Act.

"I suggest that school building has been one of the most remarkable features of post-war Britain, both for the amount of new school building and for the quality of the architectural design achieved at a reduced cost in real terms. If other Departments would copy this, and if other buildings would copy it, I think we would make a great deal more progress in some of our social building.

"Now I may be asked why all this has taken so long. In my view, looking back on it—and it is given to few people, 20 years after, to criticise their own Act—the reason is that we did not foresee two things when we planned and drafted the Education Bill.

"We did not foresee the growth in the child population nor did we forecast accurately the immense shifting of population and the growth of new housing estates.

"This in itself was one of the reasons why the grant for the Churches has had to be raised recently from 50 to 75 per cent, and why education estimates have achieved their gigantic proportions. Nor in my view can we afford to be too optimistic at the present time.

"The N.U.T. document 'Investment for National Survival' reminds us that the problem of the post-war bulge is ever with us. The idea that we shall return to a normal state of affairs and a falling birth rate is not correct. As is clearly brought out in that document, and in the supplement to it, the age of marriage is falling, more people are getting married and having larger families.

"The view is expressed there that, if this trend continues over the next 20 years, the number of children born each year, which has been about 750,000 in recent years, seems certain to go up to 850,000 and will probably go to one million. This means that more teachers and school places will be needed each year because of the population growth alone.

"When we add to the need of catering for increased child population the necessity to reduce the size of classes—the problem that was foremost in my time 20 years ago—the need for extensive teacher training and almost unlimited further education, we realize the magnitude of the task before us.

"At this stage, after mentioning the progress of reorganization, I want to say a word about teacher supply. To cope with the continuing rise in the number of children at school and to bring down the size of all classes to 40 in primary, and 30 in secondary schools by 1970—which will be quite a long time after the passage of the Act—we shall need a very substantial increase in teachers, the main pressure in this decade being on the infant and primary schools. To meet these demands a big expansion of the training colleges is being undertaken.

"A six-year programme to double the number of training college places is now in hand, and I hope myself that university expansion—which in this generation is unrivalled, will also provide more teachers. Even so, the supply of teachers is likely to remain a serious problem for at least the next decade.

"Here again we can see the effects of the trend towards earlier marriage. We cannot expect more than a few years' service from our young women teachers after they leave college. We must do all we can to attract older people from other walks of life and to persuade married women to return to teaching when their family responsibilities allow them to do so. We need these older people, not only to build up the size of the teacher force, but also for the valuable qualities of maturity and responsibility which they can bring to the schools. The schools themselves can help in this policy by making older teachers welcome and by providing opportunities for those who can only give part of their time.

"This may disturb many well-defined, old-fashioned routines and make the schools' daily life more difficult to organize. But it is really no more than enlightened self-interest for the schools to adapt themselves ahead to this changing situation.

"Now it will also be necessary for the schools to adopt a variety of technical methods. I see in the audience one or two representatives of what I call visual aids and other methods of possible future teaching and I can only express my horror at the thought of what we may have to face in the future in this respect by quoting an amusing development in Missouri described in Mr. John Vaizey's recent book, 'The Economics of Education', to which I shall be referring later. Here is his description of a school in Missouri:

"At another school I visited in St. Joseph, Missouri, a Roman Catholic nun, Mother Theresa, had managed to record an enormous number of lessons on tape which were played on a control panel (a 'console') which had replaced the teacher's desk. The children were individually 'plugged-in' (as she eloquently put it) to a tape devised for their age and ability——"

"She had copied the Butler-Ede Act—age, ability and aptitude was adapted to the teaching:

"and in front of them were books in which they wrote what the tape told them to write. At times they were required to be vocal: as the nun glided about, adjusting ear-phones, changing tapes and sharpening pencils, the class occasionally cried into the silence 'Hail Mary' or they wrote down the three reasons why the English people were anxious to welcome the Armada which was to rescue them from the heretical tyrant, Elizabeth Tudor."

"I hope that this description of what our education may come to in the years ahead is an exaggerated one, but it leads me on to what I have to say about teachers, which is that we shall have to supplement the force, whatever strides we make, in teacher training or training colleges or anything else through the old Act by technical aids.

"I said it would take a generation to carry out the 1944 Act—and thank God I had the foresight to say it, because I have already shown you that in reorganization we are running just about up to time.

"Subject to the immensely increased burden of a larger child population and new housing estates, we are now running well up to time in relation to the objective of providing a free reorganized secondary education for all within 30 years or so after the Act was passed.

"Now the very baldness of that statement shows how far we have to go with other objectives. I have particularly in mind the provision for continuing education. I want to say this: it is a great disappointment to me—and here I speak as present Home Secretary as much as a former Minister of Education—that we have not been able to bring into effect the provisions of the Act for continued part-time education of all young people not still at school.

"One of the things that troubled me most when we were framing the Act was that nine out of ten children left school at 14 at that time, and that was, generally speaking, the end of their education. We set out to remedy this by raising the school-leaving age in two stages, to 15 and later to 16, and by writing into the Act provision for county colleges which young people who had left school would attend one day a week. I daresay Mr. Ede will not forget that when we tried it on some of our educational friends, Dr. Kenneth Pickthorn said he thought the description 'county colleges' ridiculous.

"Ellen Wilkinson raised the age to 15 within the time limit specified in the Act. This was a bold decision, and I think we can look back with pride today to the work Ellen Wilkinson did for education. This decision was taken when the country was faced with the aftermath of the war but, looking back, I have no doubt that it was right.

"What made it feasible at the time, you will remember, was the Emergency Training Scheme, which drew on the talent and enthusiasm of men and women released from National Service and provided the schools with an infusion of new blood—men and women with more varied experience and wider outlook than most contemporary teachers of the time—just in time to cope with the 15-year-old age group.

"But the other step—that is, continuing education—still remains to be taken, and the Crowther Report has reminded us how far we are from providing adequately for all our boys and girls so long as so many of them finish their education at fifteen.

"I remember at the height of the war being asked to visit Chequers by Sir Winston Churchill. I drove down there with 'the Prof', Lord Cherwell—who informed me in the car that all my education statistics were wrong, and if I borrowed his slide rule I would get them right in the future.

"On arrival, Sir Winston Churchill said he wished to deliver a spiritual message to the nation and to devote a great deal of it to education. This later developed into his famous broadcast on social policy in the middle of the war—1943.

"I remember that he left me to draft the religious bit. He told me to see him at 9 a.m. when he tore it up and sent me back to London.

"I remember one phrase he used about continuing education of the boys and girls of whom I am talking. He said, 'Think of them with their jobs which begin so fair and end so foul.' And there is no doubt that at that date, when apprenticeship and so forth was not so developed as it is becoming now, there were many jobs which began fair and ended foul.

"So we wrote measures into the Act—on which practically no action has been taken—all of which rested on compulsion. What we did not foresee was the extent to which boys and girls would voluntarily stay on longer at a school. (I have not so much in mind at the moment what is happening in the grammar schools.) This is part of the great thirst for higher education which is prompting so many more of our young people to seek admission to universities—in fact, you can hardly get into a university nowadays—colleges of advanced technology and training colleges. This has been one of the most exciting developments in postwar education, and it has produced its own crop of problems, some of which the Robbins Committee is now grappling with. But we must not forget the needs of the ordinary boy and girl of no more than average ability, and children who are slow and dull. We owe all these children, too, an adequate and satisfying education.

"One of the results of the Crowther Report is that the question of giving young workers the right to claim daytime release is being discussed with both sides of industry. At present the system depends on the agreement of employers, and, although the numbers staying on are still rising, they are not rising fast enough, and not even keeping pace with the number of young people leaving school each year. More is being done, too, to link schools with technical colleges and to help school leavers to choose suitable technical courses, and so reduce the wasteful rate of failure among young students at technical colleges. And so, in one way or another, a good deal is being done to attract young people to stay on in education voluntarily.

"But, while these efforts, in my view, reduce the size of the problem, they make it, if anything, more severe, since we are left with a residue of young people who are not responding to these opportunities and who can be finding nothing meaningful in education by the age of 15.

"Observers of the social scene have called attention to the tendency for society to become stratified in bands that correspond to levels of educational achievement. This is nothing new in itself. What is new is that our educational service, by its very success in offering such widespread opportunities for advanced education at different levels, now tends systematically to winnow our young people into different grades of potentially all society. By so doing it determines broadly the kind of job they will take and their general mode of life and scale of values.

"It is obvious that we must do something for gifted and talented children—they represent our most valuable investment for future years—but I still think it is essential that we should move on as soon as possible to the principle embodied in the Act that all young people should be kept in touch with education until they reach the threshold of adult life.

"Of course it will be said that we have neither the resources nor the buildings to achieve this. Indeed, to build brand new County Colleges everywhere cannot at present be envisaged. We shall have to use the facilities of industry and of the Technical Colleges.

"I, at any rate, am convinced that the rank and file of our young people must not be put out of all touch with liberal education until they are out of their teens. The vision of H. A. L. Fisher—which, with Mr. Ede, I did no more than re-enact in a revised form in our Act—may have to be transformed."

RAB went on to claim with some pride that in his White Paper of 1943 he had emphasized the importance of far closer links between education and industry and commerce. RAB and Chuter Ede had foreshadowed the immense strides to be made in whole-time further education by the colleges of advanced technology.

Then he propounded three questions for his audience.

The first was: Should an educational system be designed to achieve a social result, and if so, what result?

The second question posed was: Does education have an effect on the country's economic future, and if so, can this be measured?

While the third question was: Should an educational system be designed to have an effect on morals?

RAB's answer to the first question was that it was not right for an educational system to depart from its primary function to "pull out" the best in men and women. He foresaw that, in fact, there would be more unified education, but he thought that the systems of the future would retain first-class educational facilities wherever they were to be found. Presumably by this he meant that the older universities and public schools would survive under Socialism as well as under Toryism, and this, it appears, they will in fact do.

Answering his second question RAB ranged abroad and examined the educational system of the Soviet Union at the time and the system previously adopted in Prussia. He thought that the big investment in money by the Soviet Union had paid off by making a backward nation in the scientific sense one of the world leaders in all scientific progress. For an attempt to analyse the real return to the nation on money invested in education, he urged his audience to read the now famous book of John Vaizey, and he outlined the spheres in which he thought that a return on the capital investment was most obvious and convincing.

Answering his third question, RAB told a story of a clergyman visiting a class of boys and girls in a school and asking the question: "What should you do to earn the forgiveness of sin?" And receiving the surprising answer: "Sin, first."

RAB, as Home Secretary, was in no doubt that there was plenty of sin about. But he continued to make a distinction between moral education and religious education.

"As for moral education, there is a broad field here for the training of what Edmund Burke called 'right character'.

"Professor Whitehead has said that the basis of experience is emotional. If that is so, then education should be concerned with the training and development of the emotion of individuals.

"As Dame Olive Wheeler has said: 'It may be that failure to recognize this has been the main reason why formal education has played so insignificant a part in the prevention of mental ill-health.'

"This is a voyage of exploration we should undertake which will concern teachers, administrators, parents, commentators and statesmen. . . ."

RAB'S basic belief that progress was good and often linked to radical reform permeates the whole of his speech.

He ended his speech with a quotation.

"I will close with the words of Thomas Wade:

> 'O for the mighty wakening that aroused
> The old time prophets to their missions high . . .
> And made our Milton his great dark defy
> To the light of one immortal theme espoused!'

"The theme which we should espouse in this first Chuter Ede Lecture is the motto we together put upon the White Paper of 1943, which launched modern education upon its great immortal theme in these words, the simple words: 'On the future education of this country the greatness of this country depends'."

I have quoted the inaugural Chuter Ede lecture so extensively for more than one reason. It gives a clear impression of the width of range of this man's mind. Just as some great pianists have an abnormal finger spread, so RAB here reveals an unusual grasp of the entire subject of education, its meaning, its importance, and its future.

The lecture also presents a combination of Party talent that would be almost impossible in most countries. Both James Griffiths, the chairman, and Chuter Ede were Labour veterans and RAB was a Tory veteran, but they were educational allies. RAB, perhaps characteristically, found himself at home with reformers and with people who knew their subject from start to finish.

It is remarkable, too, how objective is his approach. The examples range from the United States to the Soviet Union, from Prussia to Edmund Burke. There is no prejudice. Here without strain or affectation or effort is the civilized mind treating a great subject with that combination of experience and expertise, of enthusiasm and vision that reflects British public life at its best.

In his lecture RAB does not dwell on the great campaign undertaken by himself and Chuter Ede after the publication of their White Paper in 1943. This was in the nature of a crusade. By touring the country separately and together and addressing all the interested parties, school governors, teachers, the universities, local authorities and the general public, they paved the way for their Bill in Parliament which both of them, with skill and patience and tact, piloted through all its stages until it became a Statute and the Law. That the Act is generally known as the Butler Act is no misnomer.

Nye Bevan was to give the people medical care as a right in return for a weekly contribution. RAB played his part in extending education as a right to the children of England. The stature of both men, so different in background, character and method, increases year by year. In these measures they served their country well.

VI

Opposition

WITH VICTORY in the war, a victory as complete and absolute as any in history, it seemed certain that Winston Churchill, although he was now fighting as leader of the Conservative Party, rather than as a national hero and prophet, would receive the votes of a grateful public and be returned to power. Especially was this so as the war was not yet finished. Japan was still on her feet. Her empire of eight hundred million people, which she had ruled by indescribable terror and torture for four years, was almost intact, and many hundreds of thousands of troops of the Imperial Army had not yet become engaged in the battle, their duties consisting in holding down the captive territories.

Presumably the British public took the view that Japan would in the long run be no match for America, although in fact the greatest single land victory over the Japanese Forces was gained by General Slim's Fourteenth Army in Burma.

The public, especially men returning from service with the forces abroad, demanded a change. It was time for the accelerator. Hugh Gaitskell once said to the author: "When they want the accelerator, they choose us. When they want the brake, they choose the Tories." This was to be a new England, and a new England demanded a new Government.

However, there was an interval, that of the "Caretaker Government" which ruled for a couple of months until July 26, 1945, when Mr. Churchill resigned and Mr. Attlee came in on a great wave of popular approval.

The Tories were taken by surprise. RAB did not on this occasion sense the "groundswell" of mounting opposition that he was later to detect in 1964. Churchill, himself, only doubted his victory the night before the result was announced when he said he felt a stabbing pain, mental and physical, and he knew that something had gone wrong.

Probably nothing could have prevented the Labour land-slide of 1945. It was, the people thought, time for a change. But Churchill did not shine in this election. He accused the Labour Party of wishing to introduce "a Gestapo State". The people realized that this was a ridiculous charge. When Churchill followed it up by saying that the real—sinister—power behind the Labour Party was Mr. Harold Laski, at this time Chairman of the Labour Party, many a voter came to the conclusion that the old gentleman needed a rest after his tremendous exertions.

They probably expected him to retire in well-earned glory. He did not do so. Had he taken the hint, RAB's path would have been much smoother and his prospects of becoming Prime Minister much more certain than, in fact, they were. In the Caretaker Government RAB, for the first time, received ministerial rank as Minister of Labour. But this time he succeeded Ernest Bevin, one of the most powerful war leaders to a Ministry that, at this juncture, was of prime importance. The immense immobilization operation was starting and rapidly growing in momentum. RAB quickly mastered the increased responsibilities of the office with which, of course, he was already familiar.

When the Election came the issue was presented to the country as a vote of confidence in Churchill. This, it was thought, was an obvious winner. But gratitude is an elusive and often uncomfortable emotion. The Party would have done better if they had looked ahead rather than peering, however gratefully, into the past.

RAB was rising again in the political sky. He was one of the very few Tories chosen to do one of the national political broadcasts. And he was Chairman of the Conservative Party Conference in October, 1946. Moreover, as early as November, 1945, Churchill, who appears always to have regarded

RAB as a Don who had strayed into politics, and an abstemious and liberal-minded Don at that, had appointed RAB chairman of the Conservative Research Department in Old Queen Street.

So now R. A. Butler was very much at the centre of power and one of the new leaders of the Tory Party at Westminster and in the country.

The Election meant Saffron Walden again and RAB this time won a narrow fight, beating his Labour opponent, Mr. S. S. Wilson, by only just over a thousand votes. Never again was Saffron Walden to act so much out of character. RAB redoubled his ties and contacts with his constituents and then turned with relish to providing his own particular brand of opposition which was the exact opposite of the Churchillian attack.

Whereas Churchill appeared to be determined to batter Labour with his mighty armoury of invective and rhetoric, RAB had more guile. The approach was: We are all reasonable people. Let us examine this proposal a little more closely. Is it what we really want? Will it be effective?

This was an exceptionally telling approach and appealed not only to the men voters who prided themselves on their sound, middle-of-the-road common sense, but to millions of women who declared that RAB's broadcast was the best they had ever heard. In fact, at this time, RAB at forty-two was at the very height of his powers of persuasion and activity.

At this time, too, RAB was as near bridging the barrier that seemed to separate him from the general public—as opposed to his constituents who knew him—as he ever came. Later the advent of television presented him with an opportunity which he could not take. The hooded eyes, the eye pouches, the figure that had become stocky and for his height overweight, his discomfort at the whole procedure, came through so that he was never to become an effective television politician. Harold Macmillan was much better giving the impression of a good character actor playing an

Edwardian dandy, which may not have been the impression intended but was at least novel and entertaining.

It is said that the re-creation of a top-level Research Department was Churchill's idea, but, in fact, it was RAB himself who urged that the Party needed this kind of stimulation and guidance. Churchill had the foresight to put RAB in overall charge. Under him Henry Hopkinson was the first official head.

At Old Queen Street RAB soon gathered round him an exceptional team of young Tories, most of whom had not yet entered the House of Commons. Reginald Maudling, Ian Macleod and Enoch Powell were typical of the brains and originality of the men whom RAB attracted to his banner.

And Churchill, combatant in the House, was content to leave the thinking to RAB and his "backroom boys". They did their work well. Their Agricultural Charter and their Industrial Charter did set out, in terms that the public could understand, the Tory approach to the giant problems of reconstruction and domestic affairs that now absorbed the nation.

RAB was at his best in leading his Research team. If this was not teaching again as at Corpus, it was very near it. It was essentially the exercise of the mind on the problems of the present. It was not an emotionally heated conflict as House of Commons debates were apt to become. Those who worked with RAB during these years of opposition bear witness to the knack he had of getting the very best out of his lieutenants. He gave the Tory Party a new base, almost a new faith.

We have been conditioned into thinking, of recent years, that the long period of Labour Government from 1945 to 1951 was a period of restriction, frustration and failure. This is a distortion. It was one of the most dynamic periods in recent British public life. Two great countries, India and Pakistan, were created. The Health Service was introduced. The Mines and Railways were nationalized and these great measures were, on the whole, matched by the stature of the

men on the Labour Front Bench—Attlee, the best Chairman
of Committees the House had known for many years, and a
sardonic, telling debater; Ernest Bevin, who knew nothing
of the House of Commons but brought to it his own humanity
and great ability; Nye Bevan, the complex Welshman of
genius, full of virtues and failings; Hugh Dalton, the extrovert and indiscreet old Etonian; Hugh Gaitskell, the
dedicated man of Westminster, a stuffy, highly intelligent
Englishman of his type and class; Tom Williams, one of
the best Ministers of Agriculture England has had, and
many more.

Churchill was not always at his best in attacking this
formidable array of talent. And the Tory Party as a whole
could not, at first, accommodate itself to the role of opposition. This made the part that RAB could play, both in the
Research Department and as a member of the Shadow
Cabinet, all the more important.

Against the Labour big guns the Tories could muster at
least a competent team. Their casualties in the General
Election had been great, but gradually, at by-elections, they
got most of their key men back into the House.

Anthony Eden had become Deputy Leader and Harold
Macmillan was well in the running at this stage, but RAB
kept his second place quite easily and no one thought he
would lose it. He represented forward-looking Conservatism,
and with the task of turning Britain over from war to peace
and turning her vast Empire into a great Commonwealth,
any thought of going back to reactionary Toryism was not
acceptable or appropriate. The right-wing were not defeated,
but they were quiescent. It was just not their climate.

In re-reading the debates in which Attlee and Bevan
clashed with Churchill, and Ernest Bevin and Williams
clashed with RAB and Harold Macmillan, a certain un-
reality comes through.

Was nationalization, in reality, any longer a question of
principle? Was an absolute principle involved? Were there
people who still believed that all industry and service should

RAB on his wedding day in October, 1959, picks a buttonhole in the churchyard. In both his marriages, RAB has been blessed with great domestic happiness and devotion.

In full measure RAB found happiness within the family circle.
Never one to lack gallantry, he is seen at his son's wedding, kissing
the bride with characteristic aplomb.

be State owned and operated, or that none of it should be? Or was it now a matter of convenience?

The nationalization of the railways and the mines did not meet with massive public disapproval. The nationalization of steel was much more contentious and debatable. It had become a matter of emphasis. In the charters they wrote in Old Queen Street RAB and his team stressed the advantages of a free economy, the disadvantages of public ownership. They did not go so far as to say that all public ownership was bad, all private enterprise good.

In all the major debates in which RAB, as a member of the Shadow Cabinet, took part, we see that he is intensely aware that the old absolute arguments no longer apply, that in fact the people of England had settled for a free enterprise economy diluted with some Socialism especially in respect of the old, the weak and the poor. RAB seemed more aware of this than any of his colleagues.

And then, of course, there were measures which the tide of history had made acceptable to the Tory Party, but which before they had strenuously opposed. The Indian Independence Act was the most important of these measures.

Churchill, as we know, had very mixed feelings on this matter. Liberal-Imperialist that he was, he regretted to the end the passing of the glory of the British Raj and stressed the immense benefits in many directions that our rule had given the manifold peoples of India. So it was RAB who was the most effective Government spokesman on this measure.

He was effective for a number of reasons. He knew India and the peoples of India. He knew their history and their current difficulties, administrative, economic and spiritual. He had long seen that independence was the ultimate answer. If this was not so, the long period of preparatory-internal self-government had been pointless. Obviously it was all a preparation for a new nation, or as it, tragically, turned out to be, the emergence of two new nations. And RAB was perhaps the only living English Tory politician at this time whom the Indian people completely trusted and liked. He represented, in Indian eyes, all that had been best in the British Raj.

The Cabinet debated what line the Opposition should take on the Bill and RAB's view prevailed. They were to approve of it in principle, confining their attack to pointing out matters that had been overlooked, or ignored, and the undue speed which, the Opposition thought, had been insisted on in the final stages under the new Viceroy, Mountbatten.

If we follow RAB's argument in his speech in the House we see him both at his inquiring best and also revealing at times a failure to appreciate that the factor of force was to decide many issues which RAB, typically, regarded as likely to be solved by debate, reason, and, possibly, compromise.

On July 15, 1947, at 3.49 p.m., RAB caught the Speaker's eye. "We should like to make it quite clear that we support the third reading of this Bill. Indeed, I think that the business-like and friendly atmosphere which prevailed in the Committee yesterday afternoon would have proved that without any further remark from me.

"Many, many people have contributed to this ultimate result. The work of leading India towards self-government has its roots in the history of many years ago.

"We are here this afternoon to celebrate a conclusion which, in most of its aspects, can be regarded as satisfactory.

"There are one or two matters to which I shall refer in course of my remarks, but I want to voice the general sentiment which we on this side of the House feel in regard to the main objective, and that is that we should practise as well as preach the doctrine of self-government, and that I think is achieved by the passage of this Bill. We have, in fact, been true to ourselves, and by being true to ourselves, and what we believe in, we have strengthened rather than weakened the British Imperial position and improved our position generally in the world. At any rate, I have had the opportunity of obtaining the reactions to this settlement in a country, namely the North American continent, and in particular in the United States of America, which has not always been friendly to or even understanding of the efforts of the British in India.

"I was very glad to observe the almost unanimous approval with which this solution was greeted and, judging by a practical matter which is even more intense in England today, the space in the newspapers. I was very glad to see that almost the whole of the details of the solution were printed on the front pages of the main newspapers. So that, though absent, I have been fully informed, and I hope I am worthy to take part in this Debate.

"We should have liked a little longer in which to consider this Bill, and a little longer time in which the parties in India, aided by the Government, could have worked out a solution which might have been even more complete. But we understand there were grave administrative difficulties, and difficulties between those who found it difficult to work together and might be likely to split later; and it was therefore essential for a Bill to be passed through in what amounts to almost a record time for a measure of this sort.

"I believe that these decisions sprang from an original decision to abandon British recruitment to the services in India.

"I have adverted to this matter before, and there is no advantage in going over it again, but the fact is that the Administration in India was not capable of continuing indefinitely in the atmosphere which had been created.

"I, myself, do not accept responsibility for that original decision, but it was taken, and there is no doubt that to spin out the matter any longer might have been fraught with great danger.

"I should like, at this point, to pay to the Services in India a tribute which we on this side of the House feel should be paid, and to welcome the statement made by the Prime Minister on the second reading, which is a distinct advance on any previous statement made about the Services—the conditions, pensions and general desires of the Services in India—and I trust that the undertaking given by the Under-

Secretary of State in the Committee last night, that the Prime Minister's words were to be taken literally and in their full context will have been noted by the Services in India.

"I said just now that we should have liked a little more time. We should have liked certain aspects of the settlement to have been rather more satisfactory, but even we, with all the freedom of the Opposition, did not expect any easy solution for this most complex problem.

"In fact, no one who has devoted his life to this subject could imagine that any solution would be easily found.

"I believe that on one occasion in his career, Lord Curzon, perhaps our greatest proconsul, kept an official file for upwards of two months. His officials, accustomed to his regular habits, were very surprised when at last the file was returned and it had, instead of a minute couched in the Edwardian phraseology of that great statesman, the following words: 'This is a damned tough nut to crack.'

"That may well be taken by some of us, and by some in the country who read our debates, as a warning that the Indian leaders, in facing these problems, are going to have very considerable difficulties, and that this is going to be a tough nut to crack.

"It is some consolation that those of us who laboured with the Act of 1935 should find that the corpus of the Law which remains as the basis of the Bill is that of the Act of 1935.

"It is subject to considerable changes. Indeed, it was impossible in the short time in the Committee stage to elicit exactly what parts of that Act remain, and what do not, but I think it is satisfactory to claim that, at any rate, that Act forms the basis. It is not surprising, and I certainly do not complain, that the last twelve years should have resulted in a considerable departure from the general principles of the Act.

"Probably in no country have the effects of the war been felt so much as in the political life of India.

"It has been increasingly difficult to keep pace with the political changes in India.

"Among the new forces, I should like on this occasion to refer not so much to those revolutionary and other forces which may tend to threaten the régime, but to the place which I feel sure will be taken by the women of India. I myself feel certain, from my small knowledge of India, that the women have a great part to play in that Continent, whether in India or Pakistan.

"Many prominent women have taken part in our deliberations, and I hope that they will continue to mix in public life and thereby greatly enlarge the area of talent upon which the new Governments and Administrations can draw.

"I trust that they will play their part in improving social conditions in India, because, if they do, I am happy to think that those social conditions will very rapidly be improved.

"The Right Honourable and learned gentleman, the President of the Board of Trade, used some felicitous language on the subject of our Imperial relations with the new Dominions.

"I think I have stated once before in one of our Debates that we are entering upon the fourth period of Empire. That fourth period will concern itself not so much with the word Empire, but will see a development of the system within the Commonwealth which will mean that the British power of invention, of elasticity and of political wisdom will grow and expand in a manner surprising to our enemies and satisfying to our friends.

"Those of us who know some of the difficulties and sorrows of the partitions that are taking place, and in particular those in the Punjab, will realize that it is too much to hope that there will be no unfriendly gestures or no unfortunate skirmishing. But let us at least hope that, thanks to the Dominion relationship that will prevail between these two new Dominions, frontiers may be set up and observed which in time may be regarded as just as friendly as the famous frontier to which I have drawn the attention of the House.

"But we must remember that in the partition of the Punjab, which is the second partition, apart from the partition of

India itself, we have left the Sikh community, to whom the Right Honourable and learned gentleman made reference, almost exactly divided as between one side of the frontier and another.

"It is to be hoped that the Boundary Commission, on which the most serious responsibility will fall, will be able so to arrange the boundary that shrines and properties, and other things held dear to the Sikhs, may be amassed, as far as possible, in an area, provided that no violence is done to a proper division between Muslim and non-Muslim areas.

"In the same way, it is hoped that the partition of Bengal will so take place that the industrial welfare of the eastern portion may not be prejudiced, and that access may be had to the sea through the port of Calcutta in some satisfactory manner.*

"I cannot help feeling that although the partition of India appears necessary at the present time, that as history develops, certain contacts must be made between the two portions of India which have been divided, and that the conception of a greater whole will arise.

"When we come to the question of the Indian States, I maintain that the handling of this question is in marked contrast with the rest of the settlement. We, on this side of the House, have always stressed the importance of the States in India as an integral question by itself, and one which deserves the utmost consideration. Elaborate provisions were put into the Act of 1935 to provide for the accession of the States and to give them the free right to accede to the Federation.

"I am told—and the Right Honourable and learned gentleman has repeated the phrase—that the Government have been nervous about the Balkanization of India, and that, therefore, they have been nervous about giving too much opportunity to the States to establish an independent position and not to join one or other side. I am not going to claim that the States are themselves without fault. I myself

* The port of Chittagong, not Calcutta, now serves East Pakistan.

bitterly regret that they did not take advantage of the opportunities offered to them by the 1935 Act to accede to Federation on the very fair terms which were then offered. But it is no good going back on history. I remember my disappointment at the Second Round Table Conference, when the Muslims refused, through their official spokesman, an offer of provincial autonomy officially made to them.

"That was some sixteen years ago. If people had thought earlier, how easier would the government òf the world be. Now we are faced with the facts as we find them.

"The Right Honourable and learned gentleman asked us today to believe that the right policy was that the States should throw in their lot with one or other of the Indian Dominions.

"I think it is right for many States to take the decision to join one or other Dominion. But we cannot, on the information in our possession, exclude the probability that some States will desire their independence.

"All I can say therefore in reason, and maintaining the atmosphere of the Debate, as we have maintained it, is that I trust that when it becomes clear that a unit among the States, or one, or some of the States desires to maintain independence the Government will then enter into relations with that State, and will handle it with sympathy and understanding.

"I need hardly remind the House, the State of Hyderabad, for example, has more inhabitants than any British Dominion, including Canada, and is at least the size of France.

"I have had drawn to my attention by the leader of the Scheduled Castes, a man with whom we have worked in the past, and who has served their cause, namely, Dr. Ambedkar, that it would be extremely helpful if some reference could be made to this community in the course of our Debates; and I therefore say that I trust that, when the new Constitution is made, full consideration will be given to the position of the Scheduled Castes themselves. It is sometimes said that Britain has not done enough for them.

"It is well known, I think, that Queen Victoria's original proclamation—about our not interfering too much with the religion and habits of the people—has prevented the British from doing perhaps as much as they might have desired, but there is no doubt that, in later years, by a variety of devices, we have attempted to influence improvement of the position of the Scheduled Castes and have tried to mitigate the horrors of untouchability. In fact, the Franchise Committee itself recommended electorates which would have given the Scheduled Castes an opportunity for election and for looking after their own affairs.

"Unfortunately, the decisions of the Franchise Committee were abrogated by the Poona Pact, produced by one of Mr. Gandhi's longest fasts. I cannot now influence the decision of the constitution-making body, but it is quite clear that, under the Poona Pact, the Scheduled Castes do not get a chance of electing their representatives who ultimately represent their point of view. I hope that in part or parts of India it may be possible to find for them an electoral system which will be of a kind more suitable for them.

"There are many other minorities — Anglo-Indians, Christians, to whom the Right Honourable and learned gentleman referred, and many others—whose case we considered last night. We trust that in the future of India they, and those Europeans who are going to stay and practise their legitimate trade, will find free and fair opportunity, and will find happiness under the new régime.

"I remember some wording used in the Gracious Speech on the occasion of the inauguration of the Conference in the Royal Gallery of the House of Lords on November 12, 1930. These words were:

"'I have in mind the just claims of majorities and minorities, of men and women, of the town dwellers and the tillers of the soil, of the landlords and the tenants, of the strong and the weak, the rich and the poor, of the races, castes and creeds of which the body politic is composed.'

"For these things I care deeply. For these things and these

people we care deeply. They are passing out of our immediate care. We are moved on this occasion, and we wish those well who are assuming the Government and responsibility for the welfare of the Indian peoples."

This speech revealed RAB at his best. It was very much the speech of a statesman as opposed to that of a politician. What the Tory leader thought of it we do not know, but if we accept the basic thesis that the Indian peoples had the right to govern themselves, the argument is convincing and often helpful and probing. The manner was as good as the matter. It was a speech that those who heard it have not forgotten and the peroration is genuinely moving.

The defects arise from the assumption that everyone is going to play the game according to RAB's rules.

Thus on boundaries RAB sees the difficulties and dangers, both in the Punjab and in Sind, very clearly. He realizes that the minorities will need protection and his plea for the "untouchables" is wholly admirable. But when he forecasts that Moslem India and Hindu India will, some day, draw closer to each other, he is being, at any rate in the foreseeable future, unrealistic. The tendency has been for the two nations to draw farther and farther apart, not only in the aggravated sections of the frontier, such as the Ran of Kutch and Kashmir, but ideologically, politically, even economically.

Whereas India has accepted gladly the American nuclear umbrella to protect her from the recurring threat of Chinese invasion, Pakistan, under President Ayub Khan and his able young Foreign Minister, Mr. Bhutto, has accepted Chinese friendship; and the deep hatred that flares up constantly between the two nations shows no sign of abating.

To have anticipated these events would not have entailed hindsight. They could have been forecast by complete realism, by looking ahead and accepting the situation as it really was.

In the same way RAB appears to be unrealistic when he discusses the position of the great Princely States who had special Treaty relations with the British Crown. He says that

he regrets they did not take advantage of the proposals made
in the 1937 Indian Government Act to adhere to one of the
new administrative units, but he still envisages that they
will have freedom to retain their British link and not join
either Federation if they so desired. This idea had in fact
been totally abandoned. England, to put it bluntly, to secure
an overall settlement, had betrayed the Indian Princes. The
Princes were often arrogant, feudalistic and despotic, but
some were modern-minded. It was perhaps necessary to
betray them. But RAB's mind shies away from this tough
conclusion.

When the State of Hyderabad, which he specifically
mentions, attempted to remain independent, Pandit Nehru,
one of the most aggressive pacifists of recent times, settled
the matter by sending in his tanks and threatening the State
into submission.

In fact, those who controlled the armies and police forces
were the rulers. It was not played according to RAB's rules
at all. Nevertheless the speech shows very clearly the kind
of India that RAB hoped for most earnestly, a curiously
English India in which the word of the referee was law and
all the rules were observed. And in his words, spoken in the
informal style suited to the House of Commons, the sincerity,
the idealism and the knowledge do come through.

We know that here is a man who cares.

VII

Chancellor of the Exchequer

AN INDUSTRIAL nation, like ours, that produces less than
half of what it consumes, depends, for its very existence, on
exporting to all the markets of the world huge quantities
of manufactured goods either entirely made in this country
or made abroad and finished here.

London, as the centre and core of the sterling area, is the
greatest finance and insurance centre of the world, out-
rivalling New York. If the British economy waxes the country
can afford all kinds of much-needed social reform. If the
economy flags the process is apt to snowball into depression
and unemployment. We live perpetually on a knife edge
balanced between great prosperity and frightening decline.
It is now generally recognized that if unemployment in
Britain rises above the five per cent mark a dangerous
political situation is inevitable.

In Victorian times, under both Liberals and Tories, the
policy of laissez-faire was popular. Let the money fructify
in the pockets of the people. The less the Government interfered with "business" the better. But this period is long past.
We live in an age when the regulation of the economy by the
Government, its acceleration or its retarding, is taken for
granted. The economy has become the patient. The Chancellor of the Exchequer is the doctor, his the diagnosis, his
the prescription and his the annual balance-sheet we call
the Budget.

RAB, when he became Chancellor in October, 1951,
followed two very able predecessors in Sir Stafford Cripps
and Hugh Gaitskell. But they had left behind them, six years

after the war, a legacy of restriction and control that was clearly out of date. If the British economy and British trade were to recover their old rumbustious enterprise positive encouragement was now needed. RAB was well suited to give it just that.

His long-range association with the great firm of Courtaulds had taught him in a positive and practical way the kind of incentive to which business responded, the type of measure and atmosphere acceptable to the City, and the importance of instilling confidence into the economy. He took up his work with buoyancy and hope.

The period of four years from 1951 to 1955 when RAB was Chancellor of the Exchequer seem now, looking back to them, like a golden age in which free enterprise, judiciously encouraged by the Treasury, and social reform walked hand in hand, and the country advanced rapidly and with determination, led out of the maze of restrictions and priorities that had been the legacy of war.

RAB's appointment as Chancellor was not expected. In the election of February, 1950, Labour scraped home but they were handsomely defeated in October the following year. RAB had done well at Saffron Walden in both elections. In the first he had a majority of just under five thousand and in October, 1951, this had risen to over five thousand when he had a vote of over 20,000, more than the combined total of his opponents. Labour continued to poll about 15,000 votes but the Liberal vote had shrunk to under 4,000, a miserable vote for the once great Liberal Party in the former radical stronghold of Essex.

RAB, contemplating the future with his discerning eye, could not expect that he would be appointed Chancellor. It was much more likely that "the old man" would send him to the Ministry of Labour. Eden, obviously, would be the new Foreign Secretary. And Churchill was expected to pick one of the men who had "covered" finance in opposition—Oliver Lyttelton or Sir John Anderson—as the new Chancellor.

But Churchill, though he was good at nurturing his dislikes, when it came to the most decisive appointments, also was clever enough to pick for his key posts the men most likely to be acceptable to the country at large. In the case of Chancellor of the Exchequer there were a number of essential requirements: the man appointed must be young enough to carry the burden. Cripps had died of overwork. The man appointed must, if it were possible, appeal both to the "new Toryism" and to the City. And finally he should be a man sufficiently resolute and independent to be able to sweep away the frightening load of restrictive legislation necessary during the war, necessary even in the immediate post-war period when the Government in replacing a war economy by a civil economy had to exercise great powers, but now due, or, as the Tories said, overdue, for the scrap-heap.

Churchill could find no man who fitted the bill as well as RAB did. From the point of view of RAB's career this was, perhaps, high noon. Macmillan was to follow him as Chancellor. On the other hand Eden had preceded him as Foreign Secretary. The hierarchy seemed settled in their precedence. After Churchill it would be Eden and after Eden, RAB. This was certainly the form selection. RAB was forty-eight and at the height of his powers.

The new Chancellor had exceptional abilities, in part inherited, in part assiduously cultivated, to cope with the immense volume of work that came his way. He tore the heart out of a pile of correspondence or a memorandum with unerring speed. That was the gift of his intellect nurtured by long practice. He could sleep peacefully and undisturbed from eleven to eight. He cultivated a calm approach. He took things as they came, surmounting each obstacle with the practised nonchalance of a man who had mastery of his mount. He was determined not to be destroyed by the Chancellorship. "I am," as he once said, "on top of my job."

And this ability to be completely the master of his job is necessary to a Chancellor perhaps more than to any other Cabinet Minister except the Prime Minister himself. It is essential because he has to control and direct a Treasury

team consisting largely of "experts" and no Chancellor can
hope to get his own measures and ideas successfully translated into action unless the team recognizes that he is fully
in control.

The machinery is elaborate: the history impressive. The
office of the Lord High Treasurer has been continuously in
commission for well over 200 years. The Lords Commissioners
of H.M. Treasury consist of the First Lord of the Treasury
(who is also the Prime Minister), the Chancellor of the
Exchequer and five Junior Lords. This Board of Commissioners is assisted at present by a Chief Secretary, a Parliamentary Secretary, a Financial Secretary and an Economic
Secretary who are also Ministers, and joint Permanent
Secretaries. The Prime Minister and First Lord is not
primarily concerned in the day-to-day aspects of Treasury
business, and the Junior Lords and the Parliamentary Secretary are Government Whips in the House of Commons. The
management of the Treasury therefore devolves on the
Chancellor of the Exchequer and the Chief Secretary to the
Treasury. The Chancellor is responsible for the general
direction of economic and financial policy, at home and overseas. The Chief Secretary is responsible, under the general
direction of the Chancellor, for the control of public expenditure and the management of the Civil Service. The Chancellor
and the Chief Secretary are assisted at ministerial level by
the Financial and Economic Secretaries, the Financial
Secretary discharging in particular the traditional responsibility of the Treasury for the procedures for securing the
voting of funds by Parliament. Throughout history the
Treasury was always the object of a close scrutiny by the
Sovereign and by Parliament. At one time the Treasury
threatened to become so powerful that James I put the Office
of Lord High Treasurer into Commission and appointed a
Board of Lords Commissioners. The old historic link is still
kept in Treasury correspondence, formal documents running
in the name of "My Lords". The Prime Minister for over a
century has been First Lord of the Treasury and draws his

—now considerable—salary as such. This was because the post of Prime Minister and indeed the Cabinet itself was not *legally* recognized until the present century.

But nowadays the Chancellor runs the show. He even holds under a separate Patent the post of Under-Treasurer. An officer who, historically, began to operate as the person who checked the accounts of the Treasurer, has become the political and actual head of the Department.

The Office is closely linked with the mainstream of Government policy by its liaison officers. Thus the Parliamentary Secretary is Chief Government Whip; the Financial Secretary looks after the co-ordination with other Government Departments—the Treasury is the key Department of the Civil Service—and explains Treasury policy to the House when the Chancellor himself does not wish to intervene or is absent; the Economic Secretary—a post created in 1947 by the Labour Government—co-ordinates the Treasury policy with that of statistical and planning bodies within the Government.

The Treasury work itself is divided into supply, establishment and finance. The supply branch watches expenditure and is subdivided to deal separately with the various spending Departments.

From the point of view of the Chancellor of the Exchequer all this administrative complex and activity culminate in the Budget, the yearly national accounts, in which expenditure and estimates are set out with the means to be employed of balancing the entire operation. By his Budgets a Chancellor sinks or swims and it was the clear and incisive presentation of his four Budgets that made RAB an outstanding Chancellor.

There has been a tendency recently to represent the Chancellor as a mere puppet dancing to the tune currently being played by the great financial houses, the banks, both in Britain and abroad, especially in Switzerland, and the various international bodies that have been set up to cope with the increasing complexity and interdependence of nations in their economic relationships—such bodies as the

World Bank, the International Monetary Fund and the structure known as the European Common Market.

The picture is a distorted and exaggerated one. When the nation has a Chancellor who knows his job—and that is the kind of Chancellor that RAB was—there is considerable freedom of movement within the framework of all foreign commitments. And, in spite of its power, the City does not control the Government. The Government tends to control, through the Bank of England and other media, the City, the Stock Market and the factors that make for inflation or deflation.

This was the complicated world of the nation's money that RAB took over in 1951.

It soon became clear that he was a cool and calculating Chancellor, and the main outlines of his policy were made known not only to the House of Commons but to the country. His plans were based firstly on a belief that private enterprise was the best basis for a prospering economy. It followed that every inducement should be given to private interests engaged in business enterprise—with all its hazards—to make more money. It was, RAB thought, common sense. These people themselves ran all the risks. The Government could not lose. The more money they made the more the Treasury reaped by way of tax. And if they failed the Treasury was not concerned, though of course any major failure was guarded against lest it start a chain-reaction.

Britain had to export to live and pay for her enormous imports. So it followed that every possible inducement should be given to the exporter. He was the essential element who kept the whole ship afloat.

RAB combined with these twin directives a deep concern with social welfare. This was all a practical part of his house-owning, independent democracy and all his Budgets could with some minor alterations have been introduced by a radical Chancellor. Finally RAB kept the weapons that the Treasury has bright and burnished, ready for instant use in case the economy showed undue signs of over-expansion or of depression. And it was known that he was ready to act in any emergency.

This was the overall basis of his four years as a working Chancellor. Superimposed on all this was his native caution. He never, if he could help it, took any step that did not inspire confidence in Britain, confidence in sterling, confidence in British ability to meet the challenge of the new technical age of scientific advancement. He knew that confidence is a vital factor and no one can say exactly of what it consists. It is a combination of City and international talk, market trends, the content of ministerial speeches, trade figures, budget proposals and world economic and political climate. RAB was acutely aware of this and his success as Chancellor was due in no small degree to his realization that all he did in every direction should always foster confidence, never suggest that his own confidence or that of the Government had been shaken or undermined.

Churchill, during the war, had developed a system of over-lords which has perpetuated itself to the present day. These were in fact cronies of the Prime Minister who had overall supervision of sections of the national life. Lord Woolton and Lord Cherwell were the two best-known overlords. Agricultural practice and Science were their respective provinces. No Treasury overlord was appointed. If Churchill had such an appointment in mind it was made clear to him that, as far as the Treasury was concerned, there was only going to be one master.

The first test came in the presentation of the Budget of 1952. The highlights of this, his first Budget, were: to raise income tax and family allowances, to increase the benefits to the old people, to impose an excess profits duty, to put up the bank rate and to cut the food subsidies from over 400 million to around 250 million.

This was a Budget that really hit the headlines. It was extremely bold. For the member of a purely rural constituency to cut food subsidies almost in half was to hurl a thunderbolt. The raised bank rate was to cure the inflationary

tendencies that had followed the period of uncertainty during
the last short-lived Labour Government, and the excess profits
tax was something new. The Budget was both acclaimed and
attacked.

In his constituency the Labour candidate declared that
RAB had broken specific election pledges by his cut of the
food subsidies. RAB did not ignore this. He went to Saffron
Walden to explain his policy in person. In the event it did
not hurt his poll at the next election nor did it damage the
Tory national vote.

The new ceilings for income tax and the old age pensioners
provisions marked RAB's belief that the Tory Party must
always look after the weak and the aged, that they must
never forget their obligation to make a better Britain not
only for the active and the strong but for the feeble and
impoverished. It was a remarkably tough, strong budget. For
a man so intimately concerned with a great industrial empire
as RAB was with Courtaulds, the excess profits duty showed
that he was thinking purely in terms of what was right rather
than what was immediately advantageous. And his social
provisions supplied the compassion without which no Budget
can hope, in Britain, to win popular acclaim.

The public, no less than the Tory Party, thought this a
fine Budget. RAB had made a good start as Chancellor.

The years 1951-52-53 were high noon for RAB. Looking
back they were the halcyon days that could not last for ever,
but, while they lasted, were wonderful. The tenor and temper
of his Budget speeches during this period reflect the confidence both of the Chancellor and of the nation. They also
give us a good idea of the clarity of presentation and the
considerable ingenuity used in advancing a thesis and then
implementing a decision. In framing his Budget he adopted
a typically careful and legal method of presentation. The
urging of a review of the financial situation, and the imperative need for immediate new measures, are shown by the fact
that the 1952 Budget was presented on March 11, twenty
days before the end of the fiscal year.

"On Budget day the eyes of the nation are upon us as we review the state of the economy over the past year, weigh up the prospects for the coming year and decide what course we should take. This year the task is even more important than usual. The issues we face—I hope together—are serious indeed. What we do will largely determine not only our economic outlook for next year, but our entire future. This is the mood in which I have approached my task and in which I feel sure that the Commons will listen to what I have to tell them.

I propose to begin my review of the year that is just ending, the financial year 1951-52, with a short summary of the Exchequer accounts.

This summary will be brief, for the difficulties facing us today go far wider than these mere figures.

One consequence of a Budget before the end of the financial year is, of course, that final receipts and expenditure up to March 31 are not yet known.

The figures which will appear in the financial statement should prove reasonably accurate, but they must be treated as provisional. We have tried to make the Financial Statements as comprehensive as possible. I estimate that by the end of the year we shall have spent about £4,070 million. This is less than the Budget estimate by £120 million. Expenditure on Consolidated Fund Services and sinking funds is likely to exceed the estimate by some £8 million. The shortfall arises entirely in the field of supply services and is the result of a number of different factors. For reasons which the Committee know, Defence expenditure in the year coming to an end will have fallen short of the estimate. At the same time, however, Ministry of Supply expenditure will have *exceeded* the original estimate by £50 million.

A large part of this will, in due course, be reimbursed by the Services in payment for finished equipment. There have also been some supplementary estimates for strategic and trading stocks. The other supplementary estimates have been offset partly by the reduction in the Exchequer contribution to the National Insurance fund, and partly by shortfalls in a number of Departmental estimates. Thus, total revenue I now expect to be about £4,440 million, about £200 million above the Budget estimate. The biggest increase, perhaps about £100 million, is in Customs and Excise duties which are likely to yield about £1,755 million against an estimated £1,651 million. Most of this surplus is accounted for by the duties under the Import Duties Act, 1932, and the Purchase Tax, reflecting the sharp rise in prices over the year.

On the Inland Revenue side, I expect an increase of about £10 million—and out-turn of perhaps £2,370 million compared with the estimate of £1,625 million. The yield of the other Inland Revenue duties will be reasonably close to the estimates.

As a result I now expect to have at the end of March, on the conventional basis, an "above the line" surplus of over £360 million as against the figure of £39 million at which my predecessor arrived, before allowing, of course, for the reduction in the Exchequer contribution to the National Insurance Fund.

The Exchequer in a narrow sense is thus doing well. How, then, has it happened that our general economic position has declined so markedly?

I would attempt to give the impressions I received to the Committee. In January, 1951, the late Government, faced with the new and heavy burden of defence, budgeted for a significant fall in civil investment at home, and some decline in civil consumption at home. Realizing that this would not be enough, they accepted that there must be a decline in the balance of payments surplus. They set themselves, however, to maintain a balance, apart from strategic stockpiling, on the United Kingdom overall current account in the year before them.

In this year there was one serious new factor, which made the penalty of failure more serious than at any time since the war. Marshall Aid had just been suspended, and the first repayment of the United States and Canadian loans was in sight. This meant the removal of the cushion of external assistance upon which our economy had rested since the end of the war.

Failure to pay our way would quickly mean, therefore, drawing on the gold reserves.

Unfortunately, as one of my predecessors remarked, "Great

Expectations" was followed by "Bleak House". Over the year as a whole, the deficit on the balance of payments was over £400 million more than was bargained for. Some of this was due to events which could not have been foreseen. Invisible income fell below expectations, partly because of the loss of Abadan. The terms of trade proved worse than was forecast. But this is not the whole story.

The state of the national economy was such as to hamper the expansion of exports and to stimulate an increase of imports. Production did not increase so much as was expected, and the Budget failed to produce any decline in personal consumption.

Instead of falling, the volume of civil investment rose substantially. On top of the defence burdens, this put a heavy overload on the industries producing vehicles, engineering goods, and other metal products. Order books grew longer than ever, and the extra exports, which the world was ready to buy, did not go out.

At the same time, other industries met with a slack or falling demand abroad. It was thus not surprising that the total volume of exports failed to expand as fast as the situation required. This was the prospect which faced us when we took office. . . .

I announced emergency action on March 7. Imports were cut and the bank rate was raised. And it was necessary to take three steps:

1. Withdrawal of Open General Licences for a further list of selected goods to bring the trade under control.

2. Suspension of duty-free licences for the import of machinery.

3. Reduction of imports. Cut in Government civil expenditure. Increase of bank rate from 2½ per cent to 4 per cent.

We can now sum up. To meet the overriding needs of the balance of payments and in the light of the probable trend of production, we have adjusted the defence programme, reduced our civil expenditure and have taken a series of steps to bring about a major decline in investment at home. It follows that even if we attain the same increase in production as last year no more than the same amount of resources as last year can be spared for the ordinary civil consumer at home.

I judge that these changes in the distribution of our resources are both necessary and sufficient. It has been argued that we should make more severe and general cuts in consumption either instead of or in addition to the other cuts we are making. The account I have given of the external conditions facing us, especially in the sterling area, will explain why I have rejected this conclusion. The saving in resources which I have described are those which will contribute most effectively to increasing our exports.

Many industries producing consumer goods are already faced with a slack demand at home. They now face further severe cuts in their exports to the sterling area. They will have to increase substantially their exports to the non-sterling world —in difficult selling conditions—if they are to keep up their production and employment. To add to the difficulties of those industries by dispersing home demand even further would result not in still higher exports but in a further reduction of activity and employment which we would all deplore. That is why I have come to the decision which I have just stated.

I now come to the crucial question of the general strategy of the Budget itself. If our home consumer is to have no more of our resources than last year, we must see to it that his purchasing power as a whole is no more than is sufficient for this purpose.

An important level in this is the general level of taxation. This brings me to the prospect for Government expenditure and revenue in the coming year."

The Chancellor then announced:
An Excess Profits Tax from January 1, 1952.
An increase in Post Office charges.
A Tax increase on oil.
Raised Customs duty on petrol.
An increase in Motor Vehicle Duties.
A drastic cut in the agricultural food subsidies.

On the social side he announced plans to make appropriate recommendations to the Government regarding increase in National Assistance to compensate for removal of subsidy on certain foods.

He then announced:

An increase in family allowances from 5/- to 8/-.

An increase in National Insurance Benefits *and* Contributions.

An increase in War Pensions.

An increase in Industrial Injury Benefits.

An increase to Public Service Pensioners, i.e. retired school teachers, civil servants, policemen, etc.

An increase in allowances for Income Tax.

The Chancellor ended his speech by saying:

The final effect of all the changes I propose can be expressed thus: I hope to obtain in 1952-53 another £10 million from the Post Office and £66 million extra from petrol. I hope also to save about £80 million as the combined result of reducing the food subsidies, but improving social benefits.

This total of about £156 million is rather more than offset by the income tax reliefs, costing about £180 million; and allowing also for the minor proposals which I have mentioned, the final surplus above the line, to which I drew the Committee's attention earlier, becomes about £510 million, slightly less than at the outset, but still, for the reasons which I have given, approximately the amount which the situation requires, and incidentally covering—as Sir Stafford Cripps taught us to do—the liabilities below the line in the conventional accounts.

This, I think, is a thoroughly healthy and satisfactory conclusion. This, then, is my Budget, necessary, I judge, to achieve our objectives in the year ahead, and also sufficient. But, what is more, all its changes, the new revenue, and the savings from further economies are being devoted to relieving hardship, reducing inequity and providing fresh incentives.

Solvency, security, duty and incentive are our themes. Restriction and austerity are not enough. We want a system which offers us both more realism and more hope. These are the underlying purposes of the measures I have proposed, the deeper explanation of their character.

We must now set forth, braced and resolute, to show the world that we shall regain our solvency, and with it our national greatness.

I have quoted the gist of the remarkable Budget because

of its startling relevance today. Future Chancellors, faced with an economic crisis, if they had the temerity, could learn so much from the Budget of 1952.

The mastery shown in this Budget increased RAB's prestige at Westminster and in the country.

It has become the custom for British Budgets to reveal a note of great confidence and high hopes immediately before a General Election. Tory Chancellors in particular have been criticized for concealing bad news and in general dressing the shop window mendaciously in the last Budget before they have to go to the country. The charge was recently levelled against Sir Alec Douglas Home's Government who, it was charged, concealed the huge adverse trade balance which came as a most unpleasant surprise to their Labour Party successors, though the Tories staunchly maintained that the financial crisis of the summer and autumn of 1965 was due not to any chicanery on their part during the thirteen years of Tory rule but to Labour ineptitude and inexperience in the first six months of Mr. Wilson's Government.

RAB's April Budget of 1955 followed the same supremely confident note that he had struck with such success for four years. He asked the country at the Blackpool Conference of 1954 to "invest in success". He held out the promise that the standard of living could be doubled in twenty-five years. He was the golden Chancellor with the magic touch.

And then something went wrong. The British economy, always one of the most sensitive in the world, missed a beat. It may have been a mere palpitation, but it was there. Was it a passing deviation or was there an illness to be diagnosed?

The economy, if not sick, was not so well and a supplementary Budget became necessary in October, 1955. At the same time the Government had to retrench in particular to cut the housing subsidies. Just before RAB had to introduce his supplementary Budget he had to warn the Tory party conference at Bournemouth of the measures it was necessary to take. He got a poor reception. Invest in success he had said. Was this success?

There followed the battle in the House of Commons on the supplementary Budget proposals. RAB was deeply involved in these debates because he sensed that the foundation of the Opposition's case was the charge that, for electoral purposes, he had deceived the nation.

An impartial observer might think that any Chancellor who believed that the return of his Party to power was essential to national prosperity—and that is what Chancellors do believe—was entitled to put the best possible face on the national finances in the Budget of Election Year. But this is not an argument that can be advanced in the House of Commons. What stung RAB was the veiled suggestion that the last Budget had amounted to a misleading report. He met these innuendoes with real passion. The House had never seen him more moved. He was no longer cool and detached and perhaps they liked him more. It somehow made him more human, more fallible, more acceptable to the cross-section of humanity who make up the House of Commons.

The Labour Party ascribed the Tory Election win to RAB's over-optimistic Budget. They forgot that the electorate take a very broad view of politics. They forgot that the average voter—if such a man can be said to exist—asks himself no more than: How have they done on the whole? And if the answer is "not too badly" he is likely to vote the Government back again.

At least two other more important factors had contributed to the Conservative victory—the overall success of the Tory Government not least in the field of foreign affairs; and the appallingly bitter quarrel within the Labour Party between the socialist section led by Nye Bevan which was backed by at least sixty near-communists, and the majority section led by Hugh Gaitskell whose object was to destroy British socialism as it had been previously understood, for instance, by the Independent Labour Party followers, and substitute for it in a free economy society, a mildly radical philosophy, that would enable the extremes of wealth and poverty in Britain to be narrowed, and in the end result in a classless and united society in which prosperity was the rule and not the exception.

A Party rent by this dramatic and vital schism could hardly expect to be entrusted with the government of Britain.

But RAB was the target of attack not only from infuriated Labour opponents who thought the country had been tricked out of voting Labour, but, more hurtfully, by his own Party. RAB's star was shining but it had lost some of its lustre.

When the Government was reshuffled he was made Lord Privy Seal and Leader of the House of Commons. Was this demotion? Harold Macmillan was the new Chancellor. Eden made Lord Salisbury Lord President of the Council, and second man in the Government. RAB held his position as third man. This entailed a higher rating for the Office of Lord Privy Seal. We may assume then, at this point, that Anthony Eden looked upon RAB as his likely successor. Lord Salisbury as a peer was not in the race for the Premiership.

As we recall the role of recent Chancellors, Snowden, Chamberlain, Simon, Dalton, Cripps, Gaitskell, Macmillan, Thorneycroft, Amery, Lloyd, Maudling, we do not see one who, one could say with complete assurance, was better than RAB.

He was never just a Treasury man, or a City man. He bore in mind that the object of the whole exercise was to promote the welfare of the country as a whole, not to provide greater wealth for a class. As Chancellor he was a success measured by the most exacting standards. And it is hardly necessary to add that he brought to this Office that enviable quality of complete discretion that some Chancellors have found elusive.

He was at the centre and very near the top of British politics.

VIII

Suez

WE COME now to one of the most fantastic chapters in British history, the nationalization of the international Suez Canal by President Nasser of Egypt and the seizure of the Egyptian town of Suez and the invasion of Egypt by British troops acting closely in concert and in prior agreement with French and Israeli forces.

On account of the rapidly failing health of Sir Anthony Eden, RAB played a major role in this disastrous enterprise. There is no reason to doubt his word that, while admiring Eden's courage, he deplored his judgment in dealing with this whole affair. And, this being so, the question arises: Should he not have resigned in protest? His loyalty to his chief and Party impelled him to stay on and undoubtedly he rendered fine service in repairing the damage that had been done.

In order to understand RAB's position we have to go back to the genesis of the affair in Anglo-Egyptian relations.

Sir Anthony Eden had been the "golden boy" of British politics. The great Sir Winston Churchill himself had made it very plain that when he retired it was Anthony Eden who should take his place. He had been Foreign Secretary since October, 1951, and a very good Foreign Secretary, too. Churchill had encouraged and supported him. He knew all the personalities who were politically influential in both Europe and the Americas. He had supported and added prestige to the United Nations and was thought to have devoted a great part of his political life to the promotion of peace, the stimulation of prosperity, and the maintenance of

Britain's position in the world. And, on the whole, he had a fine record in all these directions.

So when he came to power as Prime Minister on April 7, 1955, the Party and the public as well as the Press were jubilant. They had said goodbye to the old man who had served his country for so long and with such distinction. They had bid farewell to the great war leader. This was a new age and it welcomed a new leader. Comparatively young, still handsome, polished, very experienced, Eden had a tremendous following within the Tory Party and outside it.

The public had not yet been told that what they wanted in their Tory and Labour leaders were a couple of clever operators who were neither aristocrats nor democrats but something delicious in-between. They rose to Eden. Here was the erstwhile young Sir Galahad who would carry on the good work that Attlee and Sir Winston had done, but who would give it a new, bright, gleaming go-ahead look that would secure Britain's place in a fast-changing world.

And Britain's place then as now was considerable and unique. The British people have been told so often in the last ten years that they are no longer a first-class power that they have, almost, come to believe it and a substantial majority in France, Italy, Germany and the United States, as well as the Soviet Union, have come to believe it to be true. There is no factual basis for this assumption. We do not have to look to past glories but to present accomplishments, as RAB pointed out in his "Great Britain" address to the notorious Tory Party Conference of 1963. Britain, as the Head of the Commonwealth, has unique links with a third of the inhabitants of the globe. No other power has this position. As the heart of much world banking, and more insurance than any other nation, as the centre of the sterling area, she occupies a special position in finance and industry. And the wisdom and experience of her statesmen are regarded by the uncommitted nations with respect which is strengthened by the fact that she is not tied—in spite of all her many Treaty commitments—to the two nuclear colossi, the Soviet Union and the United States.

Eden knew all this and inherited a great position which he seemed admirably suited to exploit. That, within two short years, his personal fortunes, his health, and his Party, as well as British prestige everywhere, should have suffered so humiliating, if temporary, a set-back and rebuff is one of the true tragedies of our times.

The part RAB played in these stirring and extraordinary events is the part he typically played throughout his career, forming and holding his own considered view, pressing it as opportunity offered, refusing to contemplate resignation if that meant splitting the party and the country.

The overthrow of King Farouk by the young officers' corps of a section of the Egyptian Army on July 25, 1952, was one of those major events that changed not only the destinies of Egypt but the whole trend and pace of Arab nationalism. This nationalism was the outward and visible sign of the feelings and aspirations of over a hundred million Moslem Arabs divided by every detail of self-interest and geographical and historical accident, but united by a common language, much common blood, by a great deal of common law and an absolutely common faith, that of Islam, which they all shared.

Now King Farouk was not the focal point of Arab nationalism. He was the rather arbitrary ruler of Egypt, but he did tolerate a Parliament, he did rule through his Ministers, and he did observe international Treaties because, perhaps, he felt that he was in no position to defy them. Unfortunately he carried on his private life largely in public and partly abroad and although that life differed not at all from the life which it was traditional for the Khedives of Egypt to enjoy, the social climate was changing and Farouk made no allowance for this. However, he had started his reign in a blaze of glory, a slim, very handsome young Prince with the world before him. And when, in World War II, the British, fearful that he was dickering with the Germans

—a well-founded fear—surrounded his Palace with tanks
and forced him to capitulate on policy, the Egyptian people,
who have always had the notion that Egypt was for the
Egyptians, revived their liking for him.

By 1952 this liking had receded. Farouk had not grown up.
He had become a womanizer with a questionable taste in
women. He had become grossly over-weight and in the hot
summer of 1952 especially he had become very rash and
unwise so that even his most loyal Ministers tired of him.

Nevertheless, when the coup came, it was a paralyzing
blow. The young officers had been humiliated and infuriated
by their defeat at the hands of the Israelis, a reverse which
they attributed largely to the inferior weapons supplied to
the Army by contractors and agents said to have the patronage of the King and his Ministers. The King was asked to
leave and was given three days to pack. A ceremony was
staged at Alexandria and in a last salute to their monarch
they let him sail off into exile, making his infant son King
for a time. This was, later, abrogated.

It was, as revolutions go, a civilized revolution. It had none
of the appalling butchery that disfigured the murdering of
young King Faisal of Iraq and his wily old Minister Nuri
Said, when baby princesses were shot and bayoneted as they
held the Koran.

But, although civilized, it was a basic revolution. After a
short spell with General Neguib, a respected senior Army
Officer, the head, the real leader of the revolution, Gamal
Abdel Nasser, emerged.

This extraordinary man, the son of a small postal official,
was very near to the Egyptian proletariat, the fellahin, the
workers, the people of Egypt who "had not spoken yet" under
four hundred years of Ottoman surpremacy and sixty-odd
years of British influence and dictation.

Nasser was determined to make the revolution a real one.
The military coup was necessary to change the régime, but
not only the régime, the whole shape of society was to
be changed. All the old Ministers and most of the former

members of Parliament were banished from public life.
Before he came to power Nasser had written his "Philosophy
of the Revolution". Egypt was to regain her former glory,
become prosperous at home, greatly industrialized, and a
power abroad, the undisputed leader of the Arab world.
That was the dream and he was determined it should come
true. Nasser was incorruptible, living in the same modest
house he had occupied as an Army Colonel and lecturer.
This side of his character brought him great prestige at home.
The Egyptian people had seldom had a leader who did not
wax rich in office.

And then came responsibility. How to make the dream
come true? One way was extensive industrialization. Egypt
had been regarded by the British as a "purely agricultural
nation". True, industry had started and started well under
Farouk, but mainly industry linked to Egypt's agricultural
produce, for instance, the textile industry linked to cotton.

Nasser decided on the greatest measures to meet the threat
of a "population explosion" that was frightening. He decided,
among other measures, to build a new Aswan High Dam that
would inundate a great lake more than sixty miles in length
so that the immense Nile waters could be stored and released
scientifically, adding at one stroke at least a third to the
natural agricultural output as well as providing huge
resources of power for industry.

America and Britain agreed to back the dam project with
the large sums required. This was a task as great in its way
as the building of the Pyramids—and much more useful, if
not equally enduring. Then, suddenly, the United States
Government withdrew its support and was followed very
shortly and, in the opinion of some observers, somewhat
slavishly, by the British Government.

For Cairo and Nasser this was a real disaster. It was a
rebuff from the West that came out of the blue and no valid
reasons were given for it. It turned Egypt towards the Soviet
Union for support, realizing the century-old Russian dream
of establishing a foothold of influence in Africa at the heart

of the principal satellite of the former Ottoman Empire in Cairo.

Nasser, sensing unerringly the feelings of his countrymen —this was, as it is now, the key to his power—decided on a stroke so bold and novel that only complete success could justify it. He decided to nationalize the Suez Canal, up to then controlled by an international company with headquarters in Paris, in which Britain held a large share. The Canal passed entirely through Egyptian territory so it was not an international waterway any more than the Panama Canal is. But the administration, the finance, the maintenance, all was in foreign hands controlled from a foreign capital.

Nasser had good reasons for wanting the Canal revenue. His sources of national income were mainly two—cotton and tourism. These were not enough. If he could have the fifty to sixty million pounds paid by the ships who used the Canal annually the financial position of Egypt would be changed overnight. It was a great gamble. If he lost, he probably lost all. If he won there was a bright future awaiting him and the people for whom he genuinely cared.

But the act of seizure—that was the word used—was at once described by the Canal users (except Greece who played a waiting independent game) as illegal. Nasser was faced with an international crisis of the first magnitude.

Britain, as one of the most influential shareholders in the Suez Canal Company and as the greatest user of the Canal, having a larger tonnage of toll-paying ships than even Greece or Norway or the United States, took a lead in the plans to bring this reckless rebel to book. Eden as Prime Minister of Britain was most deeply involved and RAB as his deputy right at the centre of the entire affair. The Government, when they heard the news, were genuinely shocked and at once set about organizing the Canal-user nations as a body who could bring their influence to bear in the matter, if necessary by refusing to use the Canal until guarantees were given, or international control was restored. The position of the United

States was a strange one. It was Eisenhower's Government who had started the ball rolling by withdrawing support for the Aswan High Dam, but now the State Department seemed, to use Lord Kilmuir's phrase, to be hedging its bet. To the school of thought who think that one of the major objectives of American foreign policy, not admitted, but nevertheless real, is the substitution of British by American influence in all countries formerly within the Empire or in close ties with Britain, this attitude caused no surprise, but to the Eden Government it must have been profoundly disturbing. The Soviet Union quite naturally decided to take the Egyptian side in the dispute as Egypt was turning to the Soviet Union for aid and money.

The Government, through the Lord Chancellor and its Law Officers, made out the case against unilateral annexation of the Suez Canal by the Egyptian Government, and in international law the case certainly had substance. But in natural justice Nasser's Government had, perhaps, an even better reply. What was being denied to Egypt, according to the Egyptian case, was the right to nationalize one of their own assets, the Canal, and its installations, all on Egyptian territory.

In fact, it was a classic dispute between the arrangements and understandings solemnly arrived at and scrupulously observed by the old imperialism and the natural, inevitable desire of the newly-liberated nations to be masters of their own house. Egypt, of course, was not an emergent nation. Her civilization was one of the oldest, her former power and empire one of the greatest. Still, for centuries she had not been fully free and it was full freedom that President Nasser was now demanding. Needless to say, the Arab nations, for the most part, took Egypt's side. But Britain started out on the Suez Canal crisis with a great deal of goodwill, especially from other large Canal users. She seemed to occupy a commanding position. How all this goodwill was dissipated and lost in a miserable and tragic adventure is the story of Suez.

Sir Anthony Eden, more even than RAB, had been conversant with the Egyptian negotiations with Britain on the Canal for a considerable period. After the defeat of the Ottoman Empire in 1918 Britain had regarded herself as custodian of the Canal for the Company and in 1935 this position was legalized for twenty years by the Egyptian Government who at that time thought that Italy had designs on the Canal. The negotiator on the British side was— Anthony Eden. In 1954 Eden negotiated a new Anglo-Egyptian Treaty and two years later the last British soldiers left the Canal Zone. One month later Nasser acted and read his nationalization proclamation to an enthusiastic meeting in Port Said.

An international conference was called in London of the principal maritime states as well as the Soviet Union, and twenty-two out of the twenty-four nations invited accepted. Mr. Dulles, since generally discredited, but at the time in the high regard of President Eisenhower, backed this approach and said that Egypt would have, as a result of this marshalling of world opinion, to accept that she must give guarantees of free passage and also accept financial control so that profits from the Canal should be ploughed back into it and not be diverted to general Egyptian Government account. This, of course, is exactly what President Nasser did not want. He needed the money, and the Canal was a flourishing business. Moreover, he had set out terms of compensation which, though not generous, were, in the opinion of some detached observers, tolerable. Britain pursued the matter through legal means, submitting the whole dispute to the United Nations after Mr. Dulles, for some reason that no one could explain, had retreated from his original stand at a press conference that followed a renewed meeting of the canal users in London on September 23. The Commonwealth, Australia—under Mr. Menzies—in particular, gave Britain much practical support on committees and in private councils.

Hugh Gaitskell told the author that on August 31, at a very critical point in the protracted negotiations, he had called on RAB in London (Eden was resting at the weekend already under strain) and asked for an assurance that Parliament would be recalled not later than September 14 to discuss Suez. RAB said he was not able to give such an undertaking. Gaitskell had no doubt that RAB, personally, took a grave view of possible developments which might land Britain in a war with Egypt and world opinion against her. That such developments were at least a possibility the public could guess, for attending the innumerable meetings the names of General Templer, the head of the Imperial General Staff, and Lord Mountbatten, the First Sea Lord, began to appear. Eden was looking ahead to military action if diplomacy should fail. With the Dulles turnabout, diplomacy did fail. It became clear that the canal users were not going to get their way and that the Egyptian Government, immensely encouraged by the Dulles new line, were going to hold fast.

RAB was not alone in opposing a resort to force. Sir Walter Monckton was equally doubtful and distrustful of the kind of operation that would have to be launched. However, Eden was advised by his Service chiefs that, given sufficiently secret preparation, the Canal could be seized and very quickly. There would be landings from the sea to capture Port Said—the French were to take Suez—and there would be parachute droppings in force along the Canal. Eden grasped at this counsel, and the real implications he seems to have ignored in spite of RAB's warnings.

He was able to do this because, distrusting the handling of so delicate an operation by a body as large as the entire Cabinet, he formed an inner Cabinet consisting of convinced Suez men who wanted to take the Canal and were sure he could do it. They were: Harold Macmillan, Selwyn Lloyd, Anthony Head, Lord Salisbury, Lord Home and, of course, the Prime Minister himself.

Of this body RAB was not a member, but he persevered and got his view through to the Cabinet on many occasions. Eden ignored RAB's views on Suez because he did not want to hear them. Eden himself had formed a most unfavourable

view of President Nasser, whom he personally disliked
intensely. The distrust was mutual, and this factor played
its part in the drama that was now unfolding. RAB stated
his views not only to his colleagues but to influential outsiders
such as two members of the Norwegian party that accom-
panied the Norwegian Prime Minister on an official visit to
London. He spoke at this time of his possible resignation,
but seemed to dread taking that awful step. In fact, had he
taken it at this time it might well have brought down the
Government, for Gaitskell, at first sympathetic to the diplomatic efforts of the Government, became actively hostile as
it became known that war was contemplated.

At this tense moment in the Suez affair the author went to
the Egyptian Embassy to deliver two copies of a book by
himself recently published and entitled *The Sphinx Awakes*.
The urbane and friendly First Secretary El Dib Benshi said:
"It is war. We leave tomorrow." And then on the steps of
the Embassy he said with much emotion: "How could you
do this to us?"

This reflected the view of many Egyptians, not of necessity
warm supporters of the revolution but patriotic and widely
read. Britain had been with Egypt for so long. Often hated,
always respected, the headmaster who intervened when
things went wrong. There was some kind of an understanding,
a toleration between the Egyptians and the British that
never contemplated the possibility of British bombs killing
Egyptians. It was just inconceivable. Yet it was going to
happen.

When thirty-four Tory Members of Parliament made it
clear that they were unable to support the Eden line, Hugh
Gaitskell offered to co-operate on a national basis with a
new leader if Eden were to go. It was the rôle that RAB
could have stepped right into. But he hesitated and was lost.

No event of recent years has been more hidden from public
probe and enquiry than the Suez affair, in particular the
invasion itself. The exercise was presented to the British
public in the press as a mere matter of form in which there

was token Egyptian resistance easily surmounted. This was not the case. It took three days to capture Port Said, and the most intense and bloody fighting took place in the city. Many paratroopers on the Canal were shot as they descended and even in the captured city of Port Said Egyptian guerrillas operated as was seen in the tragic kidnapping of Lieutenant Moorhouse.

British agents operating in Egypt had assured the Government that, with the capture of Cairo and the Canal, Nasser would flee to another Arab State taking his Cabinet with him to form a Government in exile. This did not happen. The green light had been the Dulles change-of-front. The Egyptian leaders seized on to it. Abdel Kadir Hatem, Nasser's able and energetic Minister of Information, worked with his team night and day to get the Egyptian viewpoint over to every Embassy in Cairo and every foreign government abroad. The British high explosive and fire bombs had done their dread work and it was possible to augment the verbal arguments of persuasion with some terrifying and moving photographs.

The United Nations with fifty-seven voting for the motion —though many abstained—condemned the British action and called for withdrawal and a peaceful solution.

It was decided to send a United Nations force to Egypt. The great Anglo-French withdrawal began. Eden, now very ill, flew to Jamaica leaving RAB to carry on as best he could. It was generally felt that Britain had bowed to American pressure and Sir Ian Horobin, a member of the Suez Group, asked in the House whether it would be necessary to ask American permission to bring the Prime Minister back from Jamaica. Such was the bitterness. . . .

RAB remained loyal to Eden, whose courage he admired even if he doubted his judgment. At the subsequent Tory Party Conference he paid him this tribute: "I have served under many Prime Ministers and I have never known them to possess in a more marked degree those qualities of courage and integrity that characterize the Prime Minister who is now going to address us." The Tory Party, meeting in the shambles of this great tragedy, was closing its ranks.

But RAB had lost much. He got no credit for staying in the Government. He got no credit for attempting to clear up the mess. He earned only the distrust and dislike of the Suez conspirators, who could neither forget nor forgive.

The "Not RAB" school had been founded and formed. Its cement was bitterness and frustration, but, because of its rancour, its sentiments lasted and became an enduring enmity to RAB and all he stood for. In politics, when the pack are hunting, it is necessary to hunt with the pack or quit the hunt. RAB's conviction that reason, persuasion, good sense could be more effectively exerted from within than without proved to be an illusion. There are times when a great public figure, faced with policies he knows to be wrong, has to reach out from Westminster to the people, the people who, though they may owe allegiance to one or other Party, are more concerned with peace and the acceptance between nations of the standards they try to maintain in their private lives. This is another Britain, but it is a multitude. Only the Prime Minister can reach them in office. For RAB to reach them he would have had to resign. It would have required the greatest courage.

There would have been a torrent of condemnation and abuse. It would have been said that he was seeking to under-mine the position of the Prime Minister in a crisis for personal ambition. He would have been invited, jeeringly, by the Suez Group, to join Hugh Gaitskell and the Labour Party.

His appeal to the British people would have had to give them all the facts, facts which he knew by virtue of the office he held.

He would have had to say that a great military and naval invasion of Egypt was being planned in agreement with the French. He would have to say that, although the Egyptian Government, by nationalizing the Canal, had broken pacts arrived at by former Governments, the Canal was Egyptian and the right to take over its own property was a right that all

States expected to be able to exercise. It applied to oil, and it applied to water. And he would have had to tell the English people that war, bombs, killing, invasion, terror was not the reply to this action. It was invoking too great a sanction for the crime and would lose Britain friends she had around the world.

It might well be that such a resignation followed by such an appeal by RAB would have prevented the Suez disaster. Perhaps only he could have done it, for this man, whatever his standing in his own Party, and that was unique, did appeal to that broad mass of English men and women who placed their country before their political allegiances. It was a position which, to the end, he never exploited. It was not in his nature to do so. He was all the time immensely busy. Apart from the cares of his own office and the leadership of the House, he was the only man readily available to carry the burden for an ailing Prime Minister whose judgment was failing to retain a detached approach to the great problems that seemed to press him from every side.

Egyptians' reaction to an invasion they were powerless to prevent, though fight they did, was to block the Canal by sinking ships for that purpose. This dislocated world trade by making the Canal impassable whoever ruled its banks. After Eden's departure for Jamaica RAB negotiated with Hammarskjold to use the Anglo-French forces and equipment to clear the waterway again. This was granted, but the question of crews raised immediate difficulty.

The United States refused all financial support until withdrawal had begun. On November 22 RAB had to face the House of Commons and announce that withdrawal had started. The threats of the Soviet Union to use nuclear force against Britain raised no murmur of protest from the American Government. The negotiations and the declarations that RAB had to make both to the House and to Britain's "allies" required great courage, more perhaps than his resignation would have demanded. It was only possible for him to fight this rearguard action which Nye Bevan described

as "sounding the bugle of advance to cover his retreat" if
he maintained that, broadly, the Suez operation had been
justified. He could not publicly parade the fact that, all
along, he had fought against it. That would have given the
Opposition a chance of mortally damaging the Tory Party.

Perhaps the phrase "fought against it" is an over-simplifica-
tion. He had been the creature of conflicting emotions. He
greatly admired and liked Eden. But he was quite sure his
judgment on this one great issue was at fault. He was
desperately anxious not to disrupt or to harm the Tory Party
in which he believed, and to whose aims he had dedicated
his political life. Looking back, we must feel that his position
was as difficult and as fraught with conflicting loyalties as
any a public man could be confronted with.

After the United Nations Resolution condemning Britain
over a hundred Conservative Members drafted a motion that
"this House congratulates the Foreign Secretary on his efforts
to secure international control of the Suez Canal and deplores
both the resolution of the General Assembly calling for an
immediate and unconditional withdrawal of British and
French troops from Egypt, and the attitude of the United
States which is gravely endangering the Atlantic Alliance".

RAB had to cope not only with the Labour attack but with
a greatly strengthened Suez Group that now represented
nearly a third of the Parliamentary Party. The attack from
Gaitskell was easier to counter than that of his own rebels.
When Gaitskell went on television and spoke contemptuously
of Eden as totally discredited, an almost feline note crept
into his voice. The British people did not like what they
heard. Eden might have made a major mistake, but they
did not doubt his sincerity or the gravity of the issues at
stake. They resented the exploitation of these for Party
advantage. It was a mean little tirade and it did the Labour
Party great harm.

When Eden came back from Jamaica he was met by silence
and resentment in the House. RAB at least had refused to
leave the bridge. After the Prime Minister had walked the

few steps from behind the Speaker's chair to his place on
the front bench it was obvious to those long familiar with the
peculiarities and temper of the House that he was finished
as a political force in Britain. The bright morning of two
short years ago had turned so quickly into a night of sullen
resentment.

It was the most critical time for many years for the Tory
Party. One man was largely responsible for keeping the Party
voting together—Edward Heath. This indefatigable little
man with the broad smile never let up. He was everywhere.
He rendered his Party inestimable service in a real crisis.
The situation tested the abilities of the Chief Whip to the
utmost. Edward Heath emerged triumphantly from the
struggle.

And Harold Macmillan? He kept out of the fury as much
as he could. It was easy for a Chancellor to keep to the
manifold complexities of the Exchequer. He had gone along
with Suez but little ignominy attached to him. It had not
been his decision. Selwyn Lloyd at the Foreign Office, too,
never incurred much wrath. It was not credible that Selwyn
really controlled events at the top. He was surely a camp
follower, a nice, rather pompous, completely honest support-
ing-caste actor. He was not a villain.

The rumour got around and was sedulously cultivated that
it had all been RAB's fault. He had undermined Sir Anthony.
RAB had been the Doubting Thomas from the start and
instead of getting out like a man he had used his position to
corrode the Party and the Government from within. It was
very unjust, but those who find themselves in the dock of
public opinion are apt to cast around for someone to blame.
They blamed RAB. And his only reply was that wintry and
now somewhat weary smile that said: "I've heard it all
before. Think what you like. . . ."

The whole Suez crisis has a larger than life aspect. In
retrospect it seems clear that the decisive factor that halted
the whole operation was the American refusal to support the
pound sterling in spite of pleas from Harold Macmillan over

the telephone to Washington. Sir Edward Boyle actually
resigned in protest against what he regarded as a reckless
squandering of the nation's resources. But RAB placed his
objection not on finance, which was a serious hazard, but on
principle. He held that the punishment did not fit the crime,
that the nationalization of the Suez Canal was an aggravated
international civil dispute and that to invoke the sanction of
war, the equivalent of the criminal sanction in private life,
was disproportionate, unwise, and would have the most
serious repercussions.

The cost of launching the invasion, the cost of the loss of
equipment in the former base, the loss of trade following the
closure of the Canal and the continuing loss of the Egyptian
market had amounted to well over a hundred million pounds;
probably, if secondary losses are taken into account, much
more. For this huge debt incurred at a time when Britain
could ill afford it Eden, Macmillan, Kilmuir, Selwyn Lloyd
and the other members of the inner Cabinet were to blame.
But by a feat of propaganda inspiring a tenacious whispering
campaign the blame could easily be transferred to RAB.
Sometimes politics is not a very nice business. In England
politicians are not shot in the back but they are wounded
just as effectively as if a knife was used.

The public were deeply disturbed at the repercussions of
the Suez business. They were by no means convinced that
RAB Butler was the culprit. The rumour was that he had had
reservations throughout and had expressed them forcibly.
In the House the Prime Minister was asked: Would he
appoint an official historian of the Suez affair? The answer
was: No. Then he was asked if he would appoint a Select
Committee of Inquiry along the lines of that investigating
the Dardanelles disaster. Again the answer was: No. Not at
present. When? asked members. "The time may come sooner
than you expect," said Harold Macmillan darkly. This was
pure jabberwock. There never was to be an official revelation
or explanation of the Suez disaster.

The result that chiefly disturbed the public was the

shocking blow to Britain's reputation throughout the world. In modern times we had never been the object of such universal condemnation. To ride the storm and put a brave face on matters was a dire task for our ambassadors abroad.

But the Suez Group did not relent. They made no public apology for the mistake that had cost the public so dearly. They continued to maintain they had been right. This attitude made it absolutely essential to put the blame on someone. They could not blame the French Government, who had been invited to join the adventure by Britain. They could not blame the Israeli Government, for they stoutly maintained that the Israeli attack on Egypt was just a happy coincidence planned and executed without their knowledge or consent. They could not blame Nasser for such military operations as he had undertaken were defensive. British civilians in Cairo and elsewhere had not been maltreated, in spite of great provocation. They could not blame the British public, which had been kept in the dark until the invasion was under way. They could not really blame Hugh Gaitskell except to say that he had made a whining, mischievous attack on television at the time when British paratroopers, as well as Egyptian civilians, were dying in the fighting.

RAB was the only target left. A certain amount of odium was directed by the Government against the part played by Nasser, the American Government, and the Opposition, but it was not convincing. The campaign against RAB was much more successful. They knew he was by nature vulnerable to a whispering campaign of calumny. He was most unlikely to answer back. He would just go on working. But at least, now that Eden was going, they could deprive him of the leadership. All the tension, the resentment, the frustration and the fury was channelled into one simple objective with the slogan "Not RAB"—at any price.

Had RAB become Prime Minister it would have been interpreted as a final acknowledgment of guilt by the Suez Group and the Suez Inner Cabinet. Moreover, it would have made the political futures of the gentlemen concerned much less rosy. This they were not prepared to tolerate. There was one more little conspiracy to hatch. In some way the Queen must be induced to send for Harold Macmillan and not to send for RAB Butler.

How could that be done? RAB was leader of the majority Party in the House of Commons. He had been acting as Deputy Prime Minister. How could the choice be circumvented?

It seemed certain, knowing his nature, that when Eden went RAB would make no move. He would probably go to his Essex home and wait for the summons that he would naturally expect. Or he would wait in Smith Square. Quick action by the Suez men would be necessary. Who would undertake the task? Why not the Lord President of the Council and Conservative Leader in the House of Lords— Lord Salisbury? Just the man. And backing him up with some learned explanations of the unfettered working of the Royal Prerogative, the Lord Chancellor, himself, Lord Kilmuir, the official keeper of the Queen's conscience.

With this adroit pair on the warpath RAB never had a chance. The British public were in for another surprise.

The biographer shirks his duty if he does not answer the questions he poses. We asked if RAB should not have resigned when he knew that war was being planned? This biographer, at any rate, will answer: yes. It would have indicated to the British people that a major mistake was being contemplated. RAB was the only man who could have done this at that time.

Incidentally had he done so there is little doubt that he would have been Prime Minister today. But the real motivation should have been: "I know this is wrong. It will do great harm to Britain. I must tell the people."

He could not bring himself to take this daring, dangerous and unpleasant step. As always, he stayed on the bridge.

IX

Macmillan's Triumph

JANUARY 13, 1957, was not a lucky day for RAB Butler. On that day Harold Macmillan became Prime Minister and First Lord of the Treasury. For the first time in his long career RAB had suffered a direct reversal.

He had every right to expect that he would follow Sir Anthony Eden as Prime Minister. Though not approving of the Suez operation, he had shown absolute loyalty and considerable courage in staying to repair as best he could the untold damage which that ill-starred venture had caused. He had deputized on many occasions for both Eden and Churchill. His achievements in diverse fields were second to none, his experience as long and varied as any living politician. But, when the chips were down, he was not chosen. Why?

This arose out of a sequence of events whereby the Queen sent for Harold Macmillan to form a Government instead of sending for RAB, who was Leader of the House of Commons and had been acting as Prime Minister for Sir Anthony Eden, on several occasions when for one reason or another Sir Anthony was not able to carry out his duties in person.

On the face of it, the action of the Crown in this matter is inexplicable and extraordinary. It seems certain that the outgoing Prime Minister made no firm recommendation to the Queen as to who should succeed him, and in any case the Palace must have known that Sir Anthony was so ill at the time that his judgment might well have been impaired by his illness.

It was an unexpected crisis. The Tory majority in the

House of Commons was fifty-nine, a substantial and com-
fortable working majority. After the shambles that followed
the Suez débâcle all the mopping up operations had been
in the hands of RAB. He was in fact governing Britain after
Sir Anthony's departure: Prime Minister in fact, though not
in name or in law.

In the circumstances, quite clearly, in the absence of a
firm recommendation from her outgoing Prime Minister it
was the Queen's constitutional duty to send for the Leader of
the House of Commons who was also leading the Party with
the largest number of Parliamentary seats. This applied whatever Party might happen to be in power. Instead, the Queen
sent for Lord Salisbury, who was leading the Tory Party in
the House of Lords—and for Sir Winston Churchill. To send
for the Tory Leader in the House of Lords without sending
for the Tory Leader in the House of Commons was, on the
face of it, a fantastic error of judgment. The Queen had been
ill-advised.

RAB waited for the summons to the Palace. He was
prepared to say he could form an immediate Government.
The summons never came. No meeting of the Conservative
Party was summoned. No real soundings within the Party
were made. Sir Winston Churchill was eighty-three and was
no longer playing an active part in politics. He was, of course,
a former Prime Minister. So was Lord Attlee. He was not
consulted. Lord Salisbury was still active, but he was active
mainly in the Lords. He had virtually no following in the
country. He was unpopular with the rank and file of the Tory
Party, as he was, not unnaturally, with the Labour Party.

After the visit of the two very elder Statesmen the Queen
sent for Harold Macmillan, who was Chancellor of the
Exchequer and who had married a daughter of the late Duke
of Devonshire. The present Duchess was one of the Queen's
ladies at court. There is no doubt that Churchill cast his vote
against RAB, who had crossed his path so often, and in favour
of Harold Macmillan, who had always been an admirer and
supporter. Lord Salisbury, likewise, was known to dislike

Butlerism. He was at this time tending to regard himself as a Tory oracle. Later, when he presumed on his patronage of Mr. Macmillan too much, forcing his personal views on Cyprus, Harold Macmillan, with some spirit, sent him packing. He did not emerge politically thereafter.

What really happened is so fantastic that one would not believe it if the evidence was not completely conclusive.

The strange exercise of the Prerogative, on this occasion, can only be explained by examining in some detail what went on behind the scenes. Why was Lord Salisbury called to the Palace? What mandate did he hold? And from whom?

Fortunately we have the unimpeachable word of the Lord Chancellor as to what happened at the height of the crisis:

> We then went to Downing Street and Anthony announced his resignation. . . . Thereafter Bobbety and I asked our colleagues to see us one by one in Bobbety's room in the Privy Council Offices which could be reached without leaving the building.

Very convenient and entirely private. As the Cabinet appeared one by one Lord Salisbury put the same question to each: "Well, which is it, Wab or Hawold?" My Lord Chancellor, it seems, jotted down the replies and the majority favoured Hawold. So Hawold it was. By this parody of preparatory school procedure were we governed in 1957.

This was Lord Salisbury's mandate. The Queen seems to have had some reservations as to whether the race was being run strictly according to the rules, so Sir Winston was called in to reinforce the decision of the stewards. Certainly the Chief Government Whip was briefly consulted, but no one else. It was a Cabinet decision. The Parliamentary Party, now in total control of leader-choosing, was ignored. The constituencies, of course, never heard a whisper until it was all over.

Why were Lord Kilmuir and Lord Salisbury made the referees on this occasion? Lord Kilmuir as Lord Chancellor was thought to be in over-all charge of the mystique of the

Royal Prerogative and Lord Salisbury, as Conservative Leader in the House of Lords, worked closely with him. Lord Salisbury was also Lord Privy Seal and as such had no active Ministerial duties but was close to the Sovereign and, it was said, understood all about how such matters could be arranged. He did.

Lord Kilmuir, in his captivating book, quotes a letter from Lord Salisbury congratulating him on a speech which the Lord Chancellor had made justifying Suez.

> My dear David,
>   May I most respectfully congratulate you? By jove, that was a good speech, closely reasoned, powerful, and, especially in the closing passages, extremely moving. The best I have ever heard you make.
>
> > > > Yours ever,
> > > > Bobbety.

And David Maxwell Fyfe had an equally high regard for Bobbety. David and Bobbety were, politically, David and Jonathan.

Lord Kilmuir, seeking, apparently, to justify what had been done, says quaintly that there was a "modern" precedent for the method adopted in the choice of Lord Rosebery in 1894! He seems quite unaware that the implication of this is that what was appropriate in 1894 was appropriate in 1957. Moreover, the deciding factor in 1894 was the Queen—Victoria—herself, who "hated" Sir William Harcourt—and would not have him at any price. . . .

What was behind it all? Lord Kilmuir perhaps dropped the key when he says: "RAB was in the habit of hedging his political bets. . . ." And he says this at the same time that he expresses personal affection and respect for him.

What did this really mean? If RAB had resigned because he disapproved of the Suez adventure he would have been accused of wrecking the Party, even of betraying the country. Perhaps he should have resigned and damned the consequences. Instead he urged caution and restraint not once but at over twelve Suez meetings. He made it painfully plain that, in his judgment, the venture was a major blunder and unlikely to achieve its objectives, either its first objective of seizing the Canal and restoring international control, or its secondary objective of toppling the Nasser régime and restoring King Farouk's young son as a democratic monarch in Egypt with an Egyptian Parliament. Moreover, RAB regarded with deep suspicion and foreboding the deal made with France to invade Egypt. A large number of Tories thought it would be a grand idea if the Israelis were encouraged to "go it alone"—to Cairo, but RAB was not of this school.

As it turned out, RAB was right. Bobbety, David and Anthony were wrong. Hence the wrath and the talk of bet-hedging. No impartial critic, looking back on RAB's career, can honestly say that he hedged his bets. He did not hedge his bet on India when he stood up to the bombardment of Sir Winston Churchill on the Government of India Bill before the war. He did not hedge his bets as Home Secretary when he managed to sit firmly on the police and prevent police brutality, while encouraging them, by every possible means, in their then effective fight against crime. And he did not hedge his bets as Chancellor of the Exchequer, for in all his Budgets the theme is constant—the greatest possible encouragement for free enterprise that could be achieved within the framework of a social policy that acknowledged its responsibility towards the old, the sick and the unfortunate.

What was the result of these legal machinations? The result was that the country was suddenly told: "It is not RAB, as you expected. It is Macmillan." Surprise. Surprise. The Tory Party, which has great merits, also seems to have an absolute flair for electing the leader the country does not want. Certainly the country expected RAB to take over. Quite simply he deserved it. Certainly the country was flabbergasted when Sir Alec Douglas Home—who was not even a Member of the House of Commons—emerged as the new prophet after hastily discarding his peerage. And the day before Mr. Heath was elected Leader, the public opinion polls which, as Hugh Gaitskell said, "are never quite right, but never far wrong," made it clear that the people wanted Maudling to lead the Party because they regarded him as a safer bet than Edward Heath, because of his nature, his abilities and his background. But then unregulated democracy has always been suspect in the Tory tabernacle. Even now the Parliamentary Party are the exclusive arbiters of this most important choice. Members are not obliged to take the slightest notice of any advice their constituencies give them. And on the whole they do not do so.

Sir Charles Petrie, in his excellent book on The Modern British Monarchy, puts forward the view that there was nothing strange in the Queen's action or in her nomination of Harold Macmillan. Macmillan, he suggests, had greater support within the Party. How did the Queen know this? Was it in any case true? RAB was unpopular with the "Suez Group" because, although he had not brought down the Government by resigning as perhaps he should have done, he was known to have opposed the project in the Cabinet, only bowing to a majority decision. But the Suez Group was not a large one. It represented no more than ten to fifteen per cent of the Tory Party. The Party itself and the country expected RAB to take over. The current odds quoted in his favour were four to one on. The Queen must have known this. And her advisers must have known that had RAB been summoned the Tory Party would have rallied behind him as, in fact, they rallied around Harold Macmillan.

One can only conclude that RAB was not sent for because it was realized that, had he been summoned to the Palace, he would have assured the Queen he could form a Government and that then there would have been no way out. The Queen would have constitutionally been impelled to ask him to submit his Cabinet.

The Queen's advisers must have known that, after the Suez debacle, to appoint a Minister who had backed the Suez project to the hilt, insisting that Britain could well afford it, and that it was right, must damage the name of Britain at least in the eyes of the great concourse of nations who, at the United Nations, had condemned the British action. But none of these points seems to have been considered.

This was one of the rare cases in which the Prerogative was exercised almost unfettered. Sir Anthony made no firm recommendation. In any case the Queen was constitutionally empowered to make her own choice after consulting whoever she chose. All one can say is that in the last exercise of the Prerogative in these circumstances the choice was most unfortunate. Not that Harold Macmillan made a bad Prime Minister. In many ways he was a good one. Not that RAB, of necessity, would have been better, though there were many who thought that he would have been.

What was unfortunate was that in a rare and singular case in which the Monarchy was called upon to exercise the power of choice it was exercised in such a way as to appear to be manifestly unfair. Macmillan offered to appoint RAB Home Secretary. RAB accepted and, as we shall see, was to make that office live again after a long period in the doldrums. But the shock of the passing over of RAB for the Premiership was to undermine the Tory Party and suggest to the public that Macmillan, although as a young man he had been fairly progressive, was now a member of the hard core, the old guard, who did not wish to change more than they could help. The City certainly took this view. When it was seen that Lord Salisbury had become Lord President of the Council, that Thorneycroft was at the Exchequer and that Selwyn Lloyd was at the Foreign Office the right-wing flavour of the Cabinet was reflected in a market move on the Stock Exchange. The City was quite sure that this was a defeat for the progressives. This was the all-clear to Big Business.

On this occasion RAB harboured remarkably little resentment. He was too old a trooper to expect the race always to abide by the rules. He had half expected that, at the crucial moment, the forces who suspected him and whom he had offended would bring off a lightning coup. He himself, in the vital hours, refused to make any move at all. He could have called a meeting of the Conservative Party in the House of Commons. He did not do so. He could have rallied the very powerful support he had in the House and in the party organization. He did not do so. He sat in his house attending to his papers, waiting for the call that never came.

It is customary to declare when writing of this incident that, in any case, no blame of any kind attaches to the Queen, that she was carrying out her duties as she saw them. This is a fair comment. The Queen was used in a manoeuvre to bar from the Premiership the man who was most obviously entitled to that office. It was an unfortunate lapse, all the more so as it is acknowledged in Britain that she always strives to do the right thing in the tradition in which her father brought her up.

To assess RAB's new position in the Party, in the country and at Westminster, it is necessary to know something of the character and background of Harold Macmillan, whom RAB now served as Home Secretary.

The Macmillans are an extraordinary family. Their rise has been so rapid and so well-deserved that we should know their background to appreciate the kind of man Harold Macmillan was (and is), and so have an idea of his relations with RAB and the part he was to play in RAB's career towards its end.

Over a century ago two brothers, Daniel and Alexander Macmillan, came to England from Scotland to pursue their fortunes in the book trade. They had great advantages. Coming from a poor family they knew the value of money. Brought up in God-fearing self-denial, they were much harder than the young Englishmen with whom they were to compete. And they both had integrity, astuteness and the willingness to work all hours of the day and, if necessary, the night. What they did not have was money, but this in itself was probably an advantage, because it meant that they worked hard as employees in a Cambridge bookshop and at Seeleys in the Strand, learning the trade from all angles before Archdeacon Hare and his brother lent them five hundred pounds to start in business.

They bought the Newbys bookshop in Cambridge and on account of their characters and dedication attracted the writers then resident in Cambridge—and many in London as well—to their circle as clients. Dean Stanley, Charles Kingsley, Lord Kelvin and other great names became associated with what we now know as the House of Macmillan. They published *Westward Ho!* and *John Brown's Schooldays.* They specialized in university and school textbooks. They moved to London, first to Henrietta Street and then to Bedford Street.* They became the forbears of a great publishing business still as active, as enterprising and as dedicated as it was over a hundred years ago.

This was Harold Macmillan's background. God and a profit. Integrity and astuteness. Self-denial and hard work. Prayer and progress. It was a background that stood him in good stead. He started out with no firm intention of taking part in public life. "I married a publisher," Lady Dorothy, his wife, once said, "And look what I have ended up with!"

Harold Macmillan had two assets in addition to those he inherited from his formidable grandparents. He was exceptionally handsome and distinguished-looking. Whereas RAB always looked like what he was, an intelligent and prosperous member of the British upper-class, Harold Macmillan looked every inch an aristocrat. Of course, he may have been. The Scottish clans are, or were, a closely woven society and there was no member of the clan that could not claim kinship with the laird. It was, as a rule, only a matter of tracing one's lineage but this was usually difficult. But from some ancestor or as a lucky gift from heaven Harold Macmillan looked like the historic leader of the Tory Party in person, the English country gentleman who had taken up public life. The aristocrat who had decided to work for the people.

This was not his only advantage. Beneath the charming manners and the grand public manner which characterized

* Macmillans moved in 1965 to Little Essex Street.

his later years lay a first-class brain. Like RAB, he had won
his double-first, but at Oxford. He had distinguished himself
in the First World War, had become attached to the staff of
the Duke of Devonshire on the Duke's appointment as
Governor-General of Canada, and had married one of the
Duke's daughters. His rise under Eden had been very rapid.
He had been given the vital post of Foreign Secretary which
was taken over by Selwyn Lloyd. The public could not help
comparing the nice but mediocre Mr. Lloyd with his brilliant
predecessor. And then he had been made Chancellor of the
Exchequer. RAB knew very well that Macmillan was lying
second in the race for the leadership if anything were to
happen to Sir Anthony. But RAB, typically, made no change
in his routine of dedication to his work, remaining on a
personal level amost unknown to the rank and file of the
party.

   Not so Harold Macmillan. In his club, in the smoking-room
of the House of Commons, in his constituency, Bromley
(where he maintained a huge majority), in London, in Scotland, he was always there ready to sip a sherry, ready to talk,
ready to charm. It paid dividends. And yet RAB could not
believe that his position was seriously challenged. After all,
RAB had held office in the party for twenty-five years. He
had done much more for the Tory Party than Macmillan
ever could or would do. There was one other factor that was
important in this matter. Macmillan was eight years older
than RAB. If RAB took the leadership, Harold Macmillan
might be past it when RAB was retiring. But if Macmillan
had a full term of office, RAB would still be at an age when
he could certainly take over the leadership.

   So that, on all counts, Harold Macmillan was a dangerous
rival to RAB. He was a bird of very bright plumage, as
brilliant in his own way as Oswald Mosley had been before
he began his awful flirtation with Fascism. As it happened,
Macmillan, as we have seen, owed his choice as Prime
Minister more to RAB's character and record than his own
merits.

If RAB had been able to pursue his career without offending that sometimes unforgiving old warrior Winston Churchill; if Lord Salisbury had been his personal friend although politically belonging to another wing of the party; if the Tory backbenchers had risen as one man in his support as they might well have done had he given them the opportunity of friendship, the story would have been very different. But RAB was RAB, and Harold Macmillan was himself. And the Queen's character and characteristics were also firmly resolved. The Queen always wished to do what was right. She was also most anxious not to become involved in a Party leadership clash. She read the papers submitted to her each week and understood them, but she was not, essentially, interested either in constitutional law, constitutional practice—not always identical—or in the Prerogative. It never seems to have occurred to her that in consulting Sir Winston and Lord Salisbury she was taking advice from the two men who could be guaranteed to dish RAB if they could.

One of the difficulties that arises in any exercise of the Prerogative is that the Queen has to make the approaches through her courtiers and private secretaries. When it was suggested to the Queen that she better have a word with Sir Winston it seemed a wonderful idea. The people venerated the old gentleman. He would advise what he thought was right for Britain. But human nature is not so simple. When she summoned Lord Salisbury, again, as he was leader of the House of Lords, it seemed to her a most proper move. And if the answer was Harold Macmillan, well, how suitable he was anyway, the kind of man to whom one could talk with such ease.

The Queen's mind was made up because she was told that Harold Macmillan had a firmer and larger following within the Tory Party than RAB Butler. This was not quite a lie, but it was extremely debatable. In reviewing the whole affair, it seems that only a very independent and strong-willed Monarch could have avoided being led into the choice that was made. The judgment was wrong and unjust but there was no appeal. It was Macmillan. Next day the Press were swarming round the new leader. RAB had been passed by for the first time.

At this point, an interesting turn of events occurred. Macmillan adopted exactly the same tactics in dealing with RAB as Churchill had done on forming his wartime Government. He gave him the most unglamorous high Cabinet position available. It was a difficult Cabinet-making. It was not easy to fit in all the friends of this amiable and astute new leader. But RAB had to have a post. He was too great a force in the Tory Party to be ignored or dropped. He would not, Macmillan knew, accept a post abroad however exalted. Churchill had tried that in 1941, and failed. So the Home Office? Why not?

The Home Secretary did not really have any major political decisions to make. He would not divert the spotlight from the Prime Minister. He was concerned with prisons, the police, immigration, licensing, that kind of thing and, oh yes, security. . . .

The Office was offered with a smile and accepted without one. Macmillan now reaped the full golden harvest which his friendship with Winston Churchill had been instrumental in sowing. As far back as 1946, when Macmillan had been first adopted as Prospective Parliamentary Candidate in Bromley, Churchill as Tory leader had gone out of his way to encourage and support him, sending him a carefully-worded message: "The work you did as British Resident Minister in the United Mediterranean and afterwards as Acting President of the Allied Commission for Italy during the war was important, difficult and delicate. . . ." The public had been conditioned to regard Harold Macmillan as an exceptional man. In many ways he was. RAB went to the Home Office to take up the reins there and found an organization which, in the opinion of many, was in need of inspired leadership.

Enthusiastically, RAB applied himself to the reformation

of the penal philosophy of the country just as, on being appointed Minister of Education during the war, he had turned his energies towards an educational revolution. It was no good trying to keep RAB down. Whatever job he was given to do, he did it, perhaps better than anyone else could do. His policy of "Never resign, never complain" kept him near the heart of Government in Westminster where he lived, and in the House of Commons which he loved.

The real significance of his work at the Home Office I will examine later. It is necessary now to notice that he was from the start very much more than Home Secretary. He was by far the senior member of the Cabinet. His advice on any problem arising could never be ignored. When Macmillan projected himself as a world statesman and started to travel, it was inevitable that RAB should be acting for him during his absence. And the public at any rate had no doubt that when RAB was deputizing nothing would be allowed to go wrong. Nevertheless the spotlight was firmly on Macmillan. RAB was the senior member of a supporting cast. It is to his credit that, in this position, he continued tenaciously, not yielding an inch his right to speak for the Party on matters of importance, claiming the position of a statesman with a long experience, retaining his own individual approach without at any time undermining Macmillan or detracting from the cohesion and unity of purpose in the Cabinet or in the country.

In view of the allegations that he had undermined Eden and wrecked the Suez project, it is important to note RAB's meticulous behaviour during the years of Macmillan's premiership. He was as loyal a colleague as could be wished for. If there was any treachery in the events that led up to Macmillan becoming Prime Minister, or in the years that followed, it must be attributed to a small but vociferous minority who conducted a "Not RAB at any price" campaign. Why should they do this? One answer certainly is that RAB was right about Suez, and Eden and the Cabinet and the Suez Group wrong. Their failure was mortifying and it rankled. They never forgave RAB for being right. Had he resigned he would have perhaps brought down the Government and secured his own future. Had he kept quiet, he would have been much more acceptable. On this occasion the course that was calculated to do him the most harm was the course he adopted, fighting against the Suez adventure from within. It laid him open to the unjustified suggestion that he was a wrecker who preferred to work undercover.

On 23rd January, Macmillan was presented to the Tory Party. The motion that he should be adopted as Leader of the Conservative Party was proposed by Lord Salisbury and seconded by R. A. Butler. Macmillan replied stressing Party unity. It was all over. Macmillan entered the House of Commons to great Tory cheering, but those who were there said that RAB looked pensive and aloof. Perhaps he was looking into the future, speculating when his day would come. The Labour Party secretly welcomed Macmillan. They thought him much more vulnerable than RAB whom they regarded as a formidable opponent, calculating, cautious, experienced, adroit.

Those who supported RAB and his progressive policies were, at first, inclined to think that Macmillan would not last as Premier, that the stench of Suez would drive him out of office, when RAB would take over. This was not to be. Macmillan with great astuteness consolidated his position in the House of Commons. Previously regarded as being too intolerant he became friendly, careful, sensible. He conducted himself with dignity and composure. He was, or seemed to be, as the papers said "unflappable".

Those who watched him closely during this period suggest that he was acting but that the act was so good that it was entirely acceptable. The Tory Party put themselves in the hands of a well-known publicity and public relations firm. Macmillan was built up as a television personality. He took to it with aplomb. RAB was kept in the picture by being made the housekeeper when the Prime Minister was on tour.

Macmillan showed that he had teeth. Lord Salisbury, now

Lord Privy Seal and leader of the House of Lords, said he would resign if Makarios was released. Macmillan consulted RAB. He then bid Lord Salisbury goodbye. Lord Salisbury was surprised and hurt. He had been a vital link in the chain of events that secured Harold Macmillan the Premiership. He tried to come back later over the Rhodesian Federation, but no one was listening to him any more. It was RAB who was given the impossible job of attempting to perpetuate the Federation.

Then Macmillan had to face another hurdle. His whole Treasury team—Thorneycroft, the Chancellor, Nigel Birch, and Enoch Powell resigned over the issue of economy, resisting the Premier's wish to spend an additional fifty million pounds on Defence and other services. Macmillan, as usual, was undisturbed. On the day of Thorneycroft's resignation, the Prime Minister flew off on a Commonwealth tour. The matter was debated by the Cabinet with RAB in the chair. Heathcote Amory took Thorneycroft's place. The Macmillan-Butler combination was proving to be unbreakable. In fact, between them, the two men commanded the support of ninety per cent of the Party. Only a Suez lump on the one hand and a few individualists on the other, remained as potential dangers. Macmillan could go off on the Grand Tour sublimely confident.

Although over a period of months he had gradually ousted RAB from a position that seemed invulnerable, he never entertained the idea that, when he was away, his own position might be threatened or undermined. He was completely right in relying on the loyalty both of RAB and his friends.

RAB had not changed his faith. He still believed, perhaps more firmly than before, in the unification of the "two Britains". The rich must not be allowed to become farther and farther removed from the great mass of the weekly workers in industry and the only way to prevent this was to bring the industrial worker up by making him a property owner, by raising his standards of living.

This progressive thinking was not the kind of thinking that characterized the Macmillan era. In his long spell at the head of affairs, Macmillan, himself reputedly a millionaire, encouraged free enterprise, but he also tolerated an alarmingly rapid growth of a Spiv England. The property speculators, the Stock Exchange gamblers, had the time of their lives. Luxury flat and office accommodation building easily outpaced that of homes in the London area and elsewhere where the need for cheap houses was desperate.

A suspicion grew in the minds of the people that this grandiloquent figure with his intimate fireside chats and his colleagues were very much influenced by the City. When individual members of Parliament were attacked on this score they were outraged. Lord Salisbury indignantly denied that his opposition to the breakup of the Rhodesian Federation was influenced by his South African business interests or that he represented the White minority in Rhodesia. But the public still had the impression that the strings were being pulled less by Whitehall than by Throgmorton Street.

When Macmillan went to Scotland to stay with that typical Scottish chieftain, Lord Home—of whom we shall hear more—he addressed a meeting of Scottish businessmen. He refused to release the text of his speech. His critics said that the purpose of the trip was to raise even more money for the Tory Party to ensure its return at the next General Election.

RAB, although friendly to the American Alliance, had never liked the idea that Britain might become a satellite of her powerful ally. When Macmillan allowed Polaris submarines—which had been refused much more convenient bases by the Norwegian Government—to operate without any supervision from Scottish bases it seemed as if the relationship of golden sun and pale satellite had just about been reached.

But Macmillan diverted attention from the increasing unrest at home and the growing malaise of the economy by a series of brilliant and well-advertised tours abroad. The

American President, the Soviet Leader, the Commonwealth Prime Ministers, were all treated to a flying visit from the volatile and photogenic British Premier. RAB constantly had to hold the home front. Macmillan, without any consultation, appointed Lord Home Foreign Secretary. There was uproar. A Foreign Secretary in the Lords! Unanswerable in the Commons! This ornate Victorian figure was leading us back into the 19th century with a vengeance. But Macmillan rode the storm.

In South Africa he addressed Parliament, saying that a wind of change was blowing through Africa. So it was. But there is no indication in the speech that Macmillan understood the problems of the three Africas, the Moslem Africa of the North, the negro Africa of the great Centre, or the special problems of the large white minorities of the South. Like so much else that Macmillan did it was news. It was striking, even spectacular, but it did not seem to be constructive. His one solid achievement was the Test Ban Treaty.

While all this was going on RAB did the only thing he could do. He devoted himself to the Office he ruled over. The Home Office knew from the first day he attended there that a genuine wind of change was going to blow through that establishment. The whole field of social life over which the Home Office ruled—the prisoners, the emigrants, the whores, the imbeciles as well as a far wider field of contacts with the general public through the police, law maintenance and security, was a sphere of politics that had avoided serious reform for nearly a century. RAB at once accepted the challenge that this represented. He carried on with his work at the Research Department, he retained his position as the second man in the Tory Party, he kept guard when the Prime Minister was out of the country, but, essentially, he tackled with his characteristic dedication and energy the appalling problems presented by the backwash of history, the relics of a feudal executive and the Victorian conceptions of crime, punishment, and morality, as well as the legal definition of insanity now so hopelessly outdated.

He was happy in this work. Here he could put the Butler philosophy, approach, and methods into practice. The Home Office capitulated to the impact of its masterful chief. If change had to come, it was better that it should come from RAB who would listen to advice—even if he did not always take it—and who was taking the trouble to master his brief.

X

The Home Office

IT WAS typical of RAB's resiliency and versatility that he
should survive the stresses and strains of the Suez débâcle
and come back at once to high office. True it was to the Home
Office, sometimes regarded as being a routine Police and
Security Office removed from the vital centre of political
movement. But with RAB, of course, it became an important
Office raising increasingly important questions in the rapidly
changing society of Britain.

If he knew little of penal reform when appointed, according to his permanent civil servants, he mastered the whole
problem very rapidly. Within weeks he was directing the
whole structure that covered the police, security, the prisons,
aliens, immigration and penal reform with his old consummate ease.

When RAB accepted the appointment of Home Secretary
in 1957, that Office was in a state of change with no particular
guiding principles to direct that change along modern and
profitable lines. The salaried staff lacked leadership and the
fringe of well-meaning reformers—men and women—who
dabbled in penal reform and immigration were, on the whole,
more of a liability than an asset.

It is not generally realized how important the Home Office
is in the structure of Government. The Home Secretary is
responsible for the maintenance of Law and Order and for all
home affairs not specifically assigned to other Ministers. This
makes the office an onerous one covering a very large field,
and, traditionally, the Home Secretary is not interfered with
by the Prime Minister's Office in carrying out his duties. To

this extent it is a much more independent portfolio than, for instance, the Secretary of State for Foreign Affairs has become.

Since 1886, most of the Home Secretary's duties relate to England and Wales, although he still has considerable powers in relation to Northern Ireland, and in the event of the Manx people deciding on a coup to become a fully independent member of the Commonwealth, it would be up to the Home Secretary to advise on what action, if any, should be taken. The same applies, of course, to the Channel Islands. But the bulk of work is connected not with these remnants of imperial dominion, but with affairs here in Britain.

Such affairs include overall control of the Metropolitan Police and, through the control of funds, considerable control over local police forces, overall control of fire brigades, control of immigration, of aliens and of naturalization. The Home Secretary is the overlord of bad women, innocent homeless children, intoxicating liquor, drugs, explosives and firearms.

Through the Prison Commissioners, he is responsible for the direction and control of all our prisons and for penal reform. He is responsible for civil defence in general, and when murderers, both domestic and so-to-speak public, were punished by the good, clean crack of the rope instead of being expensively imprisoned for horrifying periods, it was his duty to advise the Sovereign on the exercise of clemency. Parliamentary and local Elections are controlled by the Home Office and the right to petition the Sovereign, which is a right inherent in all Monarchies—even those former absolute monarchies common in the East as well as in Europe—was effected through the Home Secretary.

In short, the Home Secretary, though he might have little say in the political direction of Government, had more to do with the daily lives of the public than any other Minister. He was very near the homes and lives of the people.

The Home Office employs over six thousand persons

Undergraduate hooligans at Glasgow University pelt RAB with rotten fruit as he tries to make his speech on his installation as Lord Rector in February, 1958.

The Old Armoury, Saffron Walden, where, for thirty years, RAB planned his election campaigns. Now the new Member's name is to be seen in the window of the unpretentious premises.

August, 1965, and never before has the Master's Lodge of Trinity College, Cambridge, had such an energetic face-lift and overhaul in readiness for the new Master in October.

directly and through remote control and these range from the Permanent Under-Secretary of State, who is paid a very large salary, down to the most junior clerk who is not paid a penny more than the market rate.

RAB took up the Office, as was his wont, with relish. Here was a labyrinth of law and custom, of old practice and new additions, of great institutions and petty, almost parochial matters that were overnight put in his lap. The routine would be carried on by the permanent staff of the Office which, in spite of a certain amount of nepotism and old school tie-itis, managed to adminster the entire complex along the best British public school lines.

RAB, within weeks, understood the whole overall picture. He made it plain that he would tolerate no nonsense from the Police, who in Britain, as elsewhere, are apt to get above themselves when they sense a weak Home Secretary. At the same time every Commissioner and Chief Constable knew that in carrying out his duty the supreme authority in London was behind him. The morale of the Force very rapidly took an upward trend. This was not due to any special innovations —though the Home Secretary was known to favour pay revision—but to the fact that the whisper went through the Force that a good and strong man was in charge.

RAB soon saw that the most hopeless muddle was in the great area that covered prison administration and reform. And this muddle was reflected in the thinking of officialdom. That thinking did not recognize the existence of a "criminal class" who lived by crime. Criminals were merely members of the public who had committed crimes and been convicted of them in the Courts. The official thinking was blurred as to the object of imprisonment. Was it a savage act of revenge by the public? Was it a necessary protection of the public from one who broke the peace? Was it inspired by the sanctity of life? Or by the sanctity of property? Was it intended primarily to punish? Or above all to reform? If punishment was the objective then punitive measures were obviously desirable. But if reformation was hoped for then punitive measures might militate against rehabilitation.

If there were a class dedicated to crime, living by its increasingly substantial rewards, then this class was not interested in reformation, at least until they had become too old to be successful criminals. If the non-criminal classes who still committed at least one crime outside the pattern of their lives were herded with inveterate criminals might they, themselves, become hardened criminals, whereas by separation and reformatory methods they might so often re-join ordinary society? What was the effect on young people sent to Borstal institutions and prisons? Did it make them tough haters of society? Potential gangsters? These and a host of similar problems occurred to RAB soon after he took over, and his penal philosophy which he evolved in Office is a very interesting development of his mind, and still forms the basis of the painfully slow penal reform of Britain.

During RAB's tenure of this vital office an increase in crime had led to a demand for more capital punishment and the return of corporal punishment. At the 1961 Party Conference, Mr. H. P. Lucas (North Somerset) moved:

> "That this Conference is concerned at the increase in numbers of murders and other crimes of violence and calls on the Government to extend capital punishment to cover all murders where insanity is not proven and also to reintroduce corporal punishment to cover all crimes of violence."

RAB was deeply concerned. An amendment had been moved supporting the Home Secretary and RAB spoke for the Resolution as amended.

> "I think it is comparatively rare that in one of our big debates we have exactly alternative speakers pro and con. On this occasion the Chairman has given us the figures and shown that there were many more speakers who would have liked to have taken part—indeed, more for the amendment than for the motion. This debate has put the point of view, I think, of each side fairly and on the whole I think in a manner which I hope the public Press will take a little less dramatically than they

have some of our previous debates; for, if you examine the resolutions carefully, I think they are not all so extreme as public comment has made out.

"I do not pretend to agree with a good deal of what has been said but I remain and I hope I shall remain all my life long a staunch and loyal Conservative, and I do not like to see our face travestied in the public Press.

"Before I come to deal with capital punishment and corporal punishment, there is a fairly wide area of agreement but I think what I should like to do most is to ask the Conference to give me a chance to let my campaign of reform and improvements initiated since I went to the Home Office, and which is steadily growing in size, have its effect upon the crime wave. I think what has gone wrong perhaps in the past, as Miss Spinney so cleverly pointed out in her able speech, is that the reform programme appears to have been too slow. For example, the detention centres have not up till now been available, and in several other ways to which I am now immediately going to refer. This is the first occasion when I, as Her Majesty's Principal Secretary, can tell you that in my opinion we have mounted a sufficient campaign of improvement to deal with the crime wave, so I want to thank Miss Spinney for drawing our attention to that, because I believe several people have cottoned on to one remedy such as corporal punishment more or less as a symbol for saying: 'Do for goodness sake get on with the job and be strict in dealing with crime.'

"Now I propose to tell you what I am trying to do in four respects. The first is the strengthening of the police; the second, sterner and stricter penalties; the third, adequate prison and detention centres; and the fourth, a revised social legislation so that the law is respected and not abused.

"My friend Mr. Hobson, my colleague in the House, referred to Sir Robert Peel, and it is certainly true that as a Conservative Home Secretary I have tried to carry on the tradition handed down by Peel, Disraeli, Cross and many other Home Secretaries over the past years. Mr. Hobson referred to the action in 1843 under Peel's premiership and the action in 1861 under Disraeli, and if I am doing anything, I am carrying on a Conservative tradition in the action I am taking. I hope I shall not be immodest if I quote some words of Sir Robert Peel,

said when summing up his first period as Home Secretary.
These were his words: 'I have the satisfaction of reflecting that
during the past five years every institution connected with my
Office has been subject to close inspection and strict review;
and that I have been able to make such temperate and gradual
reforms as I thought consistent with the general and permanent
good.'

"Let me now make clear the various features of these reforms.
First of all, it is absolutely essential to strengthen the police.
Being caught is still and always will be the best deterrent,
whatever other punishment you bring in. Now, I have studied
this crime question in most of our big cities. I did not agree with
all Mr. Toleman said but I thought what he said about people
not wanting to come out at night is perfectly true in many of
our built-up areas. I have just received a most impressive
report on crime in Birmingham from my colleague in the House,
Mr. Cleaver, and two or three other M.P.s of that city. The
proper way to restore confidence to women and children at
night—or in the day—is to see that there is a policeman back
on the beat. Unless the force is properly staffed you cannot get
crime detected in the way in which it should be detected, and
however wonderful may be the assistance from radar and the
rest, there is nothing to replace the man who knows every
street in his beat, every person in every street and what is
happening on his beat.

"One of my chief tasks when I became Home Secretary was
to restore the strength of the police. What success have I had,
and what strength will we have? Thanks to the Royal Commission and its Report, and the acceptance of that Report by
the Government and the Authorities, the police have had the
biggest pay increase for forty years. The result is, and this is
the first time I have been able to announce these figures to the
public, that the strength has increased by over 2,360 in the first
eight months of this year, compared with a wastage in 1960
of 450. I have initiated plans for radically revising police training. I have taken into regard Lord Trenchard's reforms, though
I have not taken quite the same line. I hope that with the
improved pay and prospects and the encouragement given to
Chief Constables we shall attract the right sort of recruit and
tackle crime where it should be tackled.

"Secondly, penalties and strictness in the courts. I think that we are all agreed that crime should be punished hard and it is when the courts have imposed heavy sentences that I have been most helped. I would like to answer one or two speakers in the debate who did not think that the Government does anything in the attack on crime. Nearly all our powers are devolved on to provincial authorities so the powers of the Home Secretary are limited largely to the Metropolitan area and to general influence in the country. I hope we shall get that clear.

"What the Government can do is to give the courts added penalties, and the maximum penalties now available are much greater than generally realized. For all most serious offences— manslaughter, rape, robbery with violence, burglary and felonious wounding—there is no limit to the term of imprisonment that the courts can impose, and for other serious offences there is a maximum of between five and fourteen years. In the recent Criminal Justice Act we have added to the powers of courts to deal with young offenders by increasing the fines which may be imposed on children—and on their parents— providing for greater use of Borstal and detention centres, giving powers to deal with boys and girls in approved schools who are unruly and, what I think is more important, providing for the extension of compulsory after-care for the youth or girl who is let out of a detention centre so that they can be recalled if they misbehave again and do not do what they are told. So the courts now have most impressive powers of punishment in hand and we have seen that they recognize the deterrent value of heavy penalties in appropriate cases.

"Next—the present building programme. It is no good trying to get the courts to act, as Mrs. Roberts said, unless there are enough detention centres, buildings and institutions, and as Miss Spinney said, enough attendance centres. All I can say is that since I have been at the Home Office the Government have launched the biggest and most revolutionary building programme for over a century. All in all, our building programme provides for no fewer than forty projects and new institutions and we shall have half as many again as were previously in use when I took my office. Of these projects, ten are already in use, eleven are under construction, four at least will be started this year, and the rest are in various stages of planning. As for the detention centres, which are so vital, we have opened five this year, making nine in all. Four will be opened next year, and more are planned. Mr. Roberts made a very attractive appeal and said that we wanted 109 of these centres. That, really, would be too many. I was in Lancashire on the 2nd October and addressed the entire magistracy of Lancashire at Preston. It was not a political occasion. I was able to get their comments about the detention centre to be built at Rochdale, and they regarded that as sufficient to cover the area. I am confident that when we have twelve or thirteen it will be sufficient to help the courts. And we must add to this the £5 million programme to modernise the approved schools.

"Here I must take up what Mrs. Roberts said about the régime of the detention centres being too soft. It is not at all true that the régime in the detention centres is soft. Anybody who has visited a detention centre knows that there is plenty of hard work, but what I am pleased about, too, is that the reports I have received up to date from the penal institutions on the reform side are very encouraging, especially for first offenders. I therefore ask the Conference to give me the opportunity to test this method, and to accept my assurance that if I think that the detention centre régime wants strengthening I shall, without hesitation, strengthen it in any particular that is desirable.

"Therefore, when we look at the police, the penalties and the institutions we will see that we are making progress towards a complete policy, and if we add to that the social legislation that has been passed to deal with street offences, betting and gaming, licensing and so on, you will see that they all help to take temptation away from the police in respect of laws which were not being respected and did a great deal of harm socially in our cities.

"I think that it was Mr. Walters who asked me to mention compensation. I have published a paper which describes to you some of the difficulties of compensation, and I have received a great many comments upon it. I have asked my hon. and learned Friend, Mr. Hobson, to give me a summary of the views of himself and some friends, and if you would help with further comments I would be grateful. I believe that we would have the choice between machinery, which puts money on the stamp —an insurance scheme—and the Exchequer paying out through the courts. I have not yet got the money from the Exchequer, so please pray for me there. If I can get the money, I shall regard this matter of help to the victim as one of first-class importance in our field of reform.

"Now we come to capital punishment. Under the Act of 1957, capital punishment is kept for those types of murder which strike especially at law and order, and for which capital punishment is likely to be particularly effective as a deterrent; murder by shooting, murder in the course of theft, and murder in resisting arrest. This compromise, which is what it is, I inherited when I got to the Home Office. It has only been working for a comparatively short time, and it was arrived at only after long debates in Parliament and controversy across party lines. I want to tell the Conference quite clearly that with the present composition of Parliament it is quite uncertain whether a majority, in fact, exists to restore capital punishment for all murders, and it would be difficult to justify unless it could be shown that the 1957 Act had resulted in an increase in murders. As Mr. Hobson said, there is no evidence of this.

"The terms of the motion refer to 'the increase in the number of murders'. I was so anxious about this that I asked my research establishment at the Home Office to make a research into this, and I shall be publishing the results in the next month. This bears out exactly what Mr. Hobson said at the rostrum— namely, that any comparison of murder statistics is difficult, because under Section 2 of the 1957 Act many killings formerly classed as murder are now classed as manslaughter on the grounds of diminished responsibility. But even counting all these diminished responsibility cases, the number of murders, on an annual average, has hardly risen since the 1957 Act.

"I know what happened. There was a great burst of trouble, crime and several murders in January of this year. It gave an impression that things were getting out of hand. But, in fact, the statistics do not show that to be the case." (A representative: "Rubbish.") "Nevertheless, I will undertake to publish the statistics, so that this gentleman can read them at leisure, although they are extremely voluminous and very dull.

"I promise, however, not to talk any more about statistics,

but to keep the whole question of capital punishment under review. If a change is needed, it is not me whom you will have to press, but many of my colleagues in Parliament who would like to go the other way—namely, to abolish the death penalty. With the present composition of Parliament, I face great difficulty in giving any undertaking to change the law.

"I would like to say in passing that not only will I keep the capital punishment question under perpetual review, but also the terms of imprisonment. There has been a sort of idea that nine years is the usual term of life imprisonment. That is, of course, not so. Those released from life sentence in recent years have included men detained for much longer periods, up to twenty years. Many men must be, and have been, kept in for life. All life sentence prisoners are released on licence and can be recalled to prison by the Secretary of State at any time if this is thought desirable. And I give you a pledge that I will not hesitate to use this weapon in the public interest.

"Now, we come to judicial corporal punishment. I expressed my views on this at Blackpool three years ago and I have held to them ever since. I want to make quite clear to this Conference that the decision not to reintroduce judicial corporal punishment is the collective decision of the Government, and I do not know any of my colleagues who, were they in my shoes, would reverse the decision. I hope you will realize that this is the case. I should like to say in passing how grateful I am to the Lord Chancellor, to my predecessor as Home Secretary, who is here to support me in the course of this debate, together with my other colleagues. This is not just a personal matter or a personal feeling of my own.

"The decision has recently been upheld in both Houses of Parliament, and in the House of Lords it was upheld by such leaders of men—not exactly 'softies'—and leaders of youth, as Field Marshal Montgomery and others; Mr. Lucas suggests that I should hand over the office of Home Secretary to Field Marshal Harding. Why not hand my office over to 'Monty' and stop him journeying to China and other places? If he were handling these matters at this Conference instead of me, that would be much more fun.

"Certainly, the image of certain people in our Party has been deformed by the cartoonists. I will not mention them by name, but the best one, I think, was by Osbert Lancaster. Some of you have been depicted as armed with the lash and the knout. Conservatives have been described as sex maniacs by that inelegant female Member of Parliament of the Labour persuasion, Mrs. Eirene White. Do not let us get into that sort of exaggerated state.

"There is a motion—No. 143—by Lt. Colonel Holder. I do not happen to agree with it, but to consider the provision of corporal punishment 'under careful safeguard'. I am sure you will wish to consider this subject in that atmosphere. To discuss it in extremes, I should like to say, does not, in my opinion, do the Party or Party image any good at all.

"My reasons for not re-introducing corporal punishment judicially in a court are based on the evidence, and I cannot make it sufficiently plain that anyone who is Home Secretary must work on evidence. Heaven knows, if I was to work on emotion or because I did not like it myself, I should not be worthy of my office. Should I be worthy of that most difficult of all decisions which a Home Secretary has to make when I have to decide on questions of life and death? Whether I have the blessing of the Conservative Party or not, I shall never deviate from the path of deciding all questions strictly on the evidence that has come before me.

"If experience showed that it would help to reduce crime, and if the Government thought that it would help to reduce crime, we would not hesitate to reintroduce it, but after studying all the evidence, including records of men who had been flogged before 1948, the Committee under Mr. Justice Barry came to the unanimous conclusion that judicial corporal punishment is not an especially effective deterrent, either to those who receive it or to others, and they recommend that it should not be reintroduced.

"Lady Elliot spoke to us of her own impressions and what did she say? She said that evidence was taken from almost everybody on this subject. I have heard this evidence myself —from probation officers, with whom we have to work; from prison officers, with whom we might have to carry out the sentences; and the magistrates, who in large measure I have consulted, who are not as keen as some speakers have made out, although they are divided on the subject and some express the views which have been expressed here. In general, however, the main view of the previous Cadogan Committee of Inquiry has been supported by the evidence today.

"It is worth noting that the number of crimes of robbery with violence, which is the only offence for which in practice corporal punishment was used for adults, fell for several years after its abolition in 1948.

"I am, therefore, in the position that the inquiries set up, backed by most of the expert opinion with which I have to work—I do not mean my civil servants, but those devoted people who work in the field of youth, experienced probation officers and people of that type—believe that a sentence given impersonally on the order of a court, in a prison or a police station, with the victim very often tied to a triangle, does not produce a good result, and is not to be compared with ordinary caning in the home or by the teacher, where the person calmly bends over and 'six of the best' settle the thing easily. That is a quite different problem from the other.

"When Mr. Lucas says that he does not mind three weeks' delay, that is what I particularly object to. We could not speed up the method to such an extent that we eliminate the right of appeal which is inherent in our British judicial system. It turns the whole of this business into something nauseating instead of something done in hot blood, which, strange to relate, is the only satisfactory and sensible way to do a caning. Therefore, I am afraid, I cannot say that the Government can agree to reintroduce judicial corporal punishment.

"I will, in conclusion, give you these assurances. I will watch over and review the working of the Homicide Act, 1957. I will consider any strengthening of discipline in detention centres and other penal establishments which experience shows to be necessary. I will press ahead with the four-fold reforms which are beginning to yield results: strengthening the police; the penalties; improving the centres and institutions; and strengthening the laws. This is the best programme to deal with delinquency.

"In America and Russia, they have primarily a youth problem. In the U.S.A. the delinquency rate per size of population is several times ours. In a recent book by Mr. Fyvel, I saw it quoted as being six times ours. Much of this is due to the fact that the main influence on teenage youth, instead of being the family, religion and the teacher, is incitement to excitement, whether in films, television or commercial advertisement. . . .

"I have come to the conclusion that this is a national problem upon which a lead must be given by the Government. I therefore propose to launch this autumn an appeal to all vitally concerned and to call them together—parents, teachers, churches, voluntary societies, probation officers, and especially the B.B.C. and the I.T.A., and others concerned. For the issue is in fact far greater than could be solved by any one remedy. All this involves a mobilization of our whole society.

"I therefore ask for your support in this. I ask you to support the Amendment, to pass the Resolution as amended, to give my assurances a chance of being fulfilled, and to rally us all together in a great national campaign."

The Amendment moved by Mr. Geoffrey Howe was put to the Conference and carried by a very large majority.

The Resolution as amended was then put to the Conference and carried by an overwhelming majority.

Two considerable and, in some respects, sensational reforms had RAB's strong support. The first was the reorganization of the entire procedure for dealing with lunatics and mentally deficient persons; the second was a resolute enforcement of the law that prohibited solicitation by women on the public streets.

In the Mental Health Act the Board, as it then existed, was abolished and a whole new structure devised. The Act was very long and involved and contained ten overall sections including the functions of local authorities, Mental Nursing Homes and residential homes, compulsory admission to hospitals and guardianship, the care and treatment of patients, a most important part of the reform which dealt with great particularity on patients' rights, even protecting them from delay of communications they might wish to send to the Minister. The admission of patients "concerned in criminal proceeding" to Broadmoor and other institutions, the removal and return of patients within the United Kingdom, the care of elderly patients and of their property and estates, and a host of supplementary matters are dealt with in the Act.

The insane population of Britain remains high and is increasing; and there is no doubt that RAB's Act brought the British Law up to date and introduced humane provisions and protections hitherto undreamt of.

The care of insane and mentally deficient people had been retarded for generations by the inflexible legal definition of a madman as being one who did not know what he was doing, or, if he did know, was unable to distinguish between right and wrong. For over fifty years the alienists had asserted that this was nonsense. That insanity merged into sanity, that there were border-line cases; and that, in general, mental disbalance was one of degree. RAB's Act at least controlled the certification of persons much more carefully and protected them while they were deprived of their freedom.

As always in reforms with which RAB was concerned, the principles were laid down in the most general terms, but this did not prevent the utmost particularity on important points of detail. This is the provision of the Act that covers pocket-money for patients:

> "The Minister may pay to persons who are receiving treatment as in-patients (whether liable to be detained or not) in special hospitals or other hospitals, being hospitals wholly or mainly used for the treatment of persons suffering from mental disorder, such amounts as he thinks fit in respect of their occasional personal expenses where it appears to him that they would otherwise be without resources to meet those expenses.
>
> "For the purposes of the National Health Service Act, 1946, the making of payments under this section to persons for whom hospital and specialist services are provided under Part II of that Act shall be treated as included among those services."

This is compassionate legislation at its best, the bringing of the highest authority into immediate control so that none of the unfortunate people concerned should feel deserted, denied or abandoned.

Prostitution was another Home Office headache. The

attempt of the Home Office to clear the fifty thousand London prostitutes off the streets was successful. The Home Office controlled the Police and the prostitutes had operated in given areas with tacit police consent. Perhaps this was one of the greatest dangers of the system. The danger of police corruption was everywhere apparent, and London was notorious in Europe as the city with the most open network of street soliciting and bawdy houses. But whether the removal of the women from the streets in London—and the provincial cities—did any real good is an open question. They are now operating by telephone from houses and appear to be controlled more by gangs of pimps than was formerly the case.

Although the Home Office drove the prostitutes from the streets no effort was made to ban the homosexual other than very rare prosecutions for soliciting. The growth of homosexuality and the enticement of young men into this filthy brotherhood has not been stopped or even discouraged. The result has been that though RAB's banning of the whores from the streets has done away with London's reputation as the most wicked natural city in the world, it now has the dubious title of being the most unnatural haven of free homosexuality.

But the time at the disposal of a Secretary of State is limited. He has his chores to perform in his constituency, his Cabinet duties, his attendance in the House of Commons as well as his office work. One can only wonder that, during his tenure of the office of Home Secretary, RAB achieved so much. Certainly those who, through no fault of their own, had for a time or for good, lost their mental balance had reason to bless his name.

And it is worth mentioning here that it is in these non-contentious, non-political spheres of the public demands that RAB seems to be at his happiest, his most constructive, and his most effective. Dealing with such questions, a balanced and trained mind that could see all sides of the question directed by a heart that had genuine compassion was a great asset. In the more stormy political questions of the day this cool and analytical approach might be a positive disadvantage and lesser men, as a result, might say that, on great and explosive issues, he had "hedged his bets."

In all these movements under RAB's tenure of the Office, the Home Office was aware that the Secretary of State was very much in control. He was good at delegation, but he was quick to spot any weakness of an argument or in proposals submitted to him. He would pounce on any paragraph or idea that was weak, prejudiced or maladroit and in blue ink in the margin write the typically mild rebuke: "I don't like this. Please rethink. . . ."

If he wanted to advance an alternative he would set it out in his own hand in the margin with a knowledge that showed that he had read the whole memorandum and understood every word of it. He was an inspiring and even exciting man to work under. Only the best would do, but as a young man who had worked under him said to the author: "He made you feel that his standard was everyone's standard and that you were naturally first-class, as he was. It was a tremendous encouragement and challenge. . . ."

RAB's basic beliefs in the field of penal reform are set out with much care in his now famous Eleanor Rathbone lecture. Those who want to study the subject can hardly do so effectively without reading this illuminating and modern approach to the whole problem of penal research and reform. In delivering an Eleanor Rathbone lecture, RAB was following in the footsteps of a distinguished host. Sir Norman Angell, Hugh Gaitskell, Viscount Samuel, Lord Denning had all delivered previous lectures and the fact that RAB's lecture stands comparison with any delivered by this most distinguished galaxy speaks for itself.

At the back of most of RAB's thinking was the absolute necessity for research. Just as he had tackled the Tory philosophy by support for the Conservative Research Department, so in penal reform he did everything in his power to promote national and international research. His mind worked this way. "Let us know much more about this before we formulate our reforms."

The entire lecture is based on RAB's White Paper—Penal Practice in a changing Society—and this paper is so important in its thinking and its effect on penal reform, now and in the future, that I am quoting from it extensively in this chapter. It is, in fact, a prison and penal Charter, a Magna Carta of penal reform and represents the progressive, but practical, habit of RAB's mind, applied with absolute precision to an immensely complicated problem.

RAB, with his penchant for research, welcomed the establishment of the Institute of Criminology at Cambridge University. It was his hope and conviction that this Institute would turn out men with inventive and liberal attitudes towards the perplexing conflict between deterrence and reformation in punishment. This clash lay at the root of the difficulty in advancing penal reform and the need to study it much more closely was not the least of RAB's contribution to this cause.

RAB thought that the penal statistics published by the Metropolitan Police were wholly inadequate as a basis for study—they reflected, naturally, the police, law and order approach—and this made him favour more analytical students, both British and foreign, such as the research being conducted by the Department of Psychology at London University and the writings of Mannheim and Wilkins who invented a system of clear classifications of Borstal Boys—the embryo criminal "caught" before he has become a hardened member of the criminal fraternity.

RAB was appalled by the fact that a chronic state of affairs seemed to exist in which three prisoners were incarcerated in a small cell built for two, and built for that purpose many years ago, so that the overcrowding amounted to a perpetual, quiet cruelty.

He favoured induction units to acclimatize the new prisoner to prison life and he experimented with new "open" prisons for offenders falling within certain stated categories.

He grappled with the pressing problem of work for prisoners, trying to rid the system once and for all of punitive work designed by its nature solely to punish, and to substitute for this, active, rewarding work and even vocational training.

A scheme for housing prisoners about to be released in hostels from which they could do ordinary jobs at the current wage appealed to RAB who was struck by the awful dilemma of the ex-criminal who by having served his sentence was supposed to have paid his debt to society, but who often found that society, if it learnt of his past, solidly ranged against him. He received a report on his reforms that said:

> "The change in prison atmosphere seems clear enough: there is a feeling of enthusiasm, even of fervour, among the officers doing this work and a feeling that this may be the most important thing to happen in penology for a very long time. Hierarchies are being broken down and the ease of relationships between men of different grades has to be seen to be believed within such a traditionally rigid and authoritarian service. The prisoner thus experiences a secondary effect—that of the overall change in administration and attitude—as well as the primary one through the interactions of his group. Here he has a ready approach to authority and an opportunity to voice his grumbles: much tension is relieved which might otherwise be acted out violently and 'incidents' in prison life seem to have been greatly reduced. Numbers absconding from Pollington Borstal, the other institution where these methods were pioneered, have also fallen off. Group methods have also helped to foster a more humane approach by the staff to the prisoner, and to create the 'therapeutic atmosphere' which is essential if treatment of prisoners is to succeed. We must realize that to antagonize and intimidate a criminal still further is the very worst way to create a law-abiding citizen, and that, after all, is what matters most."

RAB's approach being what it was, GROUP COUNSELLING won his favour. This generic name covered regular meetings between the prisoners and the staff to discuss general subjects. These experiments had been carried out at both Wakefield and Pollington, and in the "Lancet" of

December, 1959, and in the "Daily Telegraph" of January, 1960, they were explained and recommended.

And the "Daily Telegraph" article added to this by stressing the new relationship induced between staff and prisoners:

> "The time to begin such observations is the beginning, and the precious chance of gaining important knowledge should not be lost.
>
> "We need to know as clearly as possible the effects of what we are doing, in both the short term and long term, in order to do better in the future; but the outlook for a service capable of throwing up a movement like group counselling must surely be very good indeed.
>
> "Apart from its therapeutic value and the new standards and values it may be fostering, the method has had a possibly even more important effect at Pollington. This is the effect of developing a remarkably confident relationship between staff and the inmates.
>
> "Two members of the staff said independently of one another: 'It's the best thing that has ever happened in the prison service.' Had it affected discipline? 'I'll tell you this,' said one of them, 'before I came here I was at a preventive detention prison. I saw more discipline here in my first ten minutes than I'd seen in ten years at the P.D. prison.'"

RAB stressed the necessity for evaluation, the correlation of the evidence, the weighing of its weight, the study of the methods by which the evidence was procured, the further study of the means by which the proposed reforms could best be implemented.

What did all this amount to? The sum total appears to be the work of a genuine reformer with no delusions—the best kind of reformer, tackling problems that for centuries had been the butt of arbitrary decisions based on outdated conceptions.

RAB was always concerned with the adoption by the Government of an Immigration Policy that would maintain the British tradition of being a host-nation while assuring that the stream of immigrants would be accommodated without conflict or hardship. At the 1962 Conference, he put forward his views:

"I had no doubt at all, after reading the forty resolutions, that it was my duty as Home Secretary to wind up this debate myself, and I propose to try to answer the very serious points which have been put forward in the debate.

"We have had a good debate. It has been divided; three speakers have been against the motion, and the others have been in favour of it. I can say straight away that the Government fully share, and have long felt, the concern which the Conference is being invited to express about the problems created by uncontrolled immigration. If you will accept that at the start, we have somewhere to start from.

"My friend Mr. Renton, who is sitting beside me, is responsible for immigration into this country. We operate a strict system against aliens, not against their countries or against them personally, but a system of control. We allow in about 16,000 aliens a year to take up permanent residence. It is a system, very carefully managed by the immigration officers, which works and is administered by my hon. friend on my right. (Mr. Renton.)

"We have no actual figures of detailed white immigration from the Commonwealth, but this is a vital question because I have no intention of introducing any legislation based on colour or race discrimination. There is some reason to think that white immigration, a figure very rarely given except by my friend Mr. Pannell, who is extremely well informed on this subject, comes to about 50,000 white immigrants a year.

"The Census of 1951, which was ten years ago, showed that about 353,000 people then living in the United Kingdom had been born in other parts of the Commonwealth and that about 573,000 had been born in the Irish Republic, which is a matter which very much complicates this question, because we need them for labour in many respects and they come here very freely at the present time.

"The most striking change in the last ten years has been the increase in the number of immigrants coming from the West Indies, India, Pakistan, and, to a lesser extent, Malta, Cyprus, Aden, Hong Kong and East and West Africa. Last year, the excess of arrivals over departures from these countries rose to 58,000, of whom some 50,000 were from the West Indies and some 8,000 from India and Pakistan. Judging from the first eight months of this year—some of the anxieties expressed at the rostrum are proving to be correct—the figure will rise, in my opinion, to well over 100,000 in the current year. The number now in the United Kingdom who emigrated from those territories is at present estimated to be about 400,000, and this is despite the restrictions on exit imposed by the Governments of India and Pakistan.

"Of course, we must recognize that the total coloured population is still a small proportion of our total—less than half a million out of 51 million, or less than one person in 100. But many—indeed, most—of these immigrants are young and, as Mr. Taylor, from Moss Side, said, many of them are married with families and are establishing them in this country, and the population is likely to increase rapidly for that reason. So these are the facts, which are very much more severe than when Mr. Pannell first moved his resolution three years ago at Blackpool.

"Now, the question arises: Do we need any immigrants? I must say definitely, after consultation with the Chancellor of the Exchequer and the President of the Board of Trade and others responsible for our economy, that these immigrants do provide a valuable contribution to our labour force, especially in certain fields, which it would be otherwise difficult to secure. I instance in particular, after consultation with the British Transport Commission, the buses and trains in London and some of our cities, and some of the girls who work in the hospitals, where we have valuable assistance from West Indian nurses. And so we must balance that in getting a balanced picture, which I am trying to give you.

"We have also to look at the housing problem. Immigrants, as I know—and I have received deputations of Members of Parliament from all over the country—are concentrated in certain cities and in certain parts of London. Their way of life is different from ours. Adjustment can only be very gradual.

"If the immigration outruns at some stage the economic capacity to absorb, we might be faced with real concentrated difficulties in certain areas, both from the social angle and from the employment angle.

"I say undoubtedly, as Home Secretary, responsible for law and order, that I take a quite serious view of the difficulty if it were intensified through any reasons of economic trouble or further housing difficulty.

"Now what remedies can we think of? I do not despair that we can find remedies which would suit Mr. Fisher, who made a very reasonable speech, Mr. Barr and perhaps, if he was in a good mood, Mr. Buck. We are not trying to be unreasonable. I have already said that much of the work done by these immigrants is invaluable to us. So let us look at some of the remedies, which I will share with the Conference to show you what is in the mind of Her Majesty's Government.

"First, will the Commonwealth and overseas Colonial Governments be able to do more to control immigration? When I first tackled this job I had a great deal of success with Mr. Nehru of India, Mr. Manley of Jamaica, and others in controlling immigration at the source. For some years immigration from India and Pakistan dwindled away to nothing. Mr. Buck can give me credit for that, because it was very successful as performed by those Governments. But our present information is that we are not likely to have very much success in those countries being able to control immigrants very much more.

"Then it is suggested—it was mentioned in the debate—that we should solve this problem by investing more money in Commonwealth countries and in the Colonies to create employment there and keep people at home. These are the figures I have been given. Apart from private capital investment in the West Indies alone, some £50 million has been granted under the Colonial Development and Welfare Act and about £13 million by the Colonial Development Corporation. But I am told that it take no less than £2,000 capital investment to provide one factory job in Jamaica, where the population is increasing at the rate of some 30,000 a year. So, however much we respond to Lord Home's appeal to tighten our belts and pay up, I think that we are going to find it very difficult to solve the matter in that way alone.

"So we must look at other remedies, although we shall always do our best to invest overseas. We must devote very anxious thought to what powers we could use to control the flow of new immigrants. Any control we judged necessary would have to be applied to Commonwealth immigration generally, with no question of control based on colour or race. I do not think that we could rely solely on a health check. I believe that the immigration authorities could use health checks aided, perhaps, by the countries from whence the immigrants come, but my advice is that we could not rely solely on a health check.

"I am sometimes urged that immigrants should make a cash deposit when they arrive, to meet the cost of the return fare. My information, in consultation with the immigration authorities and the Governments, is that we do not believe that immigrants would be likely to be very much discouraged by such an arrangement. There is no evidence that this is so.

"I have considered with the Minister of Housing, now the Chief Secretary to the Treasury, whether we could institute a control based on a certificate of available accommodation, but we have come to the conclusion as a Government that that could not be effectively enforced. It could not be done without the most intolerable supervision and regimentation, and to follow up an immigrant moving from place to place in this country would be almost impossible. We have, of course, taken steps in the Housing Bill—my right honourable friend the Minister took those steps—to deal with squalid living conditions in overcrowded houses, and that has been extremely useful. But I do not think that we could rely upon that method alone.

"I can accept immediately that if we introduce legislation we can bring in powers to deal with criminals, and I think that is vital. I can also accept that if we bring in legislation we should take powers of deportation. I already have such powers of deportation in dealing with aliens. They are performed after reference to a court. They deal with the undesirable people, some of them of a criminal character, whom we do not want to keep here, and I have already stated to a previous Conservative Conference that I myself am not against taking powers for deportation.

"This is obviously a matter in which we have to have the fullest consultations with the overseas Governments and Commonwealth Governments. This must be carried through. Also, the Conference will know that the final decision must be that of Her Majesty's Government and must be taken at the

time of year when decisions are taken about the forward
legislative programme. That is the constitutional position, and
we cannot go behind it. Meanwhile, I can give the Conference
the assurance that the fullest weight will be given to the
anxieties expressed.

"I want you now to think like a jury as to whether you are
going to support the Resolution or not. Bear in mind the
observations made by those who have opposed the Motion,
that we are departing from a great tradition. At the same time,
bear in mind that it may be that we can work out a system
which is humane, unprejudiced and sensible and which meets
some of the undoubted rising social and economic problems
which otherwise may become too much for certain parts of our
country. Bear these things in mind and, when you have taken
your decision, the Government will pay the utmost attention
to your expression of opinion."

In RAB's approach to immigration we see again his gift
for detached realism.

It may well be that if RAB was still at the Home Office
he would have been moved to take some action on the
appallingly savage sentences inflicted on the Great Train
Robbers which aroused the foreign comment that in Britain
we value property more highly than life itself.

Certainly the shocking rise to wealth and power of a small
highly organized centrally controlled gang of criminals
would have alarmed RAB, and one cannot help thinking that
he would have devised some more effective and novel means
of coping with this unheard-of phenomenon in Britain.

We are now in a position when the higher criminal
fraternity are very much on top of the Police and the building
of "maximum security prisons" broadly facing inwards
instead of outwards on the old pattern, creates its own
problems of cruelty and the "living death" which RAB would
have been quick to tackle.

When RAB went and a much less resolute Home Secretary,
the hapless Mr. Brooke, took his place the deterioration of
the standing of the Home Office was apparent to all. This
was especially noticeable in the matter of granting asylum to

foreigners, a right which, previously, the British Government had always exercised generously.

The deterioration in police discipline resulting in something like twenty serious complaints of police brutality annually is another unhealthy development, for it is this kind of savagery towards prisoners on remand that is the worst feature of the penal practice of Nazi States and at one time —though this is no longer wholly true—of communist States. The necessity for a strong Home Secretary to quell this kind of practice and support the large majority of decent police officers and constables was never more apparent than in the months that followed RAB's departure.

Still, his work lives on. All the penal reform now envisaged is based, to a large extent, on the line of thinking he impressed on the Home Office and the Prison Commissioners as well as the police and the prison staffs.

The forward movement of penal reform is always in some degree obstructed by a reactionary Bench and Lord Parker, Lord Hewart and Mr. Justice Avory are, or were, all in this tradition of applying the brake to penal reform. We must add that they do so with complete sincerity backed by great firsthand experience.

The Bar is also guilty not only of refusing to reform itself except by a façade of petty measures that have no real effect, but in failing as a great learned body closer to the criminal than any other section of the public, except the police, to urge those reforms which they must know are urgently required.

RAB is remembered at the Home Office not only because of that affection and respect he was always able to inspire in those working closely with him, but because it was generally realized that he represented that judicious blending of enlightenment and reality that was the only kind of mentality which could successfully meet the tremendous challenge that penal reform in Great Britain represents.

Less than eight years later, many connected at the highest level with the cause of penal reformation look back to RAB's period of direction as Home Secretary with a nostalgic regret.

XI

The Emergence of Sir Alec Douglas-Home

THE ILLNESS of Mr. Macmillan in the autumn of 1963 caused his retirement as Prime Minister. This led to the Blackpool Conservative Conference of October becoming a naked fight for power. RAB took no part in the canvassing or the intrigue, feeling confident that, this time, the party he had served so well for so long would call him to the leadership.

It was not to be.

In one of the most discreditable and foolish intrigues to disfigure British politics, Sir Alec Douglas-Home, who had been an efficient Foreign Secretary, but was, essentially, a Scottish landlord with no outstanding record of public service, was presented to the Party as their leader after his name had been put forward by the outgoing Prime Minister to the Queen.

The whole affair would be incredible had it not in fact happened. Its repercussions on the Tory Party are still powerful and destructive. In July, 1965, Sir Alec, under the most intense pressure from his party, resigned, but RAB's services, by then, had been lost to the nation.

The sequence of events that led up to RAB being passed over for the second time, this time by a man of obviously smaller stature, is so typical of recent British political history that it should be rewarding to trace the developments step by step.

The emergence of Alexander Frederick Douglas-Home,

the fourteenth Earl Home, P.C., K.T. (the 4th Baron Douglas in the peerage of the United Kingdom), as Prime Minister of Britain in 1963—A.D.—is perhaps the strangest story in the turbulent feudalism of Tory Party politics.

Sir Alec had sat with decorum, but without distinction in the House, while his father was still alive, as Lord Dunglass. He was regarded as a reliable border chieftain and as being firmly annexed to the well-right-of-centre group of his party. No one entertained the notion that this dessicated nobleman who looked rather like an ancestral ghost would ever become Prime Minister of Britain. A joke is a joke. The choice of Prime Minister is something else again.

True he was acceptable and accepted by the old hardcore of the Suez veterans, and Eden had appointed him to the office of Commonwealth Relations. Macmillan, when he found that Selwyn Lloyd did not really command universal awe as Foreign Secretary, promoted Lord Home and he became the first Foreign Secretary of recent times to be a member of the House of Lords, so that he could not personally be questioned on his activities by the House of Commons.

He was by no means a bad Foreign Secretary. His manners were odd in the 20th century. He dealt with any opposition rather as a sixth-form prefect might quell a new boy at school. He had, by nature, the most prodigious sneer which was well controlled so that it was able, so to speak, to hit its target without revealing itself. It was a guided missile of a rebuke. And rebuke was perhaps the operative word. Those who experienced Lord Home's displeasure felt themselves rebuked.

There was remarkably little to justify this arrogance. The Earl was a man of very simple mind. But of great natural adroitness. Like his predatory ancestors he could smell out success and treason with a primitive extra-sensory perception. His mental processes were simple—it was his habit to unravel the Budget with match sticks—but his nature was by no means simple. He was as agile as a cricket.

Lord Home, or as he was to become, Sir Alec, was definitely not in the Premier stakes as far as the public were concerned. Among Conservatives he was regarded as a reliable hack. In Labour circles he was a standing joke. But to those who followed from the beginning the tortuous tale of animosities and rivalries in British politics during the last thirty-five years, Alec Douglas-Home always represented the kind of man who might be made Prime Minister, not because anyone wanted him to receive that great office, but because they did not want anyone or someone else to achieve it. Sir Alec was always a menace if the Tory Party were forced into choosing a sour grapes candidate. This well-known manoeuvre had its precedents, the last being the disastrous choice of Stanley Baldwin because it was desired to circumvent Lord Curzon.

Lord Home was always around. When Sir Winston gave his farewell dinner at No. 10 attended by the Queen and her husband there was Alec Home and his wife, with the Duke of Norfolk, Hawold, Wab, Bobbety, Anthony, old battling Uncles Montgomery and Alexander and all. During the early autumn of 1963, it was clear, not only to those working at Westminster, but to the public at large, that the "Wondermac" of a few years before was no longer in orbit. Harold Macmillan had suddenly become an old man. Those who met him at Downing Street at this time described him as having aged rapidly, stooping with the quick shuffling gait of an elderly man and apparently very much in the hands of his Secretaries. Observers did not add, as well they might have done, that his natural mental agility and sense of occasion had not noticeably abated. But as Prime Minister, with the extraordinary pressures of that office, he was obviously drawing to an end of his innings. In speaking of Tory Premiers, the sporting metaphor is inevitable, perhaps even excusable. Nevertheless, it was a shock when the papers of Wednesday, October 9, reported the news.

"Mr. Macmillan, who is 69, entered King Edward VII Hospital for Officers, Marylebone, last night, on the eve of the Conservative Party conference, for an operation tomorrow for prostatic obstruction." A totally unexpected announcement from 10 Downing Street said:

"The Prime Minister has tonight been admitted to King Edward VII Hospital for an operation for prostatic obstruction. It is expected that this will involve his absence from official duties for some weeks and he has asked the First Secretary, Mr. R. A. Butler, to take charge of the Government while he is away."

This was followed by further details:

"The Prime Minister was taken ill early yesterday and was seen by Dr. F. L. King-Lewis. He recovered sufficiently to preside at a three-hour Cabinet meeting in the morning, but he was in considerable pain though he did not tell his colleagues.

"He took further medical advice during the day from Dr. King-Lewis, Mr. A. W. Badenoch, a Harley Street surgeon, and Sir John Richardson, his personal physician, who assisted at a gall bladder operation which Mr. Macmillan had in 1953. It was decided last night that he should undergo an operation."

The Queen conveyed her sympathy and her hopes that the operation would be an entire success.

Mr. Wilson, Leader of the Opposition, telephoned his sympathy and good wishes to No. 10. Lord Ogmore, the Liberal Party president, said he was shocked. He expressed wishes for a speedy recovery.

Prostatic obstruction is an obstruction of the bladder. It is painful and the onset is sudden. It is quite common in men of Mr. Macmillan's age. Surgical treatment is extremely safe but entails a convalescence of at least six weeks.

Press comment poured out of Fleet Street.

"It was said last night on the Prime Minister's behalf that he was naturally distressed that he will be unable to address the Conservative rally at Blackpool on Saturday. It is understood that when he entered hospital he had not drafted that part of the speech in which he intended to refer to the party leadership issue.

"It was also stated last night that the illness would have no effect on factors deciding the immediate future. Decisions on leadership, it was implied, must now depend on the outcome of the operation."

Colleagues of Mr. Macmillan realized that an illness of this nature occurring at such a time must be a big factor in Mr. Macmillan's mind in deciding his ability to continue in his office.

> "The implications must be that even if he makes a swift recovery, his absence from the House in the next few critical weeks must be an important element in the decisions facing the party in the weeks ahead."

Nearly half the Cabinet was already at Blackpool when the decision to operate was taken. But Mr. Butler was still in London. He was called to Downing Street and given the news by Mr. Macmillan personally. It was said later that Mr. Butler was distressed. The "Daily Telegraph" commented:

> "First impressions suggest that the chances of Mr. Butler of ultimately succeeding Mr. Macmillan as Prime Minister may be greatly enhanced. He will be in charge of the Government for several crucial weeks at least."

At this moment all the signs pointed to RAB. Surely the Tory Party would not harbour the old resentments and stab him in the back again? It would be inconceivably mean and petty. Besides there was no real contender. In the choice of Macmillan there had at least been a suitable and experienced alternative. Now virtually there was no one. Lord Hailsham had put himself out of the running by a remarkable television appearance during which he was questioned on the Profumo affair. His Lordship seemed at times likely to explode so angry was he, and he actually half rose from his chair as if intent on inflicting bodily harm on his irritating questioner— the clever and tenacious Robin Day. It could not, after all, be Hailsham, with or without his peerage, however clever and volatile he might appear to be.

Maudling and Heath were coming up, but the general

feeling in the party was that their time would come later. Ian Macleod was a possibility but his brains were against him. If RAB was to be "dished" once again and presumably for the last time, it had to be someone from another planet —someone from the House of Lords, perhaps?

The "Daily Telegraph", among the best informed of the great London dailies on the crisis, had these significant indicators in a feature article by Mr. T. F. Lindsay, published on the very day on which the brave, but sick, Prime Minister was admitted to hospital.

"Any party which has held power continuously for twelve years may be criticized as stale. But the injection of new and young blood by the Prime Minister, when he so drastically purged his Administration a year ago, did not give an impression of pondered rejuvenation.

"The intention, even the result, may have been good. The manner certainly was wrong. Much indignation was felt at the treatment of certain individuals, notably Mr. Selwyn Lloyd and the country, as well as Parliament, felt that the shooting of so many Admiral Byngs was hardly likely to encourage the rest.

"Certainly it would have been wrong for Mr. Macmillan to retire abruptly last June or July. Any impression that he had been driven out of office by a scandal would have been unjust and undignified.

"Yet the decision on his retirement will have to be taken, and it would be misguided to leave the party or the country too long in doubt about it. Mr. Macmillan's great strength has always been the considerable uncertainty about his successor. Although Mr. Maudling's name has often been mentioned, and often welcomed, it does not carry with it the surge of inevitability.

"Nor does Mr. Butler's taking over during the Prime Minister's absence necessarily mean that he will be the successor."

The warning is there, stark and without embroidery. Do not be shocked if there is a surprise. It may not be Butler. You have been warned.

On the same day the Gallup Poll published the largest

swing to Labour ever recorded in a National Opinion Poll, a swing to the Labour Party of over thirteen per cent.

This fantastic shift of political opinion can only be explained by the violent backwash of the Profumo affair. Jack Profumo, who was Minister of War, had had a mistress, Christine Keeler, and he had made a statement in the House of Commons denying the association. In other words, he had lied. But does not everyone lie about extra-marital intrigue? The whole fabric of established society in legally mono-gamous Britain depends on adroit lying on this one subject so that the lines may never, never become crossed. At heart the British male is as predatory and polygamous as his Arab or Chinese brother, but the façade of our society necessitates the conventions being preserved absolutely.

So that when the Profumo affair blew up, the British public lost their sense of humour naturally and absolutely. Millions of Tory women "happily married" were ready to strike a blow against "this kind of thing". An attractive, promiscuous little girl was made into a major political scandal. A passing affair was said to be pregnant with sombre and sad possibilities. Even the Russians were brought into it with the fleeting figure of an Embassy official. England reverted to Victorian-ism overnight and Harold Macmillan, who had known nothing of what was going on, had to carry the odium attach-ing to his administration.

He was never the same man again. He told his friends that if one cannot trust the word of one's friends, people one meets daily, and one's colleagues, whom can one trust? The answer appeared to be that one cannot trust anyone. It was all very disappointing. It was not the England in which he had lived and thrived. And this was not all. The most diabolical rumours spread concerning other members of the Cabinet who were said to be either homosexual or woman-chasers. There was one sinister figure in particular who simply would not be killed off. He was a naked masked man who served at an orgy said to be attended by politicians in the public eye. This man looked at one time as if he might come to life.

He never did. I wonder what became of him? The newspapers abroad wondered, too. The French press in particular
was delighted. The answer to the long-standing question:
The British: are they human? with the coming of Christine,
appeared to be a resounding: Yes!

However, the actions of gallant Jack Profumo were not the
chief concern of the Tory Party at this moment. In the
absence of the Huntsman, or perhaps the Master, the pack
split and each front runner was followed by his own
vociferous supporters, the main clamour being made by the
followers of Lord Home and Lord Hailsham (both of whom
had made it clear that they were willing to drop their
peerages for the Premiership) with a slightly more dignified
bay from RAB's supporters. The Conference was in danger
of becoming what the Tory Party had for a century avoided
—a naked power struggle.

That the gloves were off and the daggers were out was
made plain to RAB as soon as he reached Blackpool. It was
suggested that—in order to avoid controversy—Lord Home
should deputize for the Prime Minister and make the main
speech at the Conference. RAB stopped this manoeuvre in
its tracks. He insisted on making the main speech himself.

Meanwhile, at the King Edward VII Hospital for Officers,
Mr. Macmillan was facing his operation, but he was, his wife
Lady Dorothy said, "in good form". He had a meeting with
RAB and a longer meeting with Lord Home. Asked what
they talked about Lord Home replied: "Oh, we did a certain
amount of business, and had a good talk." Now Lord Home
had dined privately with the Premier some days earlier and
his friends now noted that his bearing had changed. He was
positively spry. He was jaunty and evasive in answering the
newsmen who followed him around, and he gave the
impression of a man very pleased with himself indeed.

Moreover, although RAB had managed to retain his proper
place as deputizing for the Prime Minister at the Conference
and making the chief Policy Speech, Lord Home as Chairman
of the National Union would take the Chair on the Saturday,

replacing the Conference Chairman, Mrs. T. C. R. Shepherd. It was this lady's duty and pleasure to read to the Conference the Prime Minister's message. These were its terms:

"You will have learned that I had to go suddenly to hospital for an operation. I would ask you to convey to all the members of the Conservative and Unionist Party assembled at Blackpool my deep regret that I shall not be able to be present at the mass meeting on Saturday or at any of the activities of the conference before that.

"My wife and I are very sad that we cannot attend the conference at such an important juncture in the life of the party. Please tell all those assembled under your chairmanship how deeply I appreciate the loyalty they have shown me and the affection with which they have treated my wife. We shall be thinking of you.

"I feel certain that as before in 1950, 1954 and 1958 the Conservative conference at Blackpool will be a prelude to victory."

Nothing about the leadership. No hint of who the next Prime Minister might be. No talk yet even of resignation. Just a rallying cry from the sick-bed. No mention of his deputy who was carrying on in the absence of his chief. Just a reminder that he was still Prime Minister, that he loved them all and was with them in spirit.

But the pace of events in the drama was becoming furious now. The following day Lord Home, who would not be kept in the background, read another message from the Prime Minister. This message really shook the Conference. Macmillan was going.

"I should be very grateful if you would tell the conference assembled at Blackpool, of which you are president, how sorry I am not to be with them this week. I was especially looking forward to the mass meeting on Saturday, which is a great annual event and on this occasion likely to have special significance.

"It is now clear that, whatever might have been my previous feelings, it will not be possible for me to carry the physical burden of leading the party at the next General Election.

A photograph of the young M.P. for Saffron Walden, taken when he was on the threshold of his career. Ahead lay triumph and tribulation, with total war to follow uneasy peace.

On April 19, 1961, three thousand Tory ladies unanimously demanded the return of the birch. RAB, with Mrs. Butler, tries to instil a little progressive common sense. . . .

"If the operation which I am to undergo tomorrow proves successful, it is clear that I will need a considerable period of convalescence. I would not be able to take all that is involved in a prolonged electoral campaign. Nor could I hope to fulfil the tasks of Prime Minister for any extended period and I have so informed the Queen.

"In these circumstances I hope that it will soon be possible for the customary processes of consultation to be carried on within the party about its future leadership. I am writing to you as president of the conference to ask you to announce this at the earliest opportunity."

There was loud applause when Lord Home said that Mr. Macmillan had "shown once more that his whole concern was for the nation and the party".

Lord Home managed to put so much tenderness and compassion into the reading of the Prime Minister's farewell that the Conference broke into long and sympathetic cheers. But whether the cheers were for the distinguished invalid or for the noble herald it was impossible to say.

At this point in the drama RAB was certainly still the front runner in spite of odds quoted by Sir Gerald Nabarro which gave Lord Hailsham the proud position of favourite, RAB being quoted as second favourite at two-to-one with Maudling at five-to-one and Lord Home as the rank outsider at thirty-three-to-one. It only goes to show that making a book is a very special business and is best left to the ring.

RAB, en route before the Conference, gave an interview to George Gale of the "Daily Express" in which he said that he discussed a groundswell favourable to Labour. This was pounced on as being defeatist.

The popular sentiment at this stage was that if RAB could sweep the delegates off their feet on Saturday, he was going to be hard to beat. But those who were better informed thought it most unlikely that RAB would do any such thing. Nor did they think it would have an influence on the result, for was it not all a charade?

Were not, perhaps, the most significant words spoken by

the Prime Minister's wife when she said that, in spite of all, he was in good form? And students of the Tory Party and its methods noted with interest that, for some reason, there was not going to be any repetition of the method adopted by Lords Salisbury and Kilmuir in the famous tussle between "Hawold and Wab", the method that had been sanctified by the selection of Lord Rosebery in the nineties. Why not? If it was right in 1957, why was it not applicable in 1963?

The simple answer was that this time the majority of the Cabinet were behind RAB. A substantial minority favoured Maudling. And a still smaller number were for Lord Hailsham. But the RAB supporters were about equal to the combined Maudling-Hailsham vote. So if RAB was to be ditched again another method had to be employed. This appeared to present no difficulties at all to the resilient patient of the King Edward VII Hospital for Officers.

After all, the 1957 procedure had been adopted because it was effective in advancing Macmillan and retarding RAB. It would not serve that purpose this time. So there had to be a return to the old well-tried device of the immaculate conception. Let the Conference roar and shout. Let Ian Macleod bring them to their feet with a speech of lashing rhetoric and pugnacity. Let RAB be sensible, calm, assured. It would all be of no avail. It could all be arranged between the Hospital and the Palace.

After consulting the candidates for the post, which would give a very good impression, the Prime Minister could suggest a name to the Queen, a name which could be recommended as being a desirable solution after a Conference that was rapidly becoming a shambles.

Meantime, with a flourish that was positively American in its bravura, Lord Hailsham had told a meeting of the Conservative Political Centre that he was renouncing his peerage and was going to stand:

> "I felt it would be contrary both to my duty as a colleague and my duty to the State to do any act which would be inter-

preted as an act calculated to undermine the authority of the Prime Minister of the day.

"But it must be obvious to you that that situation no longer exists. I will continue to try to serve the country honourably." To a hushed audience he continued: "But I wish to say tonight that it is my intention to disclaim my peerage."

Clapping and cheering immediately swept the hall. Conservatives swept to their feet and shouted: "We want Hailsham. We want Hailsham".

When the noise paused for a second, Lord Hailsham added: "If I can find anyone to receive me as a candidate to stand for Parliament I shall do so." Shouting lasted for more than five minutes. Later, at midnight, Lord Hailsham and his wife called at the Young Conservative Ball at the Winter Garden. Arm-in-arm they walked to the rostrum to the cheers of the Young Conservatives. He said: "This has been rather an exciting night for me. But I want to finish it off well. We have had some very serious choices to make. Last night I asked Mr. Butler if he was going to offer himself for the leadership?" He replied: "I am just going to carry out my duties as head of the Government."

"I am just going to carry out my duties as head of the Government." It was so typical a remark for RAB to make. His friends at least could say: "Well in all the clamour, he's still as he always is." And by this they meant he retained his dignity.

But the Hailsham tide ran to a roar, and suddenly was a spent force. The Tory Party woke up one morning and decided that Hailsham as Prime Minister was just an impossibility. By his nature he was precluded from that kind of supreme responsibility, despite his ability.

Lord Home was now full of fight, and on the Friday, he made a speech on Foreign Affairs. Its intellectual content may not have been high. It rang with resounding platitudes—but it did achieve at least one desirable result from its architect's point of view. It won Lord Home a standing ovation. "Alec," they said, "can rise to an occasion." But they had been saying that forty-eight hours earlier about Lord Hailsham. And Lord Hailsham was now a dead duck. But was Lord Home's timing better? Only one man could trump his card—RAB on the Saturday, the last day of the Conference. And RAB made as "popular" a speech as his conscience would allow him to without degenerating into claptrap. It was a good comprehensive summing-up. It was exactly what was needed. But the Conference crowd was deferential rather than enthusiastic. The press reported the speech without comment:

"Mr. Butler, Deputy Prime Minister, indicated yesterday that regardless of the outcome of the struggle for leadership he will continue to serve as he did when passed over in favour of Mr. Macmillan in 1957. Addressing the mass meeting at the end of the Conservative party conference, he said: 'My colleagues on whose help I have leant so much, I know that we can count on your support in pledging ourselves that our unsparing efforts will be devoted, regardless of any consideration whatever, to furthering the best interests of the country and of the party.'

"Mr. Butler paid a tribute to the Prime Minister under whose leadership there had been a great advance in both the position of the country and of the party. He has proved himself to be a greater party leader and a great Prime Minister, said Mr. Butler amid applause.

"Mr. Macmillan's decision to retire was a heavy blow. But they intended to carry on the Government of the country according to the same high standard Mr. Macmillan had maintained.

"The conference, he said, had already confounded the critics and had given the party the impetus and determination to win. It was 'a contemptuous gesture of defiance to the Opposition, who, not for the first time, are celebrating a victory before the battle has started'."

They were absolutely determined, when the opportunity came, to knock the overweening confidence out of Socialists and Liberals alike and to come through to victory in their own time. This determination came from three causes:

1. Legitimate pride in a Government which has brought nearer the goals of lasting peace and prosperity.

2. A burning enthusiasm to maintain the position of Britain in an age of change as a first-class country, politically, economically and socially.

3. A clear conviction that anything in the shape of a victory for their opponents would defeat these aims and be an unmitigated national disaster.

Mr. Butler said they had been helped and not hindered by the Denning Report. Lord Denning had demonstrated that the "scabrous rumours" about Ministers were false. The whole nation would be glad that the fogs of scandal which had befouled political life at home and Britain's reputation abroad had at last been dispelled.

Mr. Butler acknowledged the "powerful feeling" in the country that "it is time for a change". But if we regarded government as a cricket match, when each side had its innings in turn, we might well be condemned for ever to an alternation between sensible policies and silly policies.

A fourth Conservative victory would mean the end for all time of the "immature nonsense of Socialism".

He recalled his promise of nine years ago that the Conservatives would double the standard of living in 25 years. He was cheered when he said they were already ahead of schedule, with weekly earnings considerably more than personal expenditure and savings multiplied 17 times.

For years the Labour Party had been denouncing poverty. "Now that we are winning the battle against poverty they have performed a most remarkable somersault and now spend much of their time deploring the moral dangers involved in these better conditions."

Both on the land and in the towns, Britain was thriving, changing and going ahead. "It is time we answered back, good, loud and clear, the wily Wilsons and poor old Jo's who spend so much of their time cracking up other countries and running down their own."

The Wilsonian dream of automation to the accompaniment

of Socialism was the Wellsian nightmare come true. The individual in Britain was to have ample leisure and carefully controlled environment, "the exact circumstances of the battery hen."

Conservatives had used the power of the State long before the Socialists were even thought of. But they had used it to foster and preserve individual freedom. Freedom was what they cared about. The imaginative "programme for the people" which the Conservatives were putting forward would succeed only if parents and children were assured that the extra talent and skill they gained from extra education would bring them extra rewards. In a Socialist society they could never have this assurance.

On foreign affairs he said that their policy was that Britain should remain not on the sidelines, as it would under Socialism, but at the centre of international affairs.

Mr. Macmillan, as the President of the United States had testified, had played a magnificent rôle in the complex negotiations that had led to the test ban treaty. That treaty had been achieved not by agitators sitting down in the public highway, but by statesmen sitting around the conference table.

It should be remembered that Britain's views at that table derived from the policy of nuclear strength which the Conservative Party alone in Britain had consistently maintained.

For the sake of a superficial, spurious and no doubt short-lived unity, the Socialists, at their conference, had avoided the vital subjects of foreign policy and the defence of Britain. What the Socialists had accepted was that Britain should become, as it were, a camp follower in world affairs.

The next step was to extend and build on the test ban treaty, and this the Government was trying to do. It would not miss any opportunity.

They rejected the "absurd aberrations of the Left-wing mind" put forward by the Socialists, "We stand not for Little England, but for Great Britain," said Mr. Butler. "A Britain that is great in its tireless service to peace."

RAB, well pleased that the Conference was over, took the train back to London and was soon back relaxing at his Essex home. As usual, he threw off the tension, the intrigues and the whole political rat-race and was happy again.

Were they going to stab him again? He could hardly believe it. Lord Home had twice assured him that he (Lord Home) was not "running". And yet. There was a whiff of treachery in the air. After all it was not the Conference that decided the matter. The Conference only *seemed* to decide the matter. It was the Queen on the advice of the outgoing Prime Minister who made the decision. And if Harold Macmillan suggested another name it was unlikely that the Queen would over-rule him. The trend in the exercise of the prerogative was against that, and the Queen by her disposition and nature, would almost certainly take the advice proffered her. And then there was a very strange development. The Prime Minister, "rapidly recovering his strength", had all the possible contestants to see him one after the other, RAB, Home, Maudling, Macleod, Hailsham, as well as Heath, the Lord Privy Seal and Lord Dilhorne, the Lord Chancellor.

The sick room suddenly became the most important room in Britain. Visitors swarmed in and overlapped having to wait their turn in a waiting room. This was the time-table:

9.55 a.m. Mr. Butler arrived at hospital.

10.30 a.m. Mr. Butler left.

10.45 a.m.-11.00 a.m. Ministers and others who went to 10 Downing Street for Cabinet meeting were: Lord Dilhorne, Mr. Butler, Mr. Erroll, Mr. Marples, Mr. Sandys, Lord Hailsham, Mr. Maudling, Mr. Powell, Mr. Thorneycroft, Sir Edward Boyle, Lord Home, Mr. Hare, Mr. Macleod, Mr. Heath, Mr. Deedes, Mr. Soames, Mr. Brooke, Lord Dundee, Mr. Macpherson, Sir John Hobson and Mr. Redmayne.

12.26 p.m. Mr. Sandys left.

12.45 p.m. Cabinet ended. Ministers began to leave.

1.29 p.m. Mr. Butler left 10 Downing Street.

2.40 p.m. Lady Dorothy arrived at hospital.
3.05 p.m. Lord Home arrived.
3.20 p.m. Mr. Maudling arrived.
4.10 p.m. Lord Home and Mr. Maudling left.
4.36 p.m. Lady Dorothy left.
5.00 p.m. Mr. Macleod arrived.
5.15 p.m. Mr. Macleod left.
5.30 p.m. Lord Hailsham arrived.
6.00 p.m. Lord Hailsham left.
6.04 p.m. Mr. Heath arrived.
6.54 p.m. Mr. Heath left.

So it was all back in the slender but strong hands of the Prime Minister. And what did he intend to do? He intended to resign. He did so, and the Queen, as her Prime Minister could not come to the Palace, came to the hospital. She chatted for a few moments and then everyone withdrew, friends, doctors, nurses. The Queen was alone with the man who had never let the reins go.

The Queen drove back to the Palace. The crowd at the gate gave their strange little cheer, half affectionate, wholly loyal. And at this time they understood she had to carry out her duty.

She sent for Lord Home.* He did not seem unduly

* It is interesting to attempt to discover what it was exactly that made the former Tory method of the choice of a leader, either as Prime Minister, or as Leader of the Opposition, susceptible to so much abuse so that not only was injustice done, but, worse still, it was seen to be done.

Basically, in the case of recommending a name to the Queen who retained, in theory, absolute prerogative freedom of choice, the system got the worst of both worlds.

It had none of the advantages either of Absolutism or democracy. If the Queen had in fact been free to choose she could have exercised her common sense which might have been a big improvement on the outcome of Party machinations. If, on the other hand, it had been admitted that the recommendation of the outgoing Premier was final and the Queen merely fulfilled her formal function in inviting the Premier's nominee to form a Government, the public would have understood this, too, for they well comprehend the formal functions of democratic monarchy. What was fatal was to fall between the two stools. Both parties now elect their leaders by secret ballot of the Parliamentary Party—the "immaculate conception" has gone—but in the case of a new Premier being appointed in the lifetime of the former holder of that office the prerogative, presumably, is still intact. There are advantages in having an unwritten constitution. There are also grave disadvantages.

surprised, although he was most happy. It was all over. For
the second time in his career, the Tory Party, or rather its
inner oligarchy, had managed to avoid making RAB Butler
Prime Minister of England.

RAB uttered no word of reproach. His wife cried, but he
comforted her. He accepted the post of Foreign Secretary for
had he not done so the Government might well have fallen.
Iain Macleod and Enoch Powell resigned in disgust and
anger. But RAB carried on. The Queen's Government must
be carried on. It was one of the principles in this strange game
of public life.

The public was stunned. An attempt was made to present
the new Prime Minister on television but it met with little
success because the image decided upon appeared to be in
conflict with what his own family—a remarkably outspoken
lot—said when they were questioned about "Alec".

Anyway it was all over. Home was Prime Minister. And it
is fair to say that the people of England faced the future
with more equanimity because RAB was still there. A
common comment was: "They won't do anything very stupid
as long as RAB is there."

And when they spoke of RAB now they spoke of him
with a certain pride that had not been detectable before.

It is difficult to avoid the feeling that RAB's exclusion from
the supreme direction of the Tory Party and the country is
accounted for by three major factors.

The first is that he stood for a type of progressive Toryism
that the active right-wing of the Party distrusted and
despised. The second is that, during his long career at
Westminster, for a variety of reasons he managed to offend
the old hard core of the Conservative hierarchy, the
Churchills, the Cecils and others who, until the recent introduction of an elected leader, with their satellite families
such as the Macmillans, were able, in the last resort, to swing
the choice away from RAB using the Royal Prerogative for
this purpose when the new leader was, automatically, Prime
Minister. This, of course, they are no longer able to do.

And the third factor was the nature of RAB himself, his almost "civil service" approach to politics, his refusal to intrigue, his complete adherence to a code of conduct that, while it commanded wide respect, made it possible to set him aside in a leadership crisis.

In order to avoid the indictment that these charges constitute the legend was created that RAB "hedged his political bets". As we have seen this was not true. He was less bigoted than many of his contemporaries, but his basic beliefs remained remarkably constant for forty years. No one ever said that Sir Winston Churchill hedged his political bets. It was a charge reserved for someone the "hierarchy" or the establishment wished to destroy; for the innuendo was disloyalty.

The whole exercise carried on for years in an atmosphere of smiling goodwill represents one of the least attractive chapters in the long story. The charge put out to justify RAB's exclusion was extremely clever. It was so vague that no one could refute it. It exploited the willingness of the public to believe a discreditable rumour when it comes from the right quarter. And it was disseminated in the knowledge that, with clever handling, it might well snowball into a widely held conviction.

This campaign culminated in the events of 1963. The choice of Sir Alec Douglas-Home as the new leader had, in fact, been made before the Conference took place. The Conference, in debating the leadership, was discussing an issue already settled. The feudal intrigue, with its democratic charade, had proved effective again.

XII

Foreign Affairs

ALTHOUGH RAB's tenure of the Office of Foreign Secretary was not a long one it was not without interest. As always when he assumed an office, it seemed to increase in importance. Whereas under Mr. Selwyn Lloyd, the British Foreign Secretary had seemed to be dwarfed by his Prime Minister, now that RAB held the office it regained some of the enormous independent prestige which it had had in the time of such giants as Lord Curzon.

The world knew that RAB was not under the dictation of the Prime Minister or of any of his colleagues. He occupied the position that a Foreign Secretary should hold, in total overall charge of his great office subject only to Cabinet discussion, collaboration, and collective responsibility.

That this was known was in itself a great strike forward for Britain, and it was of inestimable value to RAB as he tackled, one by one, the pressing problems that piled up on his desk.

His prestige was now so generally acknowledged, his experience so long, that he was able, immediately, as he had done at the Home Office, to impose his complete authority on the permanent staff of the Ministry and, equally important, to enlist their loyalty and co-operation.

Had it not been that the swift movement of international events forced constant initiative and decision on him, he would have preferred to spend longer in mastering the great and complicated organization that the British Foreign Office now is and the even more complicated complex of bodies it has to deal with.

Britain has special treaties and relationships with over thirty foreign countries in Europe, Asia, the Americas, Africa and, of course, Australasia. The United Nations deals with the United Kingdom Government through its Secretariat, our representative at the United Nations, the International Bank, the Food Organization, the International Monetary Fund, the General Agreement on Tariffs, the Atomic Energy Agency, the Children's Fund Organization, UNESCO, W.H.O. and half a dozen other branches, departments, and semi-autonomous bodies.

The Commonwealth does not come within the orbit of the Foreign Office, but there are interwoven links with it, and it contains over sixty countries with a population of nearly seven hundred million people, about a third of the population of the world.

In sheer size then, the foreign extension of the British interest and connection far exceeds that of any other nation. In these days of derogation and self-depreciation, this is not generally realized. But RAB had not made his GREAT BRITAIN speech at the 1963 Tory Party Conference for nothing. He looked upon it as his task to nurture the total goodwill and British interest that was so extensive and so pregnant with possibilities for peace and trade.

He brought to the host of problems and situations, the same progressive, forward-looking attitude that he had constantly applied to politics for over a quarter of a century. It was based on his firm political faith. Before his appointment as Foreign Secretary, as First Secretary of State, we see him pressing for the successful outcome of the Common Market negotiations at the Tory Party Conference. The motion being debated was: "That this Conference welcomes the progress being made in the Brussels negotiations in working towards solutions of our problems of entry to the E.E.C.; expresses confidence in the Government's determination to find adequate safeguards for our special interests and those of our partners in the Commonwealth and the E.F.T.A.; and stresses the importance of a successful outcome

to the negotiations for the strength and unity of the free
world and the future prosperity of the United Kingdom, the
Commonwealth and Western Europe."

RAB made one of the best speeches of his career. It was
clearly a topic that greatly appealed to him. If Europe had
a new organization, well suited to the tremendous challenges
of a new age, Britain should play her part in it. She must
never be isolated from Europe. All his history, all his
philosophy, and his instincts told him this. He said:

"There is no issue in peacetime so vital as this one to our
future in this country or to the future of millions all over the
world. I want to make this perfectly plain from the outset that
the Government are behind this motion and ask you to vote
for it. They ask you to vote and stress the importance of a
successful outcome of the negotiations.

"I realize that it is a privilege to intervene for a few minutes,
but I have a time limit, like other speakers. I am, however, to
be allowed just a little latitude to put the Government case at
this part of the debate, and Mr. Heath will be winding up at
the end. As the Chairman of the Government Committee chiefly
involved in this, I should like us all to pay him a tribute now
for his magnificent power of negotiation, about which we shall
hear later.

"The first general reason for looking ahead with a view to
going into Europe is that the world is changing. I have been
at the spearhead of change in the Conservative Party ever
since I first spoke to you over thirty years ago. Every time we
have met and faced change, we have won through, and I think
we shall do so again in Europe, which is our greatest test.

"This Europe, which in the past has torn itself to bits and
caused our intervention, and which in the past has caused us
to lose our blood and our treasure, is now healing its ancient
quarrels and combining its wealth and resources, human and
material, to come together in unity. This is a great gain in the
quest for world peace and a step towards the ultimate vision
of a world in which unity, and not division, is the theme. It is
against that background that I now want to put a few arguments
to you.

"The advantage of quadrupling our home market and com-

peting on equal terms is, in my view, overwhelming. To this we
must add the imperative need of fresh agreements and arrangements with the Commonwealth. They need more capital. They
need more outlets for the exports for their new secondary
products. In the old days of Ottawa it was a case of the mother
country's secondary products being exchanged for overseas
primary products. Now, if you heard the last Commonwealth
Conference you know that our Commonwealth family in Asia,
Africa and the West Indies is looking for a wider market for
its own secondary industries.

"Mr. Turton asked about the negotiations. In the negotiations we have already obtained certain advantageous terms
for the African and Carribbean countries. Association gives
them free entry and a chance to protect their home industries,
but they have asked us to negotiate further. This we shall do
for them, and for India and Pakistan, who want immediate
trade agreements.

"As for the old Commonwealth countries, they see the advantage of world agreements for commodities, particularly if these
are linked up with President Kennedy's tariff initiative. The
case of New Zealand, I am sure the Conference will agree,
is a special one for which we must have special conditions.
Mr. Marshall, the New Zealand Deputy Prime Minister, has
expressed their point of view most generously. He said: 'We
realize, to put it on a level of simple self-interest, that a strong
Western Europe is to the ultimate advantage of us all. We
believe that the entry of Britain into Europe could be a tremendously important contribution to achievement of this aim, a
contribution which will be all the greater if conditions are such
that Britain is able to enter with the support of Commonwealth
countries.'

"This is our objective, and those are the sentiments we are
working for in asking you to support the Motion.

"I would sum up the economic case in this way. Modern
progressive industry must have a Continental-sized market into
which it can sell its products absolutely freely. If Britain does
not fit herself into one of the larger markets which are inevitably forming themselves, we shall have too narrow an industrial
base for our modern technological industries. If we do not urge
our economy forward, it will not grow and expand. Of course

Commonwealth trade is and remains vital to us, but we must now not be exclusive. Both we and the Commonwealth are using and in future need wider markets. Therefore, we are looking in this sense constructively to the future.

"In the last few minutes I want to deal shortly with agriculture and with the points Mr. Turton raised on the political situation. Many of us in this hall live in the country and many of us have devoted our lives to the agricultural interests and to safeguarding them. We shall never break faith. Our objectives are the same as Europe in Article 39—increased agricultural productivity, a fair standard of living, stabilized markets, and reasonable prices for the consumer. But the methods are different. In Europe the system of rewards comes from the market price. This will be by levies on imports and in other ways. We Conservatives in the 1930s introduced the Wheat Act, which involved a levy on flour. Today there is a levy on sugar. In fact, there is an advantage in the market price system over the subsidy system.

"I should say from a whole life's experience in agriculture that there probably is a need for a change in our present system anyway. If we stay outside Europe, pressures on our market by exports will grow. We shall find it difficult to maintain the system. Inside we can guard against these pressures.

"The final decision on agriculture must be made in the light of the further negotiations and must be made in the light of the economic strength of the country, because without a strong country there cannot be a strong agriculture.

"I conclude then on the political point, which I cannot go into in detail owing to the time factor. What I can say is this, and I say it quite definitely. Britain as a member of the Community would take an active and important part in shaping and directing the policies of this dynamic movement. British policy is opposed to any extinction of national identity. We shall agree to nothing which undermines the position of the British Crown. We shall agree to nothing which undermines the essential powers of Parliament or the domestic authority of our law courts in criminal and civil cases.

"I would remind you finally that any changes made have to be voted unanimously in the political field. In our opinion, Britain must be at the centre of power so as to help the

Commonwealth and to use our voice to influence events in the direction we think right.

"I therefore submit to you that the Amendment, however carefully worded, is unnecessary. We are sticking to our undertaking to negotiate further. The present negotiations do not take into account questions of political union. Any such plans would have to be decided, were we a member of the enlarged Community, by a unanimous vote.

"I ask you to accept the Motion and not to vote for the Amendment, because I think that it would mute the voice of the Party and the Conference in supporting the Government in their endeavours in Europe, and thus hamper Mr. Heath in his further negotiations. I ask the Conference to give unqualified support to the Motion. I ask the Party to take pride in the fact that after eleven years of power where we have achieved so much—one strong prosperous nation at home—we now have the life and vitality to stride out into the world of the future. I ask the country to be prepared to play a role in the development of human fortunes different from but as fine as any we have ever played in the course of our history."

In this speech RAB makes his great claim, that on which he would desire to be judged: "I have been at the spearhead of change in the Conservative Party ever since I first spoke to you over thirty years ago. . . ."

And then with pride he says: "Every time we have met and faced change we have won through. And I think we shall do so again in Europe which is our greatest test."

It was not to be for the present. President de Gaulle, consumed with his ambition to make France the leader of Europe, jealous to a degree of Britain's possible dominant intervention, closed the door which Edward Heath had his foot in. But RAB's words may yet come true. They often do. He has a gift for long-range political forecasting.

There were many other problems to be tackled. Just as in India, with the withdrawal of Britain's strong and fair hand, Moslems and Hindus, who had lived together in peace if not in amity for over a hundred years, started to kill each other in one of the bloodiest and most bestial massacres of all time, so, in Cyprus, Turks and Greeks who, under British rule, had shared the peace that Britain brought to the island and maintained, and had shared the consequent prosperity, turned on each other with a virulence and evil intent horrible to behold.

RAB, with Duncan Sandys, representing the Commonwealth Relations Office, was most concerned with the Peace Conference called in London. As had happened on innumerable occasions the children of the British Empire, now grown up, had come to try to settle their differences around a table in the quiet, unemotional and friendly atmosphere of a London Conference where the heat and hate seemed out of place and "everyone behaved a little better".

On January 14, 1964, RAB, as Foreign Secretary, was host at luncheon to Mr. Feridan Erkin, the Turkish Foreign Minister, and Mr. Christos Xanthoupulos-Palamas, the Foreign Minister of Greece. The luncheon took place at Number One Carlton Gardens. Those who watched him as he conducted this difficult and dangerous affair said that it would have taken the strength of Satan himself to have resisted the reasonableness and wisdom of RAB's approach. That he was not wholly successful at least in the immediate future was certainly not the fault of RAB, or of Sir Alec as Prime Minister, or of Mr. Sandys. Perhaps in the end their advice and proposals will form the basis of an enduring settlement the island—and the islanders—so urgently need.

The desk of the Foreign Secretary was never empty. Crisis followed crisis and new and terrible situations arose mixed with common run-of-the-mill international disputes. In November, eleven maritime nations joined Britain in protesting against the decision of the American Government that only American ships, if they were available, should carry wheat to the Soviet Union. This dispute was immediately dwarfed by the still unexplained murder of President Kennedy, on November 22, while on a visit to Dallas, Texas, with his wife. RAB had looked forward intensely to co-operating with this brilliant and progressive American who seemed to carry in his heart and his head so much promise for the future. His successor seemed to be a reversion to the old tough type of American politician, but there were still good men, enlightened and co-operative, at the State Department and at the United Nations.

The Cyprus crisis flared and President Johnson agreed to contributing, with the consent of the Cypriots, to a United Nations Peace-keeping force in Cyprus. Goldwater was chosen as Presidential candidate in the States and at one time it seemed possible that this American version of Lord Hailsham could come to power. This disaster, to RAB's infinite relief, was averted.

In January, the French Government recognized Communist China. This presented the British Foreign Office with a very difficult decision. Up to this time we had gone along with the Americans on this matter—up to a point. And our compromise solution, temporary as it was, of receiving and sending diplomatic missions to China at a Chargé d'Affaires level while refusing to admit China to the United Nations which admitted the master of Formosa, had brought us neither American goodwill, nor the great material advantages of an entrée into the rapidly expanding China market. RAB, it was known, intended to use all his powers of persuasion to rectify this situation, had his Office been continued after the General Election of 1964.

RAB based his views on this matter on the acknowledged principle of International Law that holds that one should recognize Governments who are "in effective control of the territory of that country and its government machinery". It would be a bold man who would argue that this criterion did not include "Communist" China. The retention of Formosa, for long Japanese, by General Chiang Kai-shek certainly did not make him the actual master of China. The whole trend of world power and relations seemed to centre around this matter.

Already China, now a nuclear power, had taken Pakistan under her implied protection—though Pakistan had not abrogated her membership of either CENTO, or SEATO. With China not a member of the United Nations there was nothing effective that could be done in regard to this or any future move she might make. This was the kind of basic issue fraught with danger, in which RAB's experience and gifts would, with time, certainly have been used with effective advantage. The outbreak of total war between Pakistan and India in September, 1965, highlighted the danger of China's exclusion from UN. The suspicion that the United States backed India in an attempt to topple the Ayub Khan regime in Pakistan (President Johnson was reported to be "furious" with the Field Marshal) and the certainty of Chinese support for Pakistan make China's "unanswerability" at the United Nations a real danger to world peace.

RAB watched very carefully as President de Gaulle visited Germany, and encouraged the plans for a Royal visit to that country—which turned out to be a triumphal success.

The sometimes inexplicable and odd movements of the Soviet Union constantly occupied RAB's attention. The Soviet interference with the autobahn link between West Germany and Berlin had to be strenuously resisted in conjunction with French and American Governments. And RAB had no doubt that resisted they should be.

On July 27, RAB flew to Moscow for talks with Mr. Gromyko. They were prolonged and covered the whole field of Anglo-Soviet relations in the context of the world situation. It seemed to those who made a study of the changing pattern of international postures and provocations that, after this visit, the Soviet Government adopted a less aggressive tone. How much of this could be attributed directly to RAB's persuasion we do not know, but it was noted at the time that the two men, both veterans of so much recent history, seemed to understand—and respect—one another.

Although RAB's time as Foreign Secretary was largely consumed by coping with crisis developments that would brook no delay, he did find time to outline the background of his approach to Foreign Affairs and the reasoning that impelled him to take the decisions he did take. This was the background thinking that had guided him in the past, and would certainly have directed his energies in the future had the Tory Party been returned at the 1964 General Election.

In this speech, in the House of Commons, on January 20, 1964, we see the Butler approach to the developing independence of States, and his grasp of situations as they arise to which he applies, not opportunistic solutions, but attempts at remedies based on an approach and a chain of long-held convictions all arising from his belief in progress, his vital concern with peace, and his certainty that proposals, if inherently reasonable and fair, must carry the interested parties towards a settlement of their differences. He was an optimist. The only comment appears to be that to have a Foreign Secretary, these days, who was a pessimist, would be a major disaster in itself.

The Geneva Disarmament Conference had been criticized as a "Club" which achieved almost nothing, and acted as cover for colossal increases in armament expenditure.

"My hon. Friend the Minister of State has already left for Geneva this morning and will be taking charge of the initial discussions together with the representatives of the United States and the Soviet Union and other countries concerned. . . . I shall decide what is the best moment for me to go, as I intend to. It is not impossible that a further initiative could be taken by the Government. We wish to see the introduction of the ideas of the various countries concerned in the next two or three days before making any further decision.

"As regards the British Government making proposals, I have already said that I have definitely decided that it would be better to wait for the Conference to open. A speech will be made by my hon. Friend the Minister of State and speeches will be made by other delegates, including the United States and the Soviet Union delegates. Out of that I hope we may formulate a plan for definite forward progress to be made in disarmament."

When pressed as to his proposals, RAB put forward some practical and immediate proposals:

"I list six cardinal points upon which we should try to reach agreement if we are to make practical progress:

"(1) An agreement on observation posts in the N.A.T.O. and Warsaw Pact areas.

"(2) A comprehensive nuclear test ban treaty.

"(3) An agreement to ban the further dissemination of nuclear weapons or knowledge.

"(4) The increased use of nuclear energy for peaceful purposes.

"(5) A freeze of strategic nuclear delivery vehicles.

"(6) The early physical destruction of some armaments."

He outlined three further proposals as worthy of particular attention and study:

"(1) An improved procedure for the Disarmament Conference, making use of informal working groups.

"(2) A new approach to verification.

"(3) Proposals for international peace-keeping."

This was the last great Office that RAB Butler was to hold. His acceptance of the Office and his conduct of its affairs won approval both from the public at home, from the wartime allies of Britain, the United States, the Soviet Union, and France, from our former enemies and from the Commonwealth as well as the new Afro-Asian nations.

The label of Politician no longer seemed to fit this man or describe him correctly or adequately. The hard years of varied experience and sudden fluctuations of fortune had made him a Statesman. That is what he had always wanted to become.

XIII

The Tory Party and its Leadership

THE REJECTION of RAB Butler by the Tory Party when it
came to accepting him as Leader, either Leader of the
Opposition or Prime Minister, is of such recent interest and
importance that it seems worth while to enquire how the
machinery of choice now works and whether, in fact, if RAB
had become its Leader, he could have really reshaped the
Party in a modern, progressive reality as opposed to a mere
"image".

As we have seen it has for long been the Tory practice not
to elect their leader. The leader, when he was needed, was
said to "emerge". And this doctrine of an immaculate conception was strongly defended by the Party, especially by
the upper hierarchy. In fact, of course, it enabled them to
push the candidate of their choice and by-pass the man who,
for one reason or another, they did not like or thought unsuitable.

There was a pretence, and we now see clearly that it was
little more, that the whole Tory Parliamentary Party was
consulted and that even the constituencies were allowed to
have their say. But these were merely democratic trimmings.
The real selection was by the outgoing Prime Minister—
unless he died in Office—who might or might not be
influenced by the advice of his closest political associates.

In Constitutional Law the position was clear. The retiring
Prime Minister could put forward a name to the Sovereign.
Or he could with perfect constitutional propriety submit two
names, for the choice still lay in the hands of the Sovereign.
Even if only one name was submitted, the Sovereign could

take further advice. She did not have to send for the man suggested though, during the last twenty years, the practice has grown up that the Sovereign did almost automatically call the man designated.

It is as well to remember that this restriction of the Sovereign's rôle is only a very recent development. Queen Victoria, Edward VII, George V and George VI all played their own part in the selection of "their" Prime Minister. Perhaps the present Queen has felt that the pattern was moving away from any involvement of the Crown in politics, but there are many who will regret the elimination of the rôle formerly played by the Monarch.

There is little doubt that if George VI had received the nomination of Sir Alec Douglas-Home, a perfectly "suitable" candidate, he would, nevertheless have consulted those in a position to give advice to the Crown on whether, in view of Mr. Butler's position in the Party and the country, the choice was a wise one.

As it is, we have seen the Prerogative of the Crown not exercised and, by implication or default, leaving the complete choice in the hands of the outgoing Prime Minister. This was not desirable for a number of reasons. Usually Prime Ministers do not retire, undefeated in the House of Commons, their period of office unexpired, unless illness forces them to do so. This was the case in the resignations of both Sir Anthony Eden and Mr. Macmillan. In the case of Sir Anthony, he suffered a near breakdown and had to be flown abroad on doctor's orders, and in the case of Mr. Macmillan, he had to make up his mind while undergoing an operation in hospital.

These are not situations conducive to a wise choice by a Premier lying on his sickbed, but with the apparent withdrawal of the Sovereign from active participation in the affair this was the way in which the irrevocable decision was made.

As we have seen in the case of Mr. Macmillan, it worked fairly smoothly. If there was manipulation it was done with such dexterity that the quickness of the hand deceived the public eye. But, in the notorious Blackpool Conference of 1963, it was no longer possible to conceal what was going on. The public had been surprised when Mr. Macmillan was chosen rather than RAB Butler, but the general response was: "Well, there must be some reason. Perhaps RAB lacks some quality that is essential. After all they know him best."

At the Blackpool Conference, the contenders did battle in the open and the manipulation was there for all to see. There was no illusion any more. We could see not only the puppets. We could see the strings and those who pulled them. It was, perhaps, the most disgraceful and undignified political conference ever to be held in Britain. The rumbustious clash of Party personality between Hugh Gaitskell and Nye Bevan that was said to disfigure a series of Labour Party Conferences presented nothing as sordid—or as savage—as the Tory Party Conference at Blackpool in 1963.

Clearly something had to be done; and done at once. As early as the spring of 1965, it became evident, not only to the 1922 Committee and the Party leaders, but to the Constituency Parties that Sir Alec would have to go. Various reasons were given for this. He was obviously no match for the wily and sometimes truculent Mr. Wilson in the House of Commons and the sight of their champion being regularly trounced by the man whom Mr. Macleod, in a lapse of pitiful bad taste, had described as this "shabby little man", was not at all what either the Tory front bench or their back-benches wanted to see.

In addition, the Tory Party, for the first time in its long and not undistinguished career, became "image" conscious. The people, we were suddenly told, had rejected the grouse-moor, feudal image. They did not want to be served by "gentlemen" any more. They wanted above all else to be led by clever grammar school boys who had made good. Whether any such yearning was ever expressed or felt by any considerable section of the Constituency Tory Parties is open to doubt. But there is no doubt that the Tory Central Office, who had been in cahoots with Public Relations men and other "experts", were convinced that Sir Alec was "old hat" and as such had to be sacrificed. He had served his purpose. He had sidetracked RAB Butler into the quiet and dignified shadows of Cambridge University. Now was the time for a new, vigorous leader, not quite a gentleman and not quite a working man, someone betwixt and between, whom it was argued the new technical and administrative and managerial classes would rise to as one man.

In the event, as we know, the Party, installed with brand new election machinery, chose the artistic, ebullient, cherubic, clever and classless Edward Heath. But how did this come about?

Sir Alec, after being sniped at from within the Party for six months and shot at ruthlessly by the Press, decided that the game was not worth the candle. After all, why should he expose himself to this barrage of hatred, ridicule, and contempt? He did not deserve it. He could not help his slightly supercilious manner. He had been born with it. He had done his best. He had damned nearly won the 1964 General Election and the Party had displayed remarkably little gratitude. Let one of the younger men take over. Then he could become Foreign Secretary in a future Tory administration. He liked the Foreign Office. At least one mixed with gentlemen there, and there was not all this hypocritical cant about red-brick Universities and making one's own bed.

But before he went, he took the train North to his own country to think things out. He had no intention of being bustled out of office. He thought it over for four days and decided that he would resign at once. Then the Party would have time to accept the new leader—and not time to betray him—should the alert Mr. Wilson spring an autumn election. He went on television for a last interview as Prime Minister and made it quite clear that he regarded himself as entitled to the post of shadow Foreign Secretary. He did not, of course, say this in so many words, but the implication was there. After all he had gone quietly.

Not only was he going quietly and with some dignity, he

was going to leave behind him a bequest of extraordinary interest and significance. True the idea was not originally his, but he had adopted and adapted it. It was published and distributed throughout the Party. By this, if by nothing else, would he be remembered.

This is the document headed: Conservative and Unionist Central Office: Release time: Immediate: February 25, 1965.

PROCEDURE FOR THE SELECTION OF THE LEADER OF THE CONSERVATIVE AND UNIONIST PARTY

1. There shall be a ballot of the Party in the House of Commons.

2. The Chairman of the 1922 Committee will be responsible for the conduct of the ballot and will settle all matters in relation thereto.

Nominations and Preparation of the Ballot

3. Candidates will be proposed and seconded in writing. The Chairman of the 1922 Committee and a body of scrutineers designated by him will be available to receive nominations. Each candidate will indicate on the nomination paper that he is prepared to accept nomination, and no candidate will accept more than one nomination. The names of the proposer and seconder will not be published and will remain confidential to the scrutineers. Nominations will close twenty-four hours before the first and second ballots. Valid nominations will be published.

4. The scrutineers will prepare a ballot paper listing the names of the candidates and give a copy to each voter at a meeting called by the Chairman of the 1922 Committee for the purpose of balloting and consisting of all Members of the House of Commons in receipt of the Conservative and National Liberal Whips.

First Ballot

5. For the first ballot each voter will indicate one choice from the candidates listed, and hand the ballot paper to the scrutineers who will count the votes.

6. If as a result of this ballot one candidate *both* (i) receives an overall majority *and* (ii) receives 15 per cent more of the votes cast than any other candidate, he will be elected.

7. The scrutineers will announce the number of votes received by each candidate, and if no candidate satisfies these conditions a second ballot will be held.

Second Ballot

8. The second ballot will be held not less than two days and not more than four days after the first ballot, excluding Saturdays and Sundays. Nominations made for the first ballot will be void and new nominations, under the same procedure as for the first ballot, will be submitted for the original candidates if required and for any other candidate.

9. The voting procedure for the second ballot will be the same as for the first, save that paragraph 6 above shall not apply. If as a result of this second ballot one candidate receives an overall majority he will be elected.

Third Ballot

10. If no candidate receives an overall majority, the three candidates receiving the highest number of votes at the second ballot will be placed on a ballot paper for a third and final ballot.

11. For the final ballot each voter must indicate two preferences amongst the three candidates by placing the figure "1" opposite the name of his preferred candidate and the figure "2" opposite the name of his second choice.

12. The scrutineers will proceed to add the number of first preference votes received by each candidate, eliminate the candidate with the lowest number of first preference votes and redistribute the votes of those giving him as their first preference amongst the two remaining candidates in accordance with their second preference. The result of this final count will be an overall majority for one candidate, and he will be elected.

Party Meeting

13. The candidate thus elected by the Commons Party will be presented for election as Party Leader to the Party Meeting constituted as at present.

This, then, was the end of the era of the "immaculate conception". Tory leaders in future were to be voted into office. All the pretence that the Constituencies were consulted was dropped, though Tory members were advised that it would

be discreet for them to visit their constituencies the weekend
prior to such an election to "take soundings".

The pretence that the parliamentary candidates adopted,
but not elected, were ever seriously consulted, was likewise
dropped. The choice was to be made by the Tory Members
of Parliament under the management of the Chairman of
the 1922 Committee and his acolytes and no one else. It was,
on the face of it, a frank and honest attempt to introduce fair
play and to banish once and for all the traditional "wangle"
which, married to the Royal Prerogative, had previously
governed the choice of a Tory leader.

Critics noted one or two interesting points in the new set
of rules. The first was that the document had no authors.
It was said vaguely to have emanated from the Prime
Minister. The second was that the whole procedure and
style bore a marked resemblance to the election procedures
adopted by the more exclusive West End Clubs, and the
third feature noted was the unblushing adoption of the single
transferable vote, a system long advocated by the Liberal
Party for national Elections and strenuously resisted both
by the Tory Party and by the Labour Party who were adverse
to encouraging minorities, even if they were substantial,
perhaps especially if they were substantial.

These comments are not really criticisms. The procedure
outlined is fair, sensible and effective. The provision that the
candidate elected must have an overall majority and receive
fifteen per cent more of the votes cast than any other
candidate does ensure that there should be, on the first count,
a substantial preponderance in favour of the man chosen.
If the figures show that the prerequisites for a clear cut choice
have not emerged the transferable vote or second choice
procedure is practical, easy to understand, and guaranteed
to give a clear answer with the minimum of delay.

Clause 13 is as important as any. The elected candidate is
presented to the Party Meeting at the next annual Conference. There is no intention to take into account any
opposition that might be expressed. This is an opportunity

to acclaim a leader already chosen. The rapid congealing process whereby the Tories unite behind the chosen leader as long as he is acceptable to them is given its part to play and the whole procedure is designed to avoid, for all time, the unseemly scramble for power that disfigured the Blackpool Conference of 1963.

On the surface this is an enlightened and progressive reformation of Tory Party procedure, but it does leave one pertinent question to be asked. How is the Royal Prerogative affected by the fact that both the main political parties now elect their leader by a "democratic procedure"? Does this mean that the Sovereign's undoubted constitutional right and even duty to take advice and give advice on the selection of a Prime Minister is now a mere formality? Has the electoral reformation of both parties made the prerogative in this field a mere ceremonial gesture?

The more old-fashioned constitutional lawyers still insist that the rôle of the Monarch has not been specifically infringed by any procedure adopted by either party and this is true, but our Constitution is unwritten. It can change without anyone knowing it or being able to say it changed today or it will change tomorrow. Especially is this the case in the exercise of the Royal Prerogative, that residue of executive power remaining in the hands of the Monarch after the centuries old struggle between the Crown and Parliament.

Most of the Prerogative, we know, has, in fact, passed either directly to the House of Commons or more indirectly to the Prime Minister as Chairman of the Cabinet. Of recent years the Prime Minister's Office, until so recently only legally recognized because the holder was also "First Lord of the Treasury"—under which title he still receives his salary—has quietly collected portions of the Prerogative which the Crown has seen fit to abandon.

We may take it that, whatever the technical legal constitutional position may be held to be, no Sovereign in future would feel free to question the choice as Prime Minister of the elected leader of either the Tory Party or the Labour

Party whichever commanded a majority in the House of Commons.

Progress in Britain comes from unexpected quarters and in strange disguises and it is of interest to historians to note that it was the somewhat feudal figure of Sir Alec Douglas-Home that launched this quiet, but not insignificant, little revolution.

Perhaps the most important provision in the new electoral procedure of the Conservative Party is that which gives the current Chairman of the 1922 Committee the duty of arranging with a body of scrutineers the whole electoral procedure. It is essential that we should know something of the origin and method of working of this 1922 Committee for this was the Committee with which RAB was, at times, most out of touch. He was very close to the Premiership, very close to his Cabinet colleagues, close to the Conservative Central Office, the Research Department and the Conservative Political Centre, but not nearly so close to the 1922 Committee which is essentially a Committee of all Conservative backbenchers, the basis and heart of the Tory Party who now, at last, exercise openly the power which in the past they sought to exercise by hidden persuasion.

The 1922 Committee took its name from the historic meeting at the Carlton Club called by the leader of the Tory Party in October, 1922, that led to the break-up of the Coalition Government followed by the Tory Election victory.

After the Election, Sir Gervais Rentoul, one of the recently elected members, formed a committee of friends and colleagues all recently elected as members returned to Westminster. The idea was that the "new entry" could make their ideas heard and be kept informed of events by the Party leaders. They could also tell the Party leaders what they thought.

A little over a year later, the Committee pressed for the leader or his deputy to take the chair at Meetings. This was refused. The hierarchy had no intention of becoming unduly involved with its own backbench. But a Whip was delegated to attend the weekly meetings and report to the Prime Minister's office. So, in fact, liaison was established.

The Committee, at first exclusive and select, broadened its basis to include all backbenchers. It elects its own officers and their names are published. Nothing else is published. The most careful minutes are kept but these are secret. It is said that the first minute-book has "disappeared". But then so recent a document as the report on the Blackpool Conference 1963 has in effect disappeared by becoming out of print with apparently no likelihood of ever being printed again. These quirks of character are some of the more endearing traits of the Conservative Party and its way of life.

So now under the new electoral rules this secret but comprehensive Committee is in sole charge of the election of the Party leader. If, as many people think, RAB would have been elected under such a procedure more than a decade ago, we must meet the criticism that no one was in a better position to introduce this much needed reform than RAB Butler himself, the arch-priest of progress and reform within the Party. He did not do so. It was not until the whole antiquated "emerging" procedure blew up at the Blackpool Conference, and did the Party irreparable damage, that a new procedure was adopted and election substituted for mystical preferment.

Perhaps the comment has some point in revealing a facet of RAB's character. Was his progressiveness reserved for society at large? For wide fields such as Education and Penal Reform? Did the secret machinations of the Party before Sir Alec's reform really rather appeal to him by nature? Was this all in keeping with his somewhat civil service approach to private as opposed to public affairs? And had he become so closely identified with the Conservative Party that he resented any intrusion into its domestic affairs even by back-bench members of his own Party? RAB is a strange mixture of liberal political philosophy and conservative private reaction. It may well be that his nature and outlook being what it was (and is), this may have blinded him to the need for this particular reform. If so, this may well have cost him the leadership.

When, in 1965, it was decided to get rid of Sir Alec, the procedure that had been devised for electing the leader was put into effect to choose his successor. And the drama that then unfolded is, of course, in reality the final chapter in the political life of RAB Butler. For the three candidates who were nominated were all to some extent Butler disciples though one, Enoch Powell, rejected the Butler political philosophy for a right-wing attitude. Because of this, and the fact that he was not a major figure, he received negligible support. The drama of the first Tory Election showed both the strength and weakness of the Tory Party. RAB had already been designated the new Master of Trinity.* He was out of the field, but his political children, holding his ideas, were the two chief contenders.

The Election took place on Tuesday, July 27, and the result was quickly known. It was:

> Heath 150 votes.
> Maudling 133 votes.
> Powell 15 votes.

Now this gave Mr. Heath a majority over both his opponents but it did not give him a clear fifteen per cent over his nearest rival. According to the rules there should have been a second ballot. But the Conservative Party, in the persons of Maudling and Powell, then acted with characteristic solidarity. Seeing that a new ballot would inevitably reaffirm the first result, the two "losers" withdrew, and next day Edward Heath was declared to be the official leader.

The Election had been preceded by a great ballyhoo in the Press and on television, thereby taking on, as one American commentator rather plaintively said, some of the aspects of an American Presidential Election.

How far this storming publicity influenced the result—if

---

* The Mastership of Trinity is a Royal appointment which means that the Prime Minister "suggests" the appointee to the Queen.

at all—it is difficult to say, but support for Mr. Heath came from very diverse directions. "The Times", on Monday, the 26th, came out openly and strongly for Heath. "He has shown determination and vigour. The objection that he is not married is irrelevant. What Conservative members have to choose tomorrow is a national leader not a social hostess at 10 Downing Street." The leader was almost a caricature of "The Times" leaders saying the obvious with such a panache of pomposity that the reader was left bewildered and perhaps stunned.

At the other end of the scale the "Daily Mirror" backed Heath; and the feline young gentlemen who appear to control so much on the B.B.C. were pro-Heath to a man.

Then the "Daily Mail" dropped its bomb.

National Opinion Polls decreed that in the country the voting went:

Maudling 44%

Heath 28%

Powell 3%

And the opinion poll may well have been right. The "Daily Express" did not put the pro-Maudling figures so high but came to the same conclusion. As opinion polls, though not always accurate, are seldom far out, we may conclude that the public did not want Heath and greatly preferred Maudling. But then the public were not the judges in this matter.

The candidates themselves had behaved with propriety. Mr. Maudling had submitted with good grace to being photographed with his delightful family playing ball. Mr. Heath, not to be outdone, had borrowed a couple of children and had been photographed on the beach looking benevolent as well as posing at his piano looking like a prophet, and caring for his flower pots with fussy concern.

Mr. Powell was hardly photographed at all except once with his attractive wife. He had no hope of winning, but he intended to stake a claim for those who wanted to scrap the welfare State and return to full-blooded private enterprise.

As all this was going on, RAB was quietly watching events in his home at 3 Smith Square, a very interested spectator. So they had chosen Edward Heath whom he had helped to train and bring forward as one of the bright young men, and Heath occupied the Butler position in politics, that position said by Lord Attlee to be most acceptable to the majority, the position of just left of centre.

The vote for Enoch Powell had shown that the right-wing rebels did not muster more than twenty or so votes. They were a force but not an intimidating one. The Conservative and Unionist Party—to use the old title—had adopted a middle of the road man for its new type leader.

The struggle which had been waged since 1945 between RAB and those who wanted the Conservative Party to be conservative was over, at least in the foreseeable future. It was a victory for progress. The Party would advance along the lines that RAB himself in countless speeches, papers, and addresses had laid down.

Being human he felt a great wrench at leaving Westminster and the great stage he loved so much.* But at least his ideas, his philosophy had won. The Tory Party had dismissed the master and accepted the pupil who was now the Leader. Perhaps, in RAB's memorable phrase, he would make the best Prime Minister we are likely to get.

Only one point troubled some members of the 1922 Committee, now revelling in their new-found strength and power. Edward Heath was not yet fifty. Would they be lumbered with him for fifteen or twenty years? Suppose he turned out to be not quite as virile and forceful as they hoped? Or less

---

* RAB's own statement on retirement read: "I much look forward to my new life at Cambridge, with which for several generations my family has had the closest ties. I shall dedicate my efforts to the college and to the university. This means a complete change from my political life and party politics, but I shall hope to keep in touch with national affairs through the Upper House. . . . I am not going to align myself on party lines. . . . I cannot remain a member of the Shadow Cabinet" (in which he had been Opposition spokesman for foreign affairs). At the end of his long service he emerges as an independent, free to give advice in the national interest as opposed to merely the Tory Party interest.

easy to manipulate than they liked? Could they ever get rid of him? But the answer to the unspoken question was a reassuring one. After all, no one had been happier in office than Sir Alec. He had been determined to lead the party to victory in the next General Election. And it had not been too difficult to get rid of Sir Alec. Now that the 1922 Committee had at last come into its own it did not doubt that, at a secret meeting, the fate of the Party leadership could always be debated and decided.

If RAB felt any bitterness he did not show it. "It is better for me to go to Trinity at sixty-two, when I can still talk to a thousand young men. Better than I shall be able to in ten years' time."

He was not worried about the verdict of history. He was content to "let the record speak for itself."

XIV

A Tory Who Thought

MOST OF the Conservative politicians who have loomed largely on the political stage during this century have not been conspicuous thinkers. They have been men of action and acumen, keen to implement the Party programme, quick to take advantage of their opponents, as avid for office as a healthy love of power and its trappings dictates.

In this respect RAB was different, he really did apply his mind to trying to discover a philosophic reason and justification for Toryism. And in this he achieved more success than his contemporaries. He was more in the tradition of Bolingbroke, the younger Pitt, Disraeli and Lord Randolph Churchill. He thought it important that behind the manifesto there should be a faith and, being RAB, that faith had to be both morally and reasonably defensible. The flashy, promising programme without thought behind it was anathema to him.

The real service rendered by RAB to the Conservative Party during the last two decades is that he forced the Party to think out its policies and give them a rational basis and a valid historial background.

Before Disraeli there was, in effect, little necessity for a Tory to think.

> "And if they ask us how it's done?
> We just reply: We've always won."

The English upper class, which was not a rigid body but was constantly being strengthened by new blood mainly from industry, had immense confidence in its ability to govern. And this confidence was by no means as absurd as it seemed.

Until the 20th century, England was divided into classes and the aristocracy and gentry were instantly recognized by their accent, their clothes, their air, their deportment and their mental attitudes. They were not only recognized. They were respected. In Devonshire, for instance, a Fortescue or an Acland commanded deference in all circles, in radical families almost as much as in Tory households.

To us now, this seems almost incredible but it was a fact of social life. The great families—the Cavendishes, the Cecils, the Churchills and so on—sat at the top of the intricate social system of England, near the Crown. The Dukes of Westminster drove to State Openings of Parliament in their elaborate golden coaches with their footmen and outriders. They owned—they still own through companies—large tracts of the West End of London.

The class strata of Britain went from the top to the bottom. In the houses of the gentry—and this class included retired Navy and Army Officers, retired merchants, if sufficiently civilized, lawyers, Clergy and others—there were always two entrances. One was for the family and their guests. The other was the tradesmen's entrance and it was labelled as such. It usually took a hidden and devious path directly to the kitchen door.

Until the present century, there were nearly two million English men and women "in service" in one form or another. These people ranged from the elaborate hierarchy of servants employed in the great house, each man taking the precedence of his master if there were guests, down through gamekeepers, ghillies, grooms; to the cook and two housemaids which was the amount of help thought necessary for a modest household in the country or the town.

All the great families had town houses as well as one or more country seats and these have vanished quite recently. For instance, the author as a young man looked out of his bedroom window at the New Oxford and Cambridge Club

in Stratton Street over the great garden of Devonshire House
not more than five hundred yards from Piccadilly Circus. It is
now a great motor show-room.

With a society as stratified and traditional as this, those
who lead it had every reason to believe in their innate power
to rule. After all they had been brought up to do just that.
The Public Schools aimed at turning out gentlemen who
could command obedience partly because they had learnt
to obey. The existence of a ruling upper class was taken for
granted. The school's job was to maintain a constant supply
of "the right type". The right type had no doubts at all. He
was well mannered, especially to his inferiors, not academic,
clean, robust, addicted to sport, tremendously proud of being
British, and prepared to die for his country without question
should the need arise. He was just as effective and even
ruthless a patriot as the Japanese Samurai nobles but he made
much less fuss about it. He did not believe that the King of
England was divine, but he did believe that the Crown and
all it stood for was "part of the British way of life" and a very
essential part, too. That he, and what he represented, should
puzzle or perplex foreigners troubled him not at all. Self-
doubt he seldom knew : self-confidence was an asset.

These young men did not despise the proletariat as did
the French aristocrats. They thought it very natural that the
"working class" should want to have a larger slice of the cake,
and, within reason, they were prepared to give it to them.
They were often very good, if somewhat arbitrary employers.
On the whole they suspected too much book learning. With
what quiet pride and satisfaction the tutor of the future King
Edward the Eighth had reported of his charge : "Bookish he
will never be."

The thought of having a detailed policy to which, in
changing circumstances, the Party would be more or less
tied was anathema to this generation of Tory stalwarts. What
they were really claiming in their quiet way, was the divine
right to rule by the light of nature. Mr. Disraeli himself
though he could not help thinking, being a Jew and all that,

never thought it necessary to elaborate too much on the policy of the Party at Election time:

"Gentlemen,

I shall have the pleasure of being present at the polling stations on Election Day and if you do me the honour of returning me to Westminster as your Member of Parliament, I shall endeavour to serve you diligently in the best tradition of the Party to which I belong.

Your obedient servant,

BENJAMIN DISRAELI."

After being elected on this manifesto, Disraeli did not have to worry unduly if the constantly shifting sands and the turbulent tides of politics at home and abroad necessitated changes in his tactics or even in his overall political strategy.

Perhaps this generation of politicians we are looking at were not as wrong as one might suppose in not committing themselves beforehand to detailed policies. Events are often apt to take over and make it virtually impossible for a party in office to keep its elaborate election pledges. This is especially so because of financial hazards and restrictions. For instance, the Tory Party elected on a clearly expansionist policy was soon suffering in Mr. Macmillan's administration from the ruthless credit squeeze of Mr. Selwyn Lloyd. And the Labour Party elected in 1964 on promises of lowered prices and increased social benefits found James Calaghan, the Chancellor, imposing restrictions even more severe and widespread.

But, although too great an adherence to detail in a Party's manifesto may be an embarrassment within a very short time, there clearly should be a political philosophy, "a faith" underlying the policies of any party that seeks to run a great nation with a complicated industrial and agricultural complex at home and a maze of intricate obligations in all parts of the world abroad.

The strength of the Communist Party lies in the fact that its policy, though we may disagree with it and detest its executive manifestations such as the secret police and domestic espionage, is readily ascertainable. All property belongs to the State. All men are equal. Communism is the faith that, in the end, will conquer the minds of men everywhere. This may be arrogant, even wicked. But it is a policy. It is not like any other policy. And it cannot tolerate any deviation.

The Labour Party in Britain, since it ceased to be Socialist, has suffered greatly from the loss of the hard recognizable line they formerly could boast of. After Hugh Gaitskell had torn the Socialist heart out of the Labour movement, the Labour Party had to explain with some care and ingenuity just how it differed essentially from the enlightened Conservatism favoured by RAB Butler and his supporters. And now, of course, the resemblance has become accentuated with the choice of Mr. Heath as leader for, as has been pointed out, it takes considerable concentration to decide which man is the Tory leader and which the Labour leader.

Both clever grammar school lads. Both Balliol men.

> *Balliol men and I was one,*
> *Swam together in winter rivers*
> *Wrestled together under the sun.*

Well, perhaps nothing as dangerous as that, but at least a tentative toe in the sea at holiday time with the paper bags and the family, real or related.

It was RAB's ambition to give the Conservative Party a sharp outline. Not merely an eruption of tit-for-tat manifestoes at election time cunningly designed to attract the various interests and ambitions of the community. He wanted this Party to have a real and solid faith to which they could always return if in doubt and from which their policies would naturally spring. In his view, this would give the Party authenticity and integrity. It would avoid charges of opportunism and it would attract the increasingly sophisticated and educated men and women to whom the Tories had to appeal. The plain fact was that unless they polled nearly thirty per cent of the "Working class" vote they could not be returned to Westminster. The philosophy would have to be liberal in concept, progressive in application. This was his own faith. It came to him naturally.

As a man, one can always see two streams of thought and emotion at work in his mentality. One is traditional, the quiet conviction that the lessons of history are to be learnt, that nothing is so certain as that history repeats itself; the other is an equally firm conviction that progress is the essence of life. Without progress there is atrophy and any party that does not recognize this is doomed. To these fundamental concepts he added a desire to better the way of life and leisure of the majority within the framework of a "free", non-Socialist, society. He also genuinely believed that Britain and the Commonwealth would continue to play a major and highly beneficial rôle in world affairs.

I quote from a speech he delivered at Oxford to the National Summer School in 1954. It shows very clearly the development of his thesis. It is "Butlerism" incarnate. He called this talk: "A Disraelian approach to modern politics."

"I think Disraeli was right in boasting that in the mid-nineteenth century it fell to him personally to prepare the mind of the country and to educate our Party. In the mid-twentieth century, particularly in the years of Opposition, this work of preparation and education was institutionalized. As a result we were returned to power in 1951, which proves that we were rather successful. Through the National Advisory Committee, the Conservative Research Department, the Conservative Political Centre and the Conservative College of the North at Swinton, we were able to prepare the basis of our policy with the aid of the rank and file of the Party; to disseminate our views widely; and to gain and retain the initiative in political thought.

"What is more, we have encouraged a two-way movement of ideas. Of this Disraeli would have approved, though he might have been slightly bored with some of the paper we produce. He was himself so imaginative a leader, so sparkling a speaker, so far-sighted a statesman; and his social conscience was so well attuned to the needs of his age. In his work and thought, emotion and intellect were fused into one.

"Yet many have failed to take Disraeli seriously. They admit to a sneaking feeling that perhaps Trollope was not far wrong when he complained of Disraeli's work that 'The glory has been the glory of pasteboard, the wealth has been the wealth of tinsel, the wit has been the wit of hairdressers, and the enterprise the enterprise of mountebanks.' (I need scarcely explain that Trollope's politics were Liberal.) Certainly Disraeli was somewhat too florid and satirical, and perhaps too original to suit everybody's taste. As he himself said, 'An insular country, subject to fogs, and with a powerful middle class, requires grave statesmen.' But Disraeli was not among them. Even as a septuagenarian he remained, like our beloved present Prime Minister, the enfant terrible of his century.

"When we talk of modern Conservatism, we must reflect that it emerged as a name during the period of Sir Robert Peel. (I come from another and better university where my studies were largely concerned with this period. Perhaps that is why I am sometimes accused nowadays of being a modern and inferior version of that revered figure. There was at that time a contrapuntal* movement between Disraeli's friends with their high-flown reliance upon 'the sublime instincts of an ancient people', and Peel's friends with their duller Tamworth Manifesto.

"Round about 1947, Quintin Hogg wrote to me at the Research Department and said, what the Conservative Party wants today is another Tamworth Manifesto. Whether they wanted it or not, they certainly got it. In fact, they got four. These manifestos of ours, though they admirably served their purpose, have been criticized as being too pedestrian. So perhaps we can now dismiss this approach, remembering, in Disraeli's own words, that a nation is not 'a mere mass of bipeds', but 'a work of art and a work of time'.

"We have moved into a new period. There are our Tory 'neo-Fabians' who say that Change is our ally. There are others who prefer to stress that 'the general and perpetual voice of men', the common judgment of centuries, cannot be lightly dismissed but must be treated with reverence and respect. The

* Contrapuntal means apparently, "according to the rules of counterpoint". No doubt everyone except the author knew this, but I add the note in case there should be one more ignoramus.

classical rôle of Conservatism has always been to find the right
mean between its dynamic and its stabilizing aspects.

"When there was an excess of laissez-faire we leaned towards
the authority of the State; now that we can see an excess of
bureaucracy we are leaning towards individual enterprise and
personal liberty. We should continue to lean, but without losing
our balance.

"Society is a partnership, and so underlying all our differences there should be a fundamental unity—the very anti-
thesis of the 'class war'—bringing together what Disraeli
called the Two Nations into a single social entity.

"But if Disraeli provided us with inspiration, he was no less
prescient in warning us of the pitfalls. He cautioned us, for
example, that posterity was not a pack-horse always ready to
be loaded with fresh burdens. He cautioned us no less strongly
that we should seek to secure greater equality, not by levelling
the few, but by elevating the many. I think it very important,
in looking to the future of the Welfare State, to concentrate on
these points, using the social services as a basis from which
human nature and individual enterprise can strive for better
things.

"Please remember that it will be impossible to sustain the
social service burden unless we produce more at home, and
earn more abroad, by own efforts. I was criticized for not
introducing a change in respect of old age pensions in my last
Budget.* But I was actuated by the very sober consideration
that this reform is not going to be quite so easy for the working
and insured population as some people think. The old at present
are in a ratio of about one to five of the working population, but
in less than thirty years they will be in a ratio of one to three.
The young people at work will then have to carry very largely
the burden of keeping the old. I am sorry to make things so
clear, but sometimes the realities of whom in fact pays are
conveniently forgotten in the interests of political propaganda.

"We are confronted now with the Socialist concept of the
social services as a levelling instrument, a means of securing
that everyone shall have just the same average uniform standard

* RAB was, of course, Chancellor of the Exchequer in the Churchill
Administration at this time.

of life. Wherever we meet it, we can see how self-defeating this
concept must be.

"So when I look to our future as a party and as a nation, I
rely not only upon the development of social reform, but follow
Disraeli's teaching in believing that the truest expression of our
national unity, and the real safeguard of our liberties, lies in
our national institutions. We must see that the repository of
power is not the bureaucracy, but the Ministers of the day
responsible to Parliament and sensitive to public opinion. We
must make it a major objective to strengthen personal liberty
by a further abridgement of the many Regulations still surviv-
ing under wartime emergency Acts, while noting with modest
satisfaction that over sixty per cent of them have been elimin-
ated since October, 1951. Our municipal institutions, re-shaped
and fortified by Tory Governments in 1888 and 1929, deserve
our further attention in order that they may continue to play
their indispensable part in modern domestic progress. Should
we not also widen and extend the institution and responsibilities of property, which answer to a deeply felt human need?

"The last of the institutions to which I wish to refer (which
Disraeli kept closest, perhaps, to his own heart) are the flexible
and original institutions of the British Empire and Commonwealth. It has been noted that one may read Lord Morley's
monumental *Life of Gladstone* and scarcely be reminded that
Britain possessed an Empire. You certainly cannot say that of
Moneypenny and Buckle. If he had made no other contribution
to our political life, Disraeli would still be remembered with
gratitude and esteem as the awakener of what he described
as the Imperial spirit. He foresaw what a source of incalculable
strength and hope would come to the world from our group
of free nations.

"Our aim is to develop, in a way undreamt of in Greece,
unknown to Rome, unheard of in Germany, and sometimes
misunderstood in the United States of America, institutions of
self-government which can be an example to the world.

"I should like, therefore, to end on this note, Disraeli left
us a great tradition which you are going to study, think about,
perhaps dream about during this school. But do not be satisfied
with just living in the pages of history. Society has changed.
Not all of Disraeli's ideas are applicable today. But his ideals,

translated into modern dress, can still be an inspiration. Do not worry overmuch about the Two Nations of a century ago; think of our One Nation as we see it today. Adjust yourselves to the ever-developing concepts of the Commonwealth; and think of our friends from the Colonies who now come and join in our political schools. Think of the liberty which is inherent in our institutions—and how to strengthen it. Think of our Party's conception of property in terms of ordinary men and women—and how to extend it. Don't be frightened of these things. Bring forward ideas which may help us in the future, but which are based on those inspirations of history and tradition which have made this country a great nation."

I have quoted from this speech because it reveals fairly completely the pattern of RAB's thinking. Considering that it was made by an active and important Minister in Office, it contains remarkably little invective or political back-chat. The "small change of the hustings" are ignored in the pursuit of a reasoned argument having its roots in tradition but very much attuned to the needs of the present and the future.

This is really what the struggle within the Tory Party, that denied RAB the office of Prime Minister, was all about. RAB stood for progressive liberal policies. The 1922 Committee, the heart and soul of the Conservative Party, reflected the tradition of "as little change as possible". It was a basic difference and until 1965, by and large, at crucial points in the Party history, when leaders had to be chosen, the Old Guard won.

There was, thus, a great divergence between the Party policies over which RAB and the Research Department had a large measure of control, and the actual feeling of the Party. The Party realized that they must have progressive policies—on paper. But they preferred to have an out-and-out traditionalist to execute them—or to shelve them. To have the Butler policies implemented by RAB, himself, that was too much.

The Conservative Party backbenchers are often pictured as being stupid and reactionary. They are not stupid. They are

willing to employ any acceptable device to get the Tory Party
returned to office. That—not policy statements—is the
supremely important objective. With the Tories in, according
to this creed, agriculture will be sure of reasonable patronage
and protection, business and the City can plan ahead because
they know that no inconvenient political intrusion on
industry will occur, and, indirectly, all will benefit.

The choice of Mr. Heath, who although not a RAB disciple,
has a political outlook indistinguishable from the Butler line,
raises an interesting question. Has the Tory hierarchy
capitulated at last? Or is Mr. Heath being used merely
because—ominous word—he has the "right image"? The use
of the word image is, I think, significant. What is desired is
not the reality but the appearance of change, and, of course,
if Mr. Heath's "dynamism" should flounder there is always
safe, unruffled, decent, family-man Maudling to take his place.

Certainly in basing his progressive Tory faith on the
political philosophy of Disraeli RAB was on very sure
ground. It was Disraeli who was identified with the greatest
and most glamorous period of English history. Under his
guidance the Queen became Empress of India, the patron
of all the Princes of India, with Indian and Gurkha guards
at Court on ceremonial occasions. Under Disraeli's imaginative leadership, Britain had acquired from the bankrupt
Khedive her large shareholding in the Suez Canal. Under
Disraeli Africa had become more and more an English
Colony. Under him the loss of the American colonies was
finally forgotten in the golden glory of the new-found Empire.

And how the words of Disraeli still ring out when quoted
at Tory meetings!

"The Tory Party unless it is a national party, is nothing. It
is a party formed by all the numerous classes of the realm,
classes alike and equal before the Law, but whose different
conditions and different aims, add vigour and variety to our
national life. . . ."

It was magic. The dandified figure, the black ringlets, the
great sombre eyes, the rapier wit, they might all be very

unEnglish, but the Tory Party rose to Disraeli as they never rose to RAB. For Disraeli had what RAB lacked, the gift of personal contact, instant contact. He could say two or three words to an old supporter who would remember them all his life and bore his grandchildren by relating them. Of the two men undoubtedly RAB was the more honest. Disraeli was a great man and a great opportunist. RAB never was an opportunist. He wanted the Conservative Party to have faith and policies so deeply rooted and so sensible that men would vote TORY because their reason told them that this was what they really wanted. The appeal was, almost always, to the head, and only indirectly to the heart.

RAB was not always as philosophical and as detached as he was in his Oxford speech which we have quoted. For instance, in October, 1955, he was explaining the current credit squeeze which, as Chancellor he was finding necessary, in these terms:

"We propose to make monetary and fiscal policies effective until we have cured the inflation. Of course I realize—and I come from an agricultural constituency—that a credit squeeze, unlike some other more pleasurable squeezes, is moral, in that it is a good thing to live within your means, whether as an individual or as a nation. I know that it hurts. I am bombarded and besieged with cases of difficulty. I propose to continue with the credit squeeze. I once said to you in one of my speeches some years ago, 'All change hurts', and these sorts of things do hurt. No change from one's banker is very painful, but my theme for the Party as well as the country today must be that it will be through service and sacrifice that we shall win salvation."

This is the light note on serious subjects that he often struck and which made him vulnerable to charges of flippancy. But he was not flippant. He was essentially serious. He believed in God, he believed in Britain. He believed in the Tory Party. And he believed in RAB Butler.

He also believed in an educated, property-owning democracy. He was the quietest revolutionary of them all.

XV

The Summing-up

WE COME now to the final arbitration in our attempt to assess the career of Richard Austen Butler. The jury is the British public. Their verdict is final and from it there is no appeal. The accident of a political leader becoming, or not becoming, Prime Minister is unimportant as compared to this. In politics, as in life, the race is not always to the swift, nor the battle to the strong. Lesser men than we are writing of here have filled that great office.

We are concerned with a true assessment of his accomplishment in all the diverse fields of British and imperial politics which he entered with such zest and skill. What did he achieve for India? To what extent was he really the architect of modern English education? How deeply did he change the current thinking on penal reform? How skilled and effective was his long tenure of office as Chancellor of the Exchequer? What influence did he exert and what part did he play in Foreign Affairs especially in regard to Munich, Suez and the ultimate problem of nuclear war or peace?

And, finally, this being a biography, what kind of a man was he? On the answer to all these questions the final judgment must rest.

RAB Butler, though he had been warned against becoming an intellectual by Stanley Baldwin while still at Cambridge, was the intellectual politician and statesman of his day. The honours that he gathered as he rose to a unique position in the Tory Party hierarchy were, for the most part, academic honours reflecting the kind of man he was; cultured, scholarly and profoundly interested in education, history and young people.

His old College Pembroke made him an Honorary Fellow and so did Corpus Christi, where he spent that quiet interlude lecturing on the Third Republic before taking the plunge into the turbulent seas of British politics. Now Trinity, itself, has claimed him, giving him refuge and honour and, incidentally, a vantage point from which he can express his views on any subjects that interest him, education in particular.

Universities tumbled over one another to make him an honorary Doctor of Law and Letters, and at least the latter part of this distinction well becomes him. Even in recent months, since his retirement, he has started to launch out as a writer and his style is somehow familiar to us, for it is the natural literary extension of RAB himself. In the *Sunday Times* of July 25, 1965, RAB embarked on some tentative journalism reviewing Lord Birkenhead's biography of Lord Halifax with both charm and insight. He writes: "From my memory and from my records I endorse Lord Birkenhead's findings about my then chief. I notice a quotation from John Wheeler-Bennett to sum up the Munich decision. For my own part I would like to add that the justification for Munich has still to be more elaborately set out. Under Halifax's instinct we entered the war of 1939-45 with a united Commonwealth and the framework of an air force, which defeated Hitler at the time of the Battle of Britain. We had neither of these assets at the time of Munich. I think that this account tends to under-estimate Halifax's determination to bring things to a head in the autumn of 1939. Just before war was declared, Sir Will Malkin, the legal advisor, came into my room and said: 'The right thing has been done in the right way.' This is in itself a good epitaph for Halifax."

And again, on another theme:

"For its descriptions of India and, as I shall later show, of America, this book should attract a wide reading public. The old India is recreated whether in tiger shooting at Mohand or the departure thence to Simla, 'which clings to the mountains like a swallow's nest amid fir clad peaks': or the lawns stretching down to the river at Barrackpore with memories of the Cannings, or when they were rowed up the river to Srinagar in painted barges and walked in the moonlit garden at Shalamar, and saw the Kashmir mountains with their tiara of everlasting snow. It is not for nothing that Lord Birkenhead has studied and absorbed the life and times of Kipling."

He is, of course, embarking on a part-time writing career, the easy way of exploiting his long personal knowledge of the English story at the summit, but he has every right to do this, and this review shows very clearly that he has, as one would expect, the measure of history to make for perspective in his writing. In the years to come another skilled and most persuasive pen will join those already hard at work giving us biography, travel and political revelation.

Among the universities who have honoured him are Cambridge, Oxford, St. Andrews, Nottingham, Bristol and Glasgow. No recipient of these formal accolades can have given the governing bodies of these universities less anxiety. RAB was so obviously fitted to receive what they had it in their gift to bestow.

He was made Rector of Glasgow University from 1956 to 1959. High Steward of Cambridge University and of the Town, Chancellor both of Sheffield University and of the university of his own county, Essex. This great wave of academic honour was inevitable and natural. There were not so many politicians so closely identified either with education or with the academic way of life.

His interests are shown by the societies who made him their president or chairman or otherwise honoured him, and these included the Modern Languages Association, the Royal India Society, the Anglo-Netherlands Society, the Royal Society of Literature and the National Association of Mental Health. In his little study overlooking the Square in London, invitations from one or more of these decorates the mantelpiece. RAB will never be idle, never dull.

But this spate of honours came from those who viewed his

career from afar. They were acceptable and he was grateful for them. When he had to prepare an address he always did it with meticulous care after turning the matter over in his mind for days of preparation. The tributes that touched him personally, undemonstrative as he was, were the tributes of those who worked for longest most closely to him.

The Freedom of Saffron Walden pleased him greatly, as did the presentation of gifts from his constituency where he is still held in a unique regard. These had become his people and he was very much their member.

In July, 1965, a ceremony took place at the very heart of the Tory Party, in Old Queen Street, at the Research Department where RAB had been the leading figure for twenty years. A new director had just been appointed and this young man, with tact and sensitivity, asked Mr. D. K. Clarke, who had been Director of the Department for many years under RAB, to make the presentation speech.

Mr. Clarke did so, and so charmingly that its flavour comes through to us even in cold print. Here we are in the inner circle of Conservatism and the names used are Christian names:

"Lady Butler, RAB, ladies and gentlemen, colleagues and successors. When Brendan Sewill asked me to make this presentation on your behalf he gave me a number of reasons why I should but none of them seemed to me to be very compelling. If he was looking for somebody with the earliest service in the Department he should have Henry Brooke. His work in the Department before the war and in keeping the idea alive and seeing that it was revived after the war, has not been sufficiently acknowledged. If he was looking for somebody with the longest service, nobody can beat Percy Cohen and there are many others with greater claims.

"I must say something tonight about RAB's work for nearly twenty years as Chairman of the Conservative Research Department. He is only the third chairman and has held the position longer than anybody else. It is a very important post in the Party. But it has never been bestowed as a reward for other service; it has always been regarded as a working post and RAB was chosen for the contribution he could make, and how hard he has worked. I must necessarily speak mainly of the first years during which he held it as that is the period which I knew and because what the Department has been doing since has, I believe, been made possible by the foundations which RAB laid and the standards he set in the early years of his chairmanship.

"In those days we were known as 'Mr. Butler's back-room boys'. We were very proud of that title. That phrase smacks very much of a post-war period when memories of the contribution of boffins to the war were still fresh. Today, no doubt, we should be described in some more contemporary idiom, probably that of the pop group; we might be known as 'RAB and His Researchers'! But we never shared a common uniform. We never had the same style of haircut (if you look around at Iain and others there were obvious reasons why we didn't). We have never even had that most English of institutions a common tie!

"In public there has been a good deal of misunderstanding and exaggeration about the rôle played by the Research Department. There is no doubt that it played a very important part in rebuilding the Party after 1945. But this was not because it suddenly produced a ready-made policy of its own or because it forced the views of one man on a bewildered Party. It was because it provided the Party with a centre to which ideas from every quarter could be and were brought and where they could be freely and generally discussed and evaluated.

"RAB's first contribution to the Department was that not just by his position in the Party but by the universal confidence in his integrity as a person such a centre was possible under his leadership and people were willing to accept it as such.

"Secondly (and in the long run, I believe this was his most important contribution), he brought to the work of the Department a depth of thinking about the fundamental philosophy of the Party which was never more needed than at that time. The need then to consider the whole philosophy of the Party in relation to contemporary events rather than set up a large number of committees on policy is the sign of a difference between a heavy defeat and a near miss. It is often said that politics is about power. That is true as far as it goes. But what

RAB always reminded us was that politics is also about the use of power and the purposes to which it should be put. Politics is about ideals and about the aspirations and conditions of living of ordinary men and women. He made us deeply concerned about our fundamental political beliefs and relating our policy to them. As a result we conveyed in our policy a sense of sincerity which was, I believe, an important reason why at that time many younger people gave their allegiance to the Party and played an active part in it.

"His third contribution to the Department was to stand between our political masters and the staff of the Department and to interpret one to the other. This is an essential rôle. It is all too easy for politicians to ride off on ideas which have never been tested and are only half cooked. It is equally easy for an office staff to produce ideas which are quite divorced from political reality. RAB handled this rôle with consummate skill. He had to charm a reluctant leader who at times scarcely seemed to believe in the necessity for policy. He took endless pains to see that everybody who felt he ought to be consulted was consulted, and he had to present the results of all the work to the Party and the country. That was a very heavy responsibility. He did all this by the same qualities that he has shown so often in his ministerial career in combining complete determination to maintain principles with the utmost flexibility on all details.

"The fourth thing that RAB brought to the work of the Department was a tremendous breadth of interest and knowledge and his outstanding ability to master subjects. I cannot recall here the whole of the great diversity of his interests, but they ranged from a life-long knowledge of the Indian sub-continent through a grasp of the essentials of modern economics to the Presidency of the Royal Literary Society, not to mention his abiding interest in education and mental health. He has essentially been a generalist in an age of increasing specialization, and the more specialists you have the more important does the generalist become. One sometimes wondered what there was to which he could not turn his mind and master.

"We have chosen two gifts for you, RAB. We ask you to accept them :

to record your chairmanship of the Department;

to mark our sense of your great services to the Party and the country in that post;

to express our admiration of your many qualities;

to show our gratitude for the influence you have exerted on us individually;

to give you our best wishes for your future at Cambridge."

There are, I think, some delightful touches in Mr. Clarke's speech. The line about RAB and his Researchers is so characteristic of the English upper classes condescending with genial patronage to the beat-music of the day. But the summary at the end includes a most important line: "to show our gratitude for the influence you have exerted on us individually."

This line would never have been there unless it was true and had the support of the staff working in Old Queen Street. It emphasizes once again that those close to RAB had a great respect and affection for him. It was his major failing that he was unable by nature to spread this warmth around. He could not communicate effectively outside the Ministerial file, his fellow workers, and the House of Commons, and even in the House of Commons he was never an outstanding success. His views were listened to with respect because he always had something worth while to say. But to capture the heart of the House, that was beyond him. This magic he could only exercise by close personal contacts in the day-to-day transaction of business.

So, in summing-up, the pattern of his personal relationships seems fairly clear. Here was a man capable of securing the devotion and respect of those who knew him well and worked with him closely. And here was a man who, by nature of the reservations in his make-up and character, was incapable of throwing that dazzling rainbow of friendship, transient but captivating, which the greatest public figures have been able to conjure from the overflowing humanity of their natures.

What of his work? How good was it? How much endures?

RAB served under Lord Halifax during all the time that
Edward Wood was Foreign Secretary. Lord Halifax had such
confidence in him that he gave RAB sole responsibility not
only for foreign affairs in the House of Commons but for
Britain's relations with the United Nations. Now there is a
team of Ministers to do the same work.

Again in the field of India, though RAB was officially
Under-Secretary, he remained at that vital post during the
titanic struggle on Indian independence, having to cope with
the Indian Congress Party in India and the devastating
attacks of Winston Churchill at home. His clashes with
Churchill showed the characters of the two men clearly.
RAB precise, humorous, immensely dedicated to his brief,
reaching at least to the reason of members in the benches
behind him and often crossing the floor to steal a follower
from the Opposition; Churchill, unpredictable, passionate,
capable at his best of destroying an argument, as his father
could, with a devastating whispered aside, capable, too, of
sweeping the House along on a flood of passionate exhorta-
tion until one felt that the Red Fort of Delhi would never,
never haul down its flag.

In advancing stage by stage—this method was natural and
inevitable to RAB in all his reforms—the cause of Indian
home rule and independence RAB had to fight all the way.
To the right the Tory hardcore out to frustrate, delay and,
if they could, destroy. To the left the multiple snipers at home
and in India who wanted the British link with India—which
had created India—cut without further preparation or delay.

In the reforms for which he was responsible in education
he had no such great fight on his hands. The attacks were
mainly on points of detail rather than on root principle.
Already in 1941 RAB was looking ahead to a new social
climate for a new Britain. Churchill and his closest colleagues
had taken over the war effort. On the assumption that we
won, and that was the only assumption that RAB would
contemplate—on this one issue he refused to see all sides of
the question, knowing that in war faith must be absolute—

great and far-reaching reforms would be demanded by the people. If the Conservative Party did not provide their own proposals and solutions the Labour Party would certainly do so.

Lord Kilmuir has suggested in his captivating book that only RAB and himself were looking ahead into the postwar future at this time. This is certainly true of RAB and was true, too, of Maxwell Fyfe, though he had not the vision to introduce the desperately needed reform of our judicial and legal system that might have been his special province and an abiding memorial.

RAB, made Minister of Education, ranged over the whole educational scene. His Act of 1944, with its one hundred and twenty-two clauses, swept the board, its scope was a complete reorganization of the education of Britain. And, of course, this was to be achieved in stages as the preliminary terms of reference made clear:

> "The statutory system of public education shall be organized in three progressive stages to be known as primary education, secondary education, and further education; and it shall be the duty of the local education authority for every area, so far as their power extend, to contribute towards the spiritual, moral, mental, and physical development of the community by securing that efficient education throughout those stages shall be available to meet the needs of the population of their area."

The Act ends with the words: "This Act may be cited as the Education Act 1944." In fact, the public called it the Butler Act, and the Butler Act it has remained, establishing beyond doubt RAB's permanent contribution, and perhaps we should add, continuing contribution, to English education.

In the almost unexplored region of Mental Health, too, RAB left his mark on history. This Act, with its one hundred and fifty-four sections, was as complicated in its way as the Education Act. It reconstructed and replanned the whole archaic system for treating the mentally sick and subnormal. It was and is a great human Statute and it reflects that kind of practical compassion that RAB was capable of exercising in public affairs.

He felt that the cause of the large insane and mentally deficient population was a cause that challenged his Conservative faith. If great areas of the law as it stood were harsh, based on long-discarded assumptions, and in practice ineffective, then it was up to him to rectify this and rectify it he did by applying himself to the job with an assiduity and dedication that made him a formidable champion of his cause in the House of Commons and the country.

So this man had no time for the tankard in the smoking-room of the House, or the sherry at the Carlton? Yes, that was it exactly. He had no time to spare.

How effective was RAB in spreading his own view of Toryism throughout the ranks of the Party at Westminster and in the country? Probably more successful at the centre than he was farther afield. But spread his political philosophy he did and in a practical way. He created the Conservative Political Centre, and, addressing that body in 1956, he summed up his political faith so effectively that it is best to quote his own words:

"Before we think about tomorrow . . . let us just review how far we have got today. As I see it, our achievement between 1945 and 1951 was that we showed that we were true to our Tory tradition of social progress. We gained the people's confidence because we were ready to move ahead with the times.

"Before that, I had endeavoured to indicate my own philosophy, as inherited from the Conservative tradition, namely, that of equality of opportunity in the Education Act. I wanted, and still want with all my heart, more and more of the younger generation to enjoy the good things of life and to enter into the inheritance of culture—and what goes with it, responsibility. But all that we have been working for and striving for all our lives will turn to ashes, and mock us in our old age, if the only culture we have succeeded in spreading is that of the gimmick and the gadget, the strip cartoon and the rock 'n' roll. I favour a merry England; but a merry England

and a mindless England that couldn't care less are two entirely different things.

"I am certain that we should refuse to make our Party a class Party, or identify it with this section or that section, with this class or that class. Our great strength has always been and will always be that we are a national Party. At the same time we should unite the nation by proving that we can keep a fair balance between different interests so that none feel that they are by-passed or ignored in the forward march of expansion.

"Two men of genius were contemporaries in the last century —Marx and Disraeli. One sought to divide man from man, and the other to bring them together. It always must be our aim to carry forward the mission of unification.

"Nor must we base our creed upon the materialist canon. While we cannot but be satisfied that people vote Conservative because they are more prosperous, the doctrine of 'prosperity politics', and voting Conservative because one's own position is better, or grumbling against the Government because one's own personal dividends are reduced, is neither satisfying nor satisfactory. We must not, so to speak, encourage (to borrow a term, but not analogy, from the international field) a Conservative Users' Association. People must not be led to suppose that they can simply use the Conservative Party for their own ends. Nor must anyone think that the prime task of a politician, even in a democracy, is to learn the gentle art of pleasing—as though he were a lover or an entertainer. The politician should not spend his time cajoling in the light of candelabra. He has to make his appeal not in the soft haze of artificiality but in the harsh glare of realism.

"We must base our appeal on two main and realistic principles. First, as I have said, to wield the power of the State to balance the interests within it; producing a form of society in which rewards go to those who are successful in increasing the wealth of the whole and so make it possible to help others who are in need. Second, so to organize our international and defence policies as to hold our position in the world.

"Unless our movement is deep-set in a living and spiritual philosophy it will not have the inspiration necessary to prevail."

This is the root and core of RAB's approach to politics. He wanted much more than the small change of the hustings. He wanted and insisted on having a golden thread of faith and reason to bind together all his Party stood for. At a time when that Party is being swept along on a tide of fashion that makes it ever more like its opponents in method, approach, and thinking, we may well go and drink again at the well which this wise man knew was necessary if the Conservative Party was to survive in an age of technological and social revolution.

RAB has been known to complain that critics of his career invariably dwell on Munich and Suez, when he was not in overall control, forgetting his major contributions in other directions when, as a Minister, he could direct his energy and hard work into the productive measures that moved him. It is a fair enough comment and in this book we have attempted not to exaggerate the part he played either in the immediate prewar period that led to war with the dictators or in the invasion of Egypt following the Egyptian nationalization of the Suez Canal.

I have not seen it pointed out that the very fact of this criticism is, in its way, a tribute. What other Under-Secretary or junior Minister was treated with such serious attention? The critics felt, and with some justification, that RAB was always a power, always an influence, whether he was directing events or assisting to control them. But it is fair also to say that the policy of Munich, right or wrong, was the policy of Mr. Chamberlain in which he passionately believed. In it he had the support of his ablest lieutenant, but it was support, not direction.

Again in the Suez adventure the directing force was the Prime Minister, Sir Anthony Eden, who over the years had built up a reputation as a man of peace in Foreign Affairs in Britain and throughout the world. The policy was not RAB's policy. His mistake, if mistake it was, consisted essentially in remaining loyal to his chief, staying behind to clear up the shambles that remained of Britain's foreign policy, when he disagreed with that policy and should, perhaps, have resigned. On this count we have already found against him. This was the one occasion in his long career when rebellion might have been better than Party loyalty. After all, his first loyalty was not to the Tory Party. If he was to claim the attributes of great stature his first loyalty was to the people of Britain who trusted him. But we can add this, that it is so fatally easy to have hindsight and that, at the time, it must have been an agonizing decision to make.

In summing-up we may apply another test of RAB's position in recent history and in relation to his contemporaries. Will his contribution to our public life seem larger in twenty years than it does today? And the answer must surely be that this man's achievements were so solid and diverse that the verdict will be increasingly favourable. He will increase in stature as the years go by.

Detached, urbane, quiet, scholarly, astute, immensely industrious, RAB departs for Cambridge. Many are sorry to see him go. Many felt reassured when he was near the centre of power. Will he ever come back? I do not think so. The new heroes have taken over. The ageing gladiator, still vigorous, has retired to the kind of life he loves. But to him the departure was deep sorrow for no man was more at home in the wonderful world of Westminster where he fought his battles, won his victories, and suffered his major defeats.

If this is a fair and informed summing-up of RAB's career what is the final verdict?

It is clear that he was a man who, when he disagreed with what was being done, preferred to advance his own views from within rather than by the dramatic gesture of resignation. He was not by nature a martyr. The loneliness and acrimony of exile, even for a time, dismayed him.

He was always able to see all sides of any question although personally convinced of the rectitude of his own judgment. This ability made him less emphatic—and perhaps less often wrong—than some of his contemporaries.

He was a man who found his companionship in his family

circle and he took remarkably little pains to "cultivate" the back bench Members of Parliament. He readily admits this, explaining: "I always seemed to have too much work to do." Perhaps he worked harder for longer than any other statesman of this century.

Having said this, there is another crucial test that we should apply. How much solid achievement has he left behind? And the answer must be that in all the fields of politics with which he was chiefly concerned—India, Foreign Affairs, finance, education, penal reform—he left behind him the heritage of solid and enduring achievement.

The fact that the Britain of today, for all its faults and failings, is a very much better place for the majority than the Britain of forty years ago owes more to RAB Butler than to any other living public servant.

The British people, who are not easily deceived for long, realize this and that is why, as he quits the political stage, men and women of all parties would like to salute him as an indication of their respect and gratitude.

He can look back on his long career with some pride. Being RAB it will take the form of a quiet inner satisfaction. In the end he won a position that only a very few, regardless of office, achieve.

Bibliography

Recollections of the Cambridge Union. Percy Craddock.

Macmillan. Emrys Hughes.

Richard Austen Butler. Francis Boyd.

A Source Book of Conservatism. Geoffrey Block.

Memoirs of the Earl of Kilmuir. Lord Kilmuir.

The Uncommon Commoner. John Dickie.

Tradition and Change. Conservative Political Centre.

Conservative Party Annual Conferences. Abbey House.

Sir Alec Douglas-Home. Eldon Griffiths.

The World Crisis. Winston Churchill.

Man of the Century. Gerald Sparrow.

Life of Benjamin Disraeli. Moneypenny and Buckle.

The Establishment. Hugh Thomas.

Bolingbroke and his Times. Sir Charles Petrie.

The People and the Constitution. W. I. Jennings.

Constitutional Law. A. V. Dicey.

The British Constitution. H. J. Laski.

Procedure for Electing a Leader. Conservative Central Office.

Halifax. The Earl of Birkenhead.

The House of Macmillan. C. Morgan.

Memoirs of Sir Anthony Eden. Viscount Avon.

Winston Churchill. Malcolm Thompson.

The Thousand Days. Arthur S. Schlesinger.

The Modern British Monarchy. Sir Charles Petrie.

High Tide and After. Hugh Dalton.

Conflict without Malice. Emmanuel Shinwell.

The Author's Diaries and Notes. 1925-1965.

Index